The Overland Mail

United States Troops Guarding Overland Mail
Reproduced from an old drawing

THE OVERLAND MAIL
1849–1869

Promoter of Settlement
Precursor of Railroads

by

LE ROY R. HAFEN

Foreword by David Dary

With a Note About the Author by
S. Matthew DeSpain

UNIVERSITY OF OKLAHOMA PRESS : NORMAN

Library of Congress Cataloging-in-Publication Data

Hafen, LeRoy Reuben, 1893–1985
    The overland mail, 1849–1869 : promoter of settlement, precursor of railroads / by LeRoy R. Hafen ; foreword by David Dary.
        p. cm.
    Originally published: Cleveland : A.H. Clark, 1926.
    Includes bibliographical references and index.
    ISBN 978-0-8061-3600-4 (paper)
    1. Postal service —West (U.S.)—History—19th century. 2. Coaching (Transportation)—West (U.S.)—History—19th century.   I. Title.

HE6376.A1W474 2004
383'.143'09809034—dc22

2003063439

The paper in this book meets the guidelines for permanence and durability of the Committee on Production Guidelines for Book Longevity of the Council on Library Resources, Inc.∞

Originally published by the Arthur H. Clark Company, copyright © 1926. Paperback edition published 2004 by the University of Oklahoma Press, Norman, Publishing Division of the University. Foreword by David Dary to the Oklahoma edition copyright © 2004 by the University of Oklahoma Press. Author biography by S. Matthew DeSpain copyright © 2004 by the University of Oklahoma Press. All rights reserved. Manufactured in the U.S.A.

To my wife
ANNA WOODBURY HAFEN
whose assistance and encouragement has made this
study possible and its preparation enjoyable

Contents

List of Illustrations	5
About the Author	7
Foreword	9
Preface	15
Establishment and Early Development of the Postal Service	19
The Ocean mail to the Pacific Coast, 1848–1858	37
Pioneer Monthly Mails to the inter-mountain Region, 1849–1858	53
The Butterfield Overland Mail; The South in the Ascendency	79
Extensive Increases in Mail Lines to the Pacific, 1857–1859; Testing the Routes	103
Should the Postal Service be a Pioneering Agency or a Business Undertaking? Reform and Conflict, 1859–1860	129
Mail Service to the Pike's Peak Region, 1858–1860	145
The Pony Express, Demonstrator of the Central Route	165
The Fight for a Daily Mail on the Central Route, 1859–1861	195
The Million Dollar Mail in Operation, 1861–1862	217
The Indian Peril	241
The Mail in the Middle Sixties	273
In the Days of the Stage-coach	295
Final Years and Passing of the Overland Stage	317
Bibliography of references cited	335
Index	347

Illustrations

UNITED STATES TROOPS GUARDING OVERLAND MAIL *Frontispiece*	
Reproduced by courtesy of Mr. Frank A. Root from an old drawing in his possession	
WILLIAM H. RUSSELL	167
The founder of the Pony Express	
FACSIMILE OF THE PONY EXPRESS LETTER, WHICH CARRIED THE NEWS OF ABRAHAM LINCOLN'S ELECTION	183
OVERLAND STAGE LINE RECEIPT	233
BRIDGER PASS STATION, ON THE OVERLAND STAGE ROUTE	243
From an original drawing	
BEN HOLLADAY, PRESIDENT OF THE OVERLAND STAGE LINE	297
THE CONCORD STAGE-COACH	307
The type of stage-coach used in pioneer days to transport mail. Reproduced by courtesy of Mr. E. La Forest	
MAP OF THE OVERLAND MAIL ROUTES, 1849–1869	342

About the Author

For anyone knowledgeable about western history, 1893 was some year. That year Frederick Jackson Turner unveiled his "frontier thesis," and western historian LeRoy Reuben Hafen (1893–1985) was born in Bunkerville, Nevada. Bunkerville was a small Mormon farming colony, devoutly communal and predominantly polygamist, that drew its life from the silty Virgin River—the taste of which Juanita Brooks (Bunkerville's other academic jewel) called the "Virgin Bloat." Hafen grew up in a polygamist family amid the barren range of the Great Basin, and this confluence of the Mormon church and the West would deeply influence his career.

After obtaining a B.A. in history from Brigham Young University in 1916 and an M.A. in history from the University of Utah in 1919 (his thesis, "Handcart Migration to Utah," was later revised and published as *Handcarts to Zion*), Hafen and his wife Ann Woodbury realized that academic growth meant leaving Utah for a seat at historian Herbert E. Bolton's roundtable at the University of California, Berkeley. The greatest lessons Hafen gleaned from Bolton were the importance of scouring primary sources, the value of producing readable history, and the danger of adopting the armchair historian's sedentary ways. Bolton preached what he practiced, emphasizing in his seminars geography and the utility of maps, and Hafen became a zealous disciple for life. Like his mentor, Hafen reconnoitered the terra firma connected to his research to get a feel for the land and to thicken his writings. Aided by Ann's wordsmithing, Hafen wrote *The Overland Mail, 1849–1869*, as his doctoral dissertation in 1923. As a freshly minted Ph.D., Hafen was recommended by Bolton for the position of Colorado's state historian, and

Bolton convinced the young scholar of the opportunities for research and writing there. For the next thirty years, Hafen edited *Colorado Magazine,* edited or wrote more than three dozen biographies and books on the West, wrote two textbooks, and produced some fifty articles. He was also an original founder of the Western History Association. After retiring, he returned to teach at Brigham Young University for another eighteen years and helped build the fine Western American library there.

Most of Hafen's works possess an enduring value. He was swayed little by the currents of historical fashion, choosing instead to ground his works in solid narrative and documentary sources—often reproducing key documents so that ensuing researchers could easily use them. He also established a lasting relationship with publisher Arthur H. Clark that began with the publication of *The Overland Mail* in 1926. Hafen's works are valued items, and many remain in a near perpetual state of reprint in one shape or another, including *Broken Hand: The Life of Thomas Fitzpatrick, Fort Laramie and the Pageant of the West, Ruxton of the Rockies, Life in the Far West, Old Spanish Trail, Handcarts to Zion,* and *Mountain Men and the Fur Trade of the Far West.* Because of the strong writing and even stronger grounding in primary sources, Hafen's works remain popular and his name endures as an important western historian.

Of all his own works, Hafen regarded *The Overland Mail* as among his best. Its emphasis on the role of government in transportation expansion in the West was a precursor to what William H. Goetzmann later defined as the new "Imperial School." It remains one of the foremost books on the expansion of mail and transportation in the West. Hafen, I think, would be satisfied that one of his favorite works will now win a new and widened readership.

S. Matthew DeSpain

Foreword to the Paperback Edition

Historians usually buy books for their content, while collectors seek books because of their rarity. The first edition of LeRoy R. Hafen's *The Overland Mail, 1849–1869*, is desired by both groups: by historians and students of history as the first scholarly treatment of the history of the Overland Mail, and by collectors of Western Americana for its scarcity and monetary value. Only 1,253 copies were published by The Arthur H. Clark Co. in Cleveland, Ohio, in 1926; by the 1930s they already were becoming scarce and selling for twice the original $6.00 price.

With the resurgence of interest in the history of the American West following World War II, and as Hafen's reputation as a historian and writer grew, demand for copies of his first book increased further. In today's antiquarian book trade, copies of the first edition sell for $125 to $350, depending upon condition.

The Overland Mail was an expansion of Hafen's doctoral dissertation at the University of California, Berkeley. Born in Bunkerville, Nevada, in 1893, Hafen grew up in Utah where he received his undergraduate degree in 1916 from Brigham Young University and then earned a master's degree from the University of Utah. Hafen next moved west to California and earned his doctorate at Berkeley, studying under historian Herbert E. Bolton, who favored a broader approach to writing history that incorporated and recreated the experiences and dreams of pioneers. Bolton also taught Hafen and his other students to use vigorous and colorful writing. Bolton's influence on Hafen is reflected in *The Overland Mail* and in his later books.

By the time Hafen received his doctorate, he had married Ann Woodbury and started a family. They moved to Denver where Hafen became state historian of Colorado at the Colorado Historical Society, a position he held for thirty years. During that period he also directed the Colorado State Museum and edited *Colorado Magazine,* in which approximately fifty of his articles were published.

The Overland Mail was published soon after the Hafens' move to Colorado. It contains the established facts of the history of the Overland Mail and was a pioneering account on the subject. When historian J. P. Bretz reviewed the book in the *American Historical Review* (vol. 32, no. 3) in April 1927, he noted that Hafen had produced a serious and instructive book and added, "The book as a whole tells a straightforward story and contributes not a little to a clear understanding of transcontinental communication before the coming of the railway."

Eight months later, Ralph P. Bieber, a young history professor at Washington University in St. Louis, reviewed the book in the December 1927 issue of the *Mississippi Valley Historical Review* (vol. 14, no. 3). Bieber, whose book reviews paid close attention to detail without losing the sense of a book's context and larger significance, described Hafen's book as the first scholarly work on the subject and called it "an important contribution to the history of the American frontier." Bieber noted that "the major portion of the book is devoted to a clear and well-organized description of the various mail routes in operation in the trans-Mississippi region between 1849 and 1869," and complimented Hafen for showing "that the growth and extension of the overland mail constituted an important part of our westward expansion," demonstrating that "this extension gave rise to problems which were national in their scope."

Nearly fifty years later, in 1975, Hafen, at the age of eighty-one, decided to revise *The Overland Mail*. He contacted the Arthur H. Clark Co. and asked Robert Clark, whose grandfather had started the company, to work with him on expanding and revising the book. Young Clark, then a graduate student in history, recalled: "I was busy with student teaching five classes of various history and geography courses every day, and was working harder than I knew was possible. So the project faded away, and Roy's health began to fail."

A revision was never published, but Hafen's book was reprinted in 1969 by AMS Press, by Quarterman Publications in 1976, and in an expensive edition of 150 numbered copies published in 2001 by Martino Publishing. In the meantime, it also was made available to libraries on microfiche and microfilm.

The Overland Mail reflects the influence of Herbert Bolton, who in turn was influenced by Frederick Jackson Turner, the "founding father" of western history. Turner believed the westward movement was a process that defined the American experience and left its imprint on both national character and institutions. The Overland Mail, as described in Hafen's book, was part of that process. But today some historians take the position that this approach to history belies the complexities of the West that included women, Indians, Mexicans, and the land itself. Because of these differences, these historians believe the West was a distinctive region different from the East and should be treated as such.

It was twenty-one years after *The Overland Mail* was published before another scholarly work on the subject appeared, Roscoe and Margaret Conkling's three-volume *The Butterfield Overland Mail, 1857–1869*, published in 1947 by the Arthur H. Clark Co., who had published Hafen's first book. Although the Conklings' work was comprehensive, scholarly, and definitive, it did not cover the 1849 to 1856 period included in Hafen's work. The Conklings' work also reflected the changes that had occurred in historical writing since Hafen's book was first published. The Conklings focused more on the people involved, including John Butterfield, who organized and operated the mail service over the southern route to 1861, and Ben Holladay, who purchased the Butterfield line and shifted its route north at the start of the Civil War.

Later books on the subject also emphasized the personalities involved in the Overland Mail, but none covered the 1849–1869 period that Hafen examined. J. V. Frederick's *Ben Holladay, The Stage Coach King,* published in 1947, covered 1862–1866. Since the Holladay company records were destroyed in the 1906 San Francisco fire, Frederick performed extensive research using newspapers and periodicals, private papers, and personal interviews, and his treatment of the period was far more extensive than Hafen's.

Another work on the Overland Mail was Waterman L. Ormsby's *The Butterfield Overland Mail,* edited by Lyle H. Wright and Josephine M. Bynum and published in 1942 by the Huntington Library. Ormsby was the only passenger on the westbound stage traveling the whole route to the Pacific and his recollections were first published in a series of articles by the *New York Herald* between September 28 and November 19, 1858. Hafen makes passing reference to Ormsby in *The Overland Mail* using his description of the route followed, but he did not make full use of the material.

Yet another related work was Raymond W. and Mary Lund Settle's *Empire on Wheels* published in 1949 by Stanford University. While it did touch on the Overland Mail lines, its focus was on the firm of Russell, Majors, and Waddell, who had an extensive empire in stagecoaches, freighting, and the Pony Express.

After *The Overland Mail* was published, Hafen produced a three-volume history on Colorado, a biography of Thomas

Fitzpatrick, and nearly a dozen other books by the early 1950s that he either authored or edited. Between 1954 and 1961, Hafen and his wife Ann edited the fifteen volumes in the monumental *Far West and the Rockies Historical Series, 1820–1875*. During the 1960s and early 1970s, Hafen edited another classic, the ten-volume series, *The Mountain Men and the Fur Trade of the Far West*. He and Ann then wrote their joint autobiography which was published in 1973.

Before retiring from the Colorado Historical Society in the 1950s, Hafen was visiting professor at the University of Glasgow, Scotland, in 1947 and 1948, and he spent 1950 and 1951 doing research funded by a Rockefeller fellowship at the Henry E. Huntington Library at San Marino, California. After retiring from the Colorado Historical Society, Hafen and his wife moved to Utah, where he joined the faculty of Brigham Young University and taught until 1971.

Many of Hafen's later works were collaborations with his first wife, Ann Woodbury Hafen. After her death in 1970, Hafen, as she wished, married her sister, Mary Woodbury. LeRoy Reuben Hafen died at age 91 on March 8, 1985, at his winter home in Palm Desert, California. The publication of this reprint edition is long overdue and gives persons interested in its content an opportunity to own a copy of the book at a fraction of the cost of the scarce first edition.

David Dary

Preface

The permanent settlement of the Trans-mississippi region had hardly begun before the question of regular communication between the older and the newer regions was raised. Then when the frontier of settlement was thrust suddenly to the Pacific Coast, leaving the intervening section largely unoccupied, the problem of communication was proportionately increased. The postal service became an important political agency binding the western pioneer to his government and his home in the East.

The ocean steamer was the first agency of regular communication with the Pacific Coast. But much of the emigration went overland and people came to look more and more favorably upon the land routes as avenues for mail service. Pioneer monthly mails were projected to the inter-mountain region at the beginning of the fifties, and toward the end of the decade, through lines were established. Competition immediately ensued to determine what course these lines should take. The mail stage was looked upon as the precursor of the railroad and a promoter of settlement; hence, the concern manifested as to whether the stage-coach should follow a northern or a southern route.

Another question that attracted the attention of Congress was whether the Post Office Department should be strictly self-supporting, or whether, in its western lines especially, it should act as a pioneering agency, leading the emigration, encouraging settlement, and making safe the routes of travel. Each side had its vigorous advocates, and the governmental attitude was not always consistent; but in general, the liberal policy prevailed. The growth and extension of the overland mail service is a reflection of the conquest of the West. In tracing this topic one encounters most of the agencies of frontier expansion and sees at work the processes of empire building.

The packhorse and the stage-coach were but temporary expedients in the western mail service, as the railroad age had hardly begun. But in the growth of the West they played their part, humble and transient though it was. Along with the buffalo and the wild Indian the overland stage has gone, but for the history of the fifties and sixties it will remain as one of the typical and significant institutions of the Trans-mississippi West.

In this study my chief reliance has been upon the government documents and the newspapers of the period; but very valuable assistance was also derived from the personal narratives of travelers and from accounts given by participants in the scenes described. To Professor Herbert E. Bolton the writer wishes to acknowledge his indebtedness for aid and encouragement given. To my wife, also, much credit is due for assistance at all stages of the study.

Chapter I

Establishment and Early Development of the Postal Service

The story of the extension of the postal service into the Trans-mississippi region and to the Pacific Coast would come rather late in a general chronicle of the development and extension of the postal service in English North America. In such a larger story considerable space would be devoted to colonial beginnings and to the first half century of our national history. For our present purposes, however, a brief survey of this earlier period must suffice.

The English colonies in America were founded independently, and their early dealings were with the mother country rather than with each other. The first postal facilities were trading vessels. No post offices existed during the early years, but gradually certain taverns came to be employed to fill the need. In 1639 the General Court of Massachusetts issued an ordinance directing that all letters arriving at Boston from beyond seas, or those intended for transmission thither, should be taken to Richard Fairbanks's Tavern.[1] This, perhaps, is the official beginning of a postal system in the colonies.

The first step towards a domestic post connecting the several colonies was taken in 1672, when Governor

---

[1] See William Smith's "Colonial Post Office" in *American Historical Review*, vol. xxi, 258. These data are given as coming from Massachusetts Historical Society, *Collections*, third series, vol. vii, 48. Fairbanks was authorized to charge a penny for each letter delivered.

Lovelace of New York decreed that a post should go monthly between New York and Boston.[2] It was not successful.[3] Other attempts were made to establish postal facilities before 1691, but nothing of an enduring nature resulted.

The real beginning of postal service in the English colonies was made when King William III granted a patent to Thomas Neale, empowering him to establish a postal service between the colonies, and to open post offices in the chief places. This patent had a duration of twenty-one years and gave Neale the exclusive privilege of letter conveyance throughout the British possessions in North America. Neale appointed Andrew Hamilton as his deputy in America. Hamilton was a man of energy and ability. He prepared a bill and was successful in getting its essential features enacted by the Colonial legislatures. These colonial acts fixed the postage rates, which varied from colony to colony; and also appropriated money in payment for the conveyance of public letters. Maryland and Virginia did not join with the northern colonies in establishing this service. The line of posts established by Hamilton extended from Portsmouth, New Hampshire, to Philadelphia, and the mails were carried over it weekly each way.[4]

In 1698 Hamilton returned to England and reported to Neale. The total expense had been 3,817 pounds and the revenue but 1,457 pounds. However, the bus-

---

[2] Roper, Daniel C. *United States Post Office*, 17. See also Channing, E. *History of United States*, vol. ii, 474.

[3] Bayles, W. "Postal Service in the Thirteen Colonies," in *Journal of American History*, vol. v, 430.

[4] Smith, W., in *American Historical Review*, vol. xxi, 261-266. Neale paid only a nominal sum of six shillings and eight pence for his Patent. See also Rich, W. E. *History of United States Post Office to Year 1829*, pp. 12-22.

ESTABLISHMENT OF POSTAL SERVICE

iness was improving. Neale relinquished his postal service and assigned his rights to Andrew Hamilton and a Mr. West. Hamilton died in 1705, and was succeeded by his son, John Hamilton, who operated the system until 1707, when the British government paid him 1,664 pounds and took over the Colonial Post.[5]

In 1710 Parliament passed a comprehensive post office act which, for the first time, included the colonies. The whole system throughout the empire was placed under the direction of the Postmaster-general of England, who appointed deputies for the different colonies. Postal rates were fixed by this act, and were no longer left to the decision of the several colonies. One purpose of the act was to raise revenue to help defray the expenses of the War of the Spanish Succession, so there was a general augmentation of the rates.[6]

For a time an undistinguished line of Postmasters-general administered the postal system,[7] and there was but little development during the period, 1711 to 1753. In this latter year Benjamin Franklin was appointed jointly with William Hunter as deputy Postmaster-general. Franklin improved the service and put it on a paying basis. Although the American post office had ceased to be a burden upon the Treasury in 1721, it was not until 1764 that the first surplus was transmitted to London.[8] Thereafter it was an annual occurrence.

---

[5] Roper, Daniel C. *United States Post Office*, 24

[6] Smith, W., in *American Historical Review*, vol. xxi, 268. The charge on a letter from New York to Philadelphia was raised from 4½ to 9 pence, that from Boston to Philadelphia from 15 to 21 pence. Overseas postage was raised from two pence to a shilling.

[7] Roper, *op. cit.*, 25. J. Hamilton was continued by the Crown as deputy Postmaster-general until 1721, when he was replaced by John Lloyd of South Carolina. He was succeeded by Alexander Spotswood in 1730. Head Lynch occupied the office, 1739-1743, and Elliot Benger, 1743-1753.

[8] Smith, *op. cit.*, 270.

Franklin says that the net revenues of the British post office from 1754 to 1773 amounted to about 250,000 pounds, of which about 3,000 pounds a year was contributed by the American posts.[9]

It was during the first part of the eighteenth century that wheeled vehicles began to come into general use in America.[10] During the seventeenth century the horse and rider had been the postal carrier.[11] Now, big awkward wagons came to be used for transportation of freight and passengers. Their wheels had tires from six to ten inches wide, made of hard wood or thin iron. These famous Conestoga wagons introduced between 1750 and 1760[12] were to remain in persistent use for over a century, and as the "prairie schooner," to form the caravans to the Pacific. During the second half of the eighteenth century the stage-coach service was inaugurated and soon it replaced the post-rider on all the more important routes.[13]

The earliest stages that made through trips from Boston to New York were more than a week on the way. Washington was twelve days in going from Philadelphia to Boston in 1775 to assume command of the Continental Army.[14] When Mercereau's stage-wagon

---

[9] Franklin, B. *Autobiography*, edited by Bigelow, vol. i, 241.

[10] Dunbar, Seymour. *History of Travel in America*, vol. i, 179. Many of the two-wheeled carts used throughout the colonies at an early day had wheels that were sections sawed bodily from a round tree trunk. See p. 176.

[11] These post-riders often made a business of hiring horses for travelers to ride, and in the earlier years acted as guides to travelers. They often took horses or oxen from place to place and performed other commissions. When approaching a post office or inn the rider blew his horn. See account of ride of Mrs. Knight from New York to Boston in the year 1704, by Bayles in *Journal of American History*, vol. v, 442.

[12] Dunbar, S., *op. cit.*, vol. i, 204.

[13] Bayles, W., in *Journal of American History*, vol. v, 455. Facsimile of a stage-coach advertisement.

[14] Dunbar, Seymour. *History of Travel in America*, vol. i, 187.

in 1771 reduced the time between Philadelphia and New York to a day and a half, it was advertised as the flying machine.[15] But even after the introduction of wagons, a predominant part of the land traffic of the country, except on the highways connecting the principal cities, was carried throughout the eighteenth century by packhorses.[16]

A survey of the postal service in the colonies can be extracted from the Journal of Hugh Finlay, surveyor of Post Roads in the colonies in 1773.[17] The most frequent service was from New York to Philadelphia, running tri-weekly; from Philadelphia to Suffolk, North Carolina, trips were made weekly; from Suffolk to Charleston, fortnightly; and from the latter city to Savannah and Saint Augustine, monthly service only was maintained.

As the friction which was to precipitate the Revolution increased between the colonies and the mother country, the Royal postal system felt the ill effects. In 1774 the Committees of Correspondence began to suggest the establishment of an independent postal system, since they were distrustful of, and antagonistic towards the existing system.[18] The Continental Congress took up the question in May, 1775, and a committee, of which Franklin was the leading member, was directed to make a report.[19]

With the report of the committee before it, the Congress resolved, on July 26, 1775, to appoint a Postmas-

---

[15] — *Idem*, vol. i, 174.

[16] — *Idem*, vol. i, 194. The packhorse men were often strongly opposed to road building, as that would result in the replacement of their packhorse trains.

[17] Journal published by Frank H. Norton, Brooklyn, 1867. Finlay succeeded Benjamin Franklin who was dismissed January 31, 1774.

[18] Smith, *op. cit.*, 274.

[19] *Journals of Continental Congress*, vol. ii, 71.

ter-general for the united colonies, with headquarters at Philadelphia. Benjamin Franklin received the appointment. A line of posts was to be established from Falmouth (Portland) to Savannah, with as many cross posts as the Postmaster-general thought desirable.[20]

The Royal postal system decreased in favor until it became practically inoperative in 1775. On Christmas day of this year the New York post office gave notice of the suspension of the inland service.[21]

In the conduct of the war an improved postal service was much needed. To aid rapid communication Congress resolved in August, 1776, that a rider be employed for every twenty or thirty miles on the post roads, and that the mail go tri-weekly, going night and day with the greatest dispatch. Some towns kept special riders in readiness to convey important messages. Additional riders were employed between Philadelphia and the headquarters of the army. But despite these efforts the irregularity of the posts was the cause of much complaint.[22] However, feeble and imperfect as the service was, it was, nevertheless, a great aid to the cause of independence and was a prominent factor in the promotion of union among the colonies.

The Articles of Confederation provided that "The United States in Congress assembled shall (also) have the sole and exclusive right and power of . . . establishing and regulating post offices from one State to another, throughout all the United States, and exacting such postage on the papers passing through the same as may be requisite to defray the expenses of said office."[23]

---

[20] *Laws of United States from 1789 to 1815*, vol. i, 649.
[21] Force, Peter. *American Archives*, fourth series, vol. iv, 453.
[22] Bayles, *op. cit.*, vol. v, 458.
[23] *Articles of Confederation*, Art. ix. The law passed by Congress October 18, 1782, fixed the postage rates on single or four-ounce letters as follows:

The activity of this federal post office was limited to inter-state mails. Under this restricted authority and in the disordered condition of the country little improvement was made in postal facilities before the adoption of the Constitution.[24]

The Constitution gave Congress power "to establish post offices and post-roads."[25] During those first years when the strict and loose construction views as to the proper interpretation of the Constitution were in conflict, this clause played its part in the controversy. Did "establish" mean to *make* or merely to *select*? Liberal construction prevailed. In 1792 a post road was established between Richmond, Virginia, and Danville, Kentucky, and federal money was spent to put it in fit condition.[26] Government aid has been employed to a greater or less degree ever since.

During the first three sessions of Congress no postal legislation was passed except brief temporary measures continuing in effect the law of October 18, 1782.[27] But on February 20, 1792, a more adequate law was enacted.[28] It established and enumerated the post roads; provided the death penalty for robbing the mails; defined the powers and duties of the Postmaster-general, and fixed his salary at $2,000; fixed the rates of postage; and provided in general for the conduct of the service.

". . . in pennyweights and grains of silver . . . For any distance not exceeding sixty miles, one pennyweight eight grains; upwards of sixty and not exceeding one hundred, two pennyweight; upwards of one hundred and not exceeding two hundred, two pennyweight sixteen grains, and so on, sixteen grains advance for every hundred miles . . ."

[24] Roper, *op. cit.*, 39.
[25] U. S. *Constitution*, Article i, section 8.
[26] Roper, *op. cit.*, 94.
[27] U. S. *Statutes at Large*, i, 70, 178, 218.
[28] — *Idem*, i, 232.

Samuel Osgood of Massachusetts was appointed by President Washington as the first Postmaster-general under the Constitution.[29] He was not a member of the cabinet and his report was submitted to the Secretary of the Treasury. It was not until 1829, when William T. Barry was appointed to the office by President Jackson that the Postmaster-general became a cabinet officer.

There is perhaps no better register of the growth of our country than the record of the expansion of the postal service. The opening of a post office in some remote section of the West is proof sufficient of the presence of the pioneer. The establishment of a post road is the official marking of the pioneer trail.

During the period immediately following the Revolution, when the "Shadow of Europe"[30] was cast heavily upon the Trans-allegheny country, the postal service was a political as well as an economic necessity. With Spanish, English, and French intrigues working for alienation; with a feeling often present among the pioneers that the West was being ignored or sacrificed for the sea-board colonies, a real political menace was evident. The National Government was cognizant of this situation and early directed its attention to the needs of the West. The success of the Union, it was generally understood, would in some measure depend upon the diffusion of information throughout the land. President Washington in his address to Congress in

---

[29] U. S. Senate. *Executive Documents*, 32d congress, first session, no. 1, vol. ii, p. 423. Thirteen other persons occupied the office before 1849. Of this number three were from Kentucky; two each from Connecticut, Ohio, and New York; and one each from Pennsylvania, Georgia, Tennessee, and Vermont.

[30] An expression used by Professor Herbert E. Bolton in his lectures on the History of the Americas.

ESTABLISHMENT OF POSTAL SERVICE 27

1791 referred to the "instrumentality (of the posts) in diffusing a knowledge of the laws and proceedings of the Government," [31] and advocated the establishment of additional cross posts to the western section of the Union. Congressmen also, were inclined to be liberal in dealing with the West, and while in general they wanted the post office establishment to be self-supporting they preferred extension of service to a surplus for the general treasury. They did not expect all western routes to pay for the cost of operation, but looked for ultimate reimbursement in terms other than postal receipts.[32]

The early postal legislation fixed low rates for newspapers and provided for the free exchange of papers among all editors and publishers. The dissemination of news and the rise of a local press, it was believed, would have a patriotic, nationalizing effect.

The admission of newspapers to the mails had an important influence upon the mode of transportation. Horseback service soon became inadequate upon the principal routes across the mountains; stage carriage and the improvement of highways were the inevitable results. In 1806 and 1807 coach service was established in Ohio, Kentucky, and Tennessee, and rendered a valuable assistance in the development of this western country.

An express service was authorized by Congress in 1836.[33] This was to expedite the transmission of news and was to be introduced upon the principal post roads

---

[31] Richardson, J. D. *Compilation of Messages and Papers of Presidents, 1789-1897*, vol. i, 107.

[32] Bretz, J. P. "Some Aspects of Postal Extension into the West," in American Historical Association *Report*, 1909, p. 145. Also, Rich, *History of United States Post Office*, 71.

[33] U. S. *Statutes at Large*, vol. v, 80.

at the discretion of the Postmaster-general. The express mails were to consist of newspaper slips, stock quotations, letters at triple rates of postage, and public dispatches. The carriage was to be on horseback at the rate of eleven to twelve miles an hour, night and day, with the briefest possible pauses. Such service was installed to Saint Louis, New Orleans, and Nashville during 1836 and 1837 and reduced the usual time of transmitting intelligence by about one-half.[34] This was the last notable improvement in postal service to the interior before the coming of the railroads.

At the beginning the Post Office Department was intended to be, and was, self-supporting. Until 1838, with slight exceptions, there was an excess of receipts over expenditures. During the next eight years there was usually a slight deficit.[35] This was due to the high cost of railway and stage-coach service; to the high rates of postage which limited correspondence by mail; and to the operation of numerous private expresses which, in spite of the law, carried letters and papers outside of the mails. The postage revenue per capita declined from twenty-six cents in 1837 to twenty-two cents in 1845.

The postal rates on land fixed by the general law of 1792 were as follows: for single letters going under thirty miles, six cents; between thirty and sixty miles, eight cents; between sixty and one hundred miles, ten cents; between one hundred and one hundred fifty miles, twelve and one-half cents; between one hundred fifty and two hundred miles, fifteen cents; between two hundred and two hundred fifty miles, seventeen cents;

---

[34] Bretz, *op. cit.*, 148.

[35] U. S. Senate. *Executive Documents*, 32d congress, first session, no. 1, vol. ii, 448. (Serial 612.)

between two hundred fifty and three hundred fifty miles, twenty cents; between three hundred fifty and four hundred fifty miles, twenty-two cents; and over four hundred fifty miles, twenty-five cents.[36] Newspapers were to circulate free among publishers; while to subscribers, the rate was one cent when sent under one hundred miles, and one and one-half cents when going beyond that distance.

These rates continued practically unaltered until 1814, when fifty per cent was added as a war revenue measure.[37] This war measure was repealed by the act of February 1, 1816, and the old rates, approximately, were restored by the law of April 9, 1816.[38] The general act regulating the Post Office Department, enacted in 1825, continued the rates of 1816.[39] With these high charges in effect, many letters were sent by private expresses.

Agitation began for cheaper postage. England in 1840 adopted a uniform two-cent rate for half ounce letters throughout England and Ireland. The success of this cheap postage policy gave impetus to the movement in the United States. The Postmaster-general, Wickliffe, recommended a moderate reduction and legislatures passed resolutions instructing their congressmen to adopt measures for reduction. The agitation culminated in the passage of the act of March 3, 1845.[40] It provided that half-ounce letters going under three hundred miles should pay five cents, over three hundred miles, ten cents; and that an additional rate should be

---

[36] U. S. *Statutes at Large*, vol. i, 235.
[37] — *Idem*, vol. iii, 159.
[38] — *Idem*, vol. iii, 252, 264.
[39] — *Idem*, vol. iv, 105.
[40] — *Idem*, vol. v, 733. This act appropriated $750,000 to make up the deficit anticipated by the postage reduction.

collected for every additional half-ounce. Newspapers of no greater size than 1,900 square inches could be sent by the publisher within a radius of thirty miles free of postage. Those going beyond thirty and under one hundred miles were to pay one cent postage; and those going more than one hundred miles, one and one-half cents.

When postal service with the Pacific Coast was established in 1847, the rate was fixed at forty cents "to or from Astoria, or any other place on the Pacific Coast, within the territory of the United States." [41] This year, also marks the adoption of the postage stamp by the United States government.

The reduced postage inaugurated in 1845 had a stimulating effect upon the correspondence of the country. Although there was a temporary deficit the department was on a self-supporting basis by 1848. This was in part due to economies effected in the transportation of the mails,[42] but in large measure was the result of increased correspondence encouraged by cheap postage. The success which attended the operation of the law of 1845 caused agitation for further reduction. Cheap postage associations were formed, and Congress, during the session of 1849-50 was beset with petitions and memorials. They came from four state legislatures,

---

[41] — *Idem*, vol. ix, 200. Act creating post routes, and for other purposes, approved March 3, 1847. This act also authorizes the Postmaster-general to prepare postage stamps and provides a penalty for forgery of these stamps.

[42] Section 18 of the act of 1845 required the Postmaster-general to accept the lowest bid which in his judgment secured the requisite certainty, security, and celerity in the transportation of the mail. Previously, extensive service was maintained on certain routes for the convenience of passengers rather than for the transportation of the mail only. Under this new rule, the cost of transportation was reduced from $2,905,504 in 1845, to $2,577,407 in 1849; although the extent of the mail routes was increased during the same period from 143,940 to 167,603 miles. – Postmaster-general's *Report*, 1851, in U. S. Senate. *Executive Documents*, 32d congress, first session, no. 1, 430.

from faculties of ten colleges and universities, from chambers of commerce, banks, and hundreds of citizens.[43] It was stated during the discussion in Congress that while ten cents was the postage on a letter from Detroit to Buffalo, a barrel of flour was carried between the two cities on the same conveyance (by steamboat) for the same compensation.[44]

The cheap postage advocates were successful and the act passed by Congress March 3, 1851, made a further postal reduction. It provided that half ounce letters going less than three thousand miles should be charged three cents and those over three thousand miles, six cents.[45] This reduction from five and ten cents to three cents applied to practically all of the domestic letters. It introduced a decided postal deficit which together with other causes, ushered in an era of postal deficits that continued for more than sixty years.[46] The authors of the law recognized that a deficit would result, but they did not purpose to have that fact retard the extension and development of the system. The act declared that "no post office now in existence shall be discontinued, nor shall the mail service on any mail route in

---

[43] McMaster, J. B. *A History of People of United States*, vol. viii, 113.

[44] Rhodes, J. F. *History of United States since Compromise of 1850*, vol. i, 216.

[45] U. S. *Statutes at Large*, vol. ix, 587. Section 2 provides that "newspapers published weekly only shall circulate in the mail free of postage within the county where published." Postage on weekly papers sent within fifty miles beyond the county was to be five cents per quarter; from fifty to three hundred miles, ten cents per quarter; from three hundred to one thousand miles, fifteen cents; from one thousand to two thousand miles, twenty cents; from two thousand to four thousand, twenty-five cents; and beyond four thousand miles, thirty cents per quarter (three months). Monthly newspapers were to pay one-fourth this amount; bi-weekly, one-half; semi-weekly, double; tri-weekly, treble; and those published oftener than tri-weekly were to pay five times the weekly rates.

[46] Roper, *op. cit.*, 67.

any of the States or Territories be discontinued or diminished in consequence of any diminution of the revenues that may result from this act; and it shall be the duty of the Postmaster-general to establish new post offices, and place the mail service on any new mail route established, in the same manner as though this act had not passed." [47]

The growth of the Post Office Department to this point is graphically shown by a table prepared by the Postmaster-general in 1851:

Year	No. of Post Offices	Length of Post Roads	Receipts	Expenditures
1790	75	1,875	37,935	32,140
1795	453	13,207	160,520	117,893
1800	903	20,817	280,804	213,994
1805	1,558	31,076	421,373	377,367
1810	2,300	36,406	551,684	495,969
1815	3,000	43,748	1,043,065	748,121
1820	4,500	72,492	1,111,927	1,160,926
1825	5,677	94,052	1,306,525	1,229,043
1830	8,450	115,176	1,919,300	1,959,109
1835	10,770	112,774	3,152,376	2,585,108
1840	13,468	155,739	4,543,521	4,718,235
1845	14,183	143,930	4,439,841	4,320,731
1850	18,417	178,672	5,499,984	5,212,953

This table is the skeleton outline of sixty years of remarkable growth. Seventy-five offices had multiplied to over eighteen thousand. The length of post roads had increased ninety-five fold. The Post Office Department was now (1851) a five million dollar business and was reaching the homes of about twenty-five million Americans.

During the next twenty years it was to continue its

---

[47] U. S. Senate. *Executive Documents*, 32d congress, first session, no. 1, vol. ii, 424.

work upon an even grander scale. It was to penetrate and serve the western half of our commonwealth. It was to be a promoter of settlement and a precursor of railroads through the Trans-mississippi region and to the Pacific Coast.

Chapter II

The Ocean Mail to the Pacific Coast
1848-1858

During the first decade following the acquisition of California by the United States, the great agency for intercourse between the eastern states and the Pacific Coast was the ocean steamer. Much emigration went overland, but for regular communication the ocean route was preferred.

Even before the Mexican War had given us California and the greater part of the inter-mountain region, the problem of regular communication with the Oregon country was presented to Congress. The joint occupation treaty with Great Britain in reference to the Oregon country was terminated in the summer of 1846, and we came into complete possession of the southern portion of that region.[48] President Polk, in a message to Congress August 5, 1846, recommending certain legislation for Oregon, said:

"It is important that mail facilities, so indispensable for the diffusion of information, and for binding together the different portions of our extended Confederacy, should be afforded to our citizens west of the Rocky Mountains."[49]

Accordingly, in January, 1847, Senator Niles of the Committee on Post Offices and Post Roads reported a

---

[48] The Convention with Great Britain was concluded June 15, 1846, and the ratifications were exchanged at London July 17, 1846. – U. S. *Congressional Globe,* 29th congress, first session, 1199.

[49] — *Idem,* 1199.

bill to provide for a mail to Oregon.[50] Such a mail was very much needed, he said, "the commerce with that territory employing five or six hundred vessels and forty thousand persons." [51]

The Post Route bill, enacted March 3, 1847, authorized the Postmaster-general to contract for the transportation of the mail from Charleston, South Carolina, to Chagres, across the Isthmus of Panama, and from thence to Astoria, Oregon, or the mouth of the Columbia River. The mail was to be transported each way once every two months, or oftener, but the expenditure was not to exceed $100,000 per annum.[52] The Postmaster-general made the usual advertisement for the service but reported in December of the same year that no acceptable bid had been received, and that most probably the service to Oregon would cost more than double the amount provided.[53]

While the measures mentioned above proved ineffectual, a practical plan was being evolved from another angle. The first mail service to the Pacific Coast was provided for by an act concerned primarily with naval development. The object of Congress was to build up a steam-marine, capable of conversion into warships in case of need. "An Act providing for the Building and Equipment of four naval steamships," [54] approved March 3, 1847, declared it to be the duty of the Secretary of the Navy to contract for the transportation of the United States Mail from New York to Chagres and back, twice a month. The mail was to be transported in at least five steamships of not less than

---

[50] U. S. *Congressional Globe*, 29th congress, second session, 183.
[51] — *Idem*, 480. The measure passed the Senate February 23, 1847.
[52] U. S. *Statutes at Large*, vol. ix, 200.
[53] Postmaster-general's *Report*, 1847.
[54] U. S. *Statutes at Large*, vol. ix, 187.

fifteen hundred tons burden and propelled by engines of not less than one thousand horse-power each, to be constructed under the superintendence of the Navy Department, in such a manner as to render them convertible, at the least possible expense, into war steamers of the first class. The steamships were to be commanded by officers of the United States Navy. The compensation for this service was not to exceed $290,000 per annum. The Secretary of the Navy was also to contract for the transportation of the mail from Panama to some port in the territory of Oregon, once a month each way. This mail was to be transported in either steam or sailing vessels, as should be deemed most practicable and expedient. The Navy Department was at all times to exercise control over these ships, and at any time have the right to take them for exclusive use and service to the United States upon making proper compensation to the contractors.

In conformity with the above law the Secretary of the Navy made a ten-year contract with A. G. Sloo of Ohio for transportation of the mail from New York to Chagres, and with Arnold Harris of Arkansas, for the service from Panama to Astoria.[55]

A. G. Sloo transferred his contract to George Law, Marshall O. Roberts, and Bowers McIlvaine of New York, September 3, 1847. The agreement with them provided that two of the steamships should be ready for service by October 1, 1848; and should a smaller vessel be permitted from Havana to Chagres (of 600 tons burden), then the two remaining vessels should be com-

---

[55] U. S. Senate. *Executive Documents*, 32d congress, first session, no. 50, vol. viii, p. 3. "Report of the Secretary of the Navy and the Postmaster-general, communicating in compliance with a resolution of the Senate, information in relation to the contracts for the transportation of the mails by steamships, between New York and California."

pleted by October 1, 1849. The steamships were not completed on time but a temporary arrangement was made whereby an inferior vessel, the *Falcon*, was accepted, and postal service was begun in December, 1848.[56]

The contractor for the Panama-to-Oregon mail transferred his contract to William H. Aspinwall of New York, November 19, 1847. The contract was to run for ten years from the first of October, 1848, and the service to be performed "in not less than three sea-steamers, two of which shall be of not less than one thousand tons burden, and the other of not less than six hundred tons burden."[57] The compensation for this monthly service was to be $199,000 per annum. Through Aspinwall's exertions the Pacific Mail Steamship Company was incorporated on the 12th of April, 1848, with a capital stock of $500,000.[58] The three vessels were built with dispatch, and on the 6th of October, 1848, the first of these, the *California*, sailed from New York for the Pacific Coast. Rumors of the discovery of gold in California had reached the eastern states but as yet had attracted little attention, and the *California* sailed away

---

[56] — *Idem*, 4, 5. The first steamship built and accepted under the contract was the *Georgia*, accepted January 26, 1850. The *Ohio* was at first rejected, but was later (January, 1851) accepted. The *Illinois* was accepted September, 1851. The Secretary of the Navy had been directed by the act of August 3, 1848, to advance to the contractors one year's pay to assist them in the completion of their ships. This amount was subsequently deducted from the compensation allowed them. Some doubt was entertained as to whether full pay should be given for the service before all five steamships were constructed, but since the Attorney-general was of the opinion that full compensation should be paid it was done accordingly.

[57] — *Idem*, 6.

[58] Bancroft, H. H. *History of California*, vol. vi, 129. The company had a remarkable growth. In 1850 the capital stock was increased to $2,000,000; in 1853 to $4,000,000; in 1865 to $10,000,000, and in 1866 to $20,000,000. This company closed its remarkable career in 1925.

carrying no passengers to the land of gold.[59] But upon reaching Callao, Peru, December 29th, the gold fever was encountered and the rush for passage began. The Isthmus of Panama was found to be fairly swarming with gold-seekers when the *California* arrived there January 30, 1849. With accommodations for little over a hundred people, the vessel took on board four hundred. "Many a one, glad to make his bed in a coil of rope, paid a higher fare than the state-room holder; for steerage tickets rose to very high prices, even, it is said, to $1,000 or more."[60] The scramble for passage was even fiercer upon the *Oregon* and the *Panama* in March and May.

After a voyage of four weeks the *California* entered San Francisco Bay February 28, 1849. The reception was cordial, all was excitement. The siren call of gold carried all hands from the ship except the engineer, and prevented the making of the return voyage. When the *Oregon* arrived her captain anchored the vessel under the guns of a man-of-war and arrested the most rebellious of the crew. "The refractory sailors were kept in irons until they submitted to accept an increase of pay from $12 to $112 per month."[61] Consequently, the *Oregon* was able to make its return trip April 12th, and thus carried the first eastbound mail in conformity with the contract. Hereafter, these three steamships with occasional extra vessels, continued to make their trips with fair regularity.[62]

In March, 1851, Congress authorized an increase in

---

[59] — *Idem*, 129. The *California* was the third steamship to thread the Straits of Magellan, having been preceded in 1840 by the *Peru* and the *Chili*, built by an English company.

[60] — *Idem*, 134.

[61] — *Idem*, 137, footnote.

[62] U. S. Senate. *Executive Documents*, 32d congress, first session, no. 50,

the Pacific Coast mail service to a semi-monthly schedule, and a seventy-five per cent increase in compensation was granted.[63] During the remainder of the ten-year term of the contract the service continued semi-monthly and the compensation was $348,250 per year.

The mail at first, was transported across the Isthmus of Panama by the New Granada Government under treaty of March 6, 1844.[64] Twelve cents per pound was allowed for this service.[65] Later, in conformity with the Naval Appropriation Act of March 3, 1851, the Postmaster-general made a temporary contract with the Panama Railroad Company (before the railroad was constructed), for transporting the mail across the Isthmus. This arrangement dates from December 1, 1851, and the compensation allowed was twenty-two cents per pound.[66] At first the mail was rather light, and was carried in canoes and by mules. As the weight increased the cost to the government grew in proportion. Although the annual compensation had increased from $40,387 in 1851 to $119,727 in 1854,[67] no attempt was made to reduce the rate until the Panama railroad was completed in January, 1855.[68] Inasmuch as the charge for express freight on passenger trains was now fixed at ten cents per pound, the Postmaster-general attempted to get a more favorable rate for the mail transportation,

---

pp. 42-44. A table is here given of the sailings of these vessels during 1849-1850.

[63] U. S. *Statutes at Large*, vol. ix, 623.

[64] U. S. Senate. *Executive Documents*, 32d congress, first session, no. 50, p. 193.

[65] Postmaster-general's *Report*, 1850, p. 440. "Thirty dollars per trip for the first 100 pounds of each mail, and $12 for each succeeding 100 pounds."

[66] U. S. Senate. *Executive Documents*, 32d congress, first session, no. 50, p. 193.

[67] Postmaster-general's *Report*, 1856, p. 766.

[68] Bancroft, H. H. *History of California*, vol. vi, 139.

but the Company insisted upon the old rate of twenty-two cents.[69] With this rate the sum of $160,321 was paid during the year preceding April, 1857. But a new contract was now made wherein a straight rate of $100,000 per year for the Panama service was agreed upon.[70] This continued in effect until October, 1859.

After the first years, few passengers reached California by the route around South America, but various routes across Central America and Mexico were explored, and employed in competition with the one via Panama. Cornelius Vanderbilt and other American capitalists obtained concessions from Nicaragua during 1849-50, and established a transit company operating steamers between New York and California. For a time the Nicaragua route came to be a favorite, inasmuch as it offered better scenery and climate and shorter distance than did the Panama route.[71] The Nicaragua Steamship line advertised in 1855 as follows:

"Through ahead of the mails! Only twelve miles land carriage. Macadamized road. Shortest and quickest route. . . this route 700 miles shorter than any other. The trip through to New York is generally made in less than 21 days." [72]

But since the route was hampered by the disturbed condition of Nicaragua and was at a disadvantage in having no mail contract or government subsidy,[73] the line

---

[69] U. S. Senate. *Executive Documents*, 34th congress, third session, no. 5, p. 767. The Postmaster-general ordered that 18 cents per pound be paid, but the company refused to carry the mail unless the old rate was restored and the Postmaster-general was forced to submit.

[70] Postmaster-general's *Report*, 1857, p. 968.

[71] Bancroft, *History of California*, vol. vi, 140.

[72] San Francisco *Bulletin*, November 2, 1855.

[73] Vanderbilt made an offer to carry the United States mail between New

did not persist. A number of other opposition lines sprang up from time to time, but they were usually forced out or bought out by the Pacific Mail Steamship Company.

In February, 1853, a conditional contract was made for a semi-monthly mail service from New Orleans to San Francisco by way of the Isthmus of Tehuantepec.[74] The contract was made upon the condition that Congress would appropriate the $424,000 per year called for by the contract. The incoming Postmaster-general, Mr. Campbell, disapproved of the proposition and did not order service on the route, and as Congress did not appropriate the necessary funds, the line was not established.[75] This shorter route, therefore, was not put into use until 1858, even though the United States had been given rights over the Isthmus of Tehuantepec by the Gadsden Treaty of December 30, 1853.[76]

The ocean mail service to the Pacific Coast, begun in

York and California for $300,000 per year. – Postmaster-general's *Report*, 1854.

[74] U. S. Senate. *Executive Documents*, 34th congress, third session, no. 5, p. 806 (serial 876). The contract is here given in full.

[75] The contractors, Carmick and Ramsey, went to considerable expense to equip the line and were greatly disappointed and financially involved when the contract did not materialize. They presented their case to Congress and a law was passed August 18, 1856, requiring the Comptroller of the Treasury to adjust the damages due them. The Attorney-general advised that their contract had not been abrogated, had never gone into effect, and therefore there was nothing due them. A long document (221 pages) gives the history of the case and all the papers and correspondence involved. This is found in U. S. House. *Executive Documents*, 35th congress, second session, no. 30.

[76] One section of this treaty with Mexico provides: "The United States, by its agents shall have the right to transport across the Isthmus (of Tehuantepec) in closed bags the mails of the United States not intended for distribution along the line of communication; also the effects of the United States government and its citizens, which may be intended for transit, and not for distribution on the isthmus, free of custom-house or other charges by the Mexican government. Neither passports nor letters of security will be required of persons crossing the isthmus and not remaining in the country."

the latter part of 1848, continued in operation during the ten succeeding years. It was the great link connecting the gold seekers and pioneers with relatives and friends in the "States." The semi-monthly arrival and departure of the mail steamship was an occasion of importance. Preparations were made days in advance for "Steamer Day" – the day of the mail steamer's *departure*. A fortnightly summary of news was condensed in the "Steamer Papers" for transmission eastward. The mercantile class exerted itself to collect debts and make proper remittances. At the wharf strutted coarsely-clad miners – some, girdled with well-filled belts, their complacent faces turned eastward; others, soured by disappointment, looked haggard and dejected.[77]

The *coming* of the mail steamer was for most people, undoubtedly, a more important occasion. Its approach was announced by the hoisting of a large black ball on Telegraph Hill in San Francisco.[78] Upon its arrival, reporters of the various journals who had previously gone out to meet the vessel hurried from the wharf with their budget of news for the press.[79] "Extras" were immediately published, while the month-old eastern newspapers sold readily for a dollar apiece.[80] To obtain letters, positions were taken in the long line before the delivery window of the post office. The line began to form the day or night before receipt of the mail and late comers often purchased front positions from men

---

[77] Bancroft, *History of California*, vol. vi, 236.

[78] Communication by signal was had between Telegraph Hill and Fort Point and Point Lobos. – Bancroft, *Chronicles of the Builders of the Commonwealth*, vol. v, 363.

[79] Kuykendall, R. S. *History of Early California Journalism*, 94. (M.A. thesis, University of California.)

[80] Bancroft, *History of California*, vol. vi, 235.

and boys who made a business of coming early to hold a place that would subsequently demand a good price. This long line of expectant faces, this drawn-out agony of suspense, the strong demonstrations of joy or of sorrow upon receipt of the long-delayed news from loved ones – are dramatic pictures of the days when the mail service was the only connecting link between the East and the West, the old home and the new.

The first postage rate to the Pacific Coast, that provided by the act of March 3, 1847, was forty cents for single letters.[81] With the general reductions of postage in 1851 the rate to California was reduced to six cents.[82] This was raised in 1855 to ten cents,[83] and remained at that rate until 1863.

The amount of mail sent by the ocean steamers gradually increased during the period under consideration. The first steamers in 1849 brought about six thousand letters and a large newspaper mail. The number increased to thirty thousand letters in November, and throughout 1850 this was the average monthly mail. The Sacramento *Placer Times* of April 29, 1850, says that the steamer *Panama* on her preceding trip to San Francisco brought upwards of ninety five mail sacks, each containing an average of two bushels of letters, and other mailable matter. In July, 1852, sixty thousand letters were carried on the *Oregon*.[84] The Postmaster-general reported in 1859 that 2,006,662 letters and 3,914,868 newspapers were carried in the California mail by ocean steamer during the preceding year.[85]

The mail from New York to San Francisco was

---
[81] U. S. *Statutes at Large*, vol. ix, 200, 320.
[82] — *Idem*, 587.
[83] — *Idem*, vol. x, 641.
[84] Bancroft, *Chronicles of the Builders*, vol. v, 283, 287.
[85] Postmaster-general's *Report*, 1859. (Serial 1025.)

usually about four weeks in transit. During the early fifties the average time taken was from twenty-six to thirty days.[86] Not much improvement in time was made during the first decade. On February 26, 1858, the steamer *Golden Age* arrived at San Francisco completing what was said to be the quickest passage yet made from New York — twenty-one days, two hours, and thirteen minutes from dock to wharf.[87]

The ocean mail service was not always praised. During the year 1849 and through the early fifties the rush was so great that over-crowding of the steamers was frequent, and dangers and abuses were the inevitable results. The legislature of Maine passed a resolution in 1852 requesting its representatives in Congress to secure legislation to prevent the abuses of excessive crowding, neglect of proper ventilation, unwholesome provisions, and the like, that were alleged to exist in the conveyance of passengers to California.[88] But despite the complaints against the ocean service, it was the quickest and easiest mode of reaching California during the decade following the gold discovery. The passenger and mail steamers usually carried a good complement of passengers. Horace Greeley, upon his visit to the Pacific Coast in 1859, gives the following as the official returns of arrivals at, and departures from San Francisco by water:[89]

Year	Arrivals	Departures
1849	91,415	no returns
1850	36,462	no returns

[86] Kuykendall, *History of Early California Journalism*, 96.
[87] San Francisco *Alta California*, February 27, 1858.
[88] U. S. Senate. *Miscellaneous Documents*, 32d congress, first session, no. 63.
[89] Greeley, Horace. *An Overland Journey from New York to San Francisco in the Summer of 1859*, 368.

Year	Arrivals	Departures
1851	27,182	no returns
1852	66,988	22,946
1853	33,232	30,001
1854	47,531	23,508
1855	29,198	22,898
1856	28,119	22,747
1857	22,990	16,902
Total	381,107	139,002

During this first decade there had been some competition with the governmentally subsidized line, but it was usually short-lived. In 1857 the Pacific Mail Steamship Company connecting with the Panama railroad and the United States Mail Steamship Company was looked upon as a gigantic monopoly making great profits, charging exorbitant prices and giving inferior accommodations to the public. The loss of the *Central America* September 12, 1857, increased the criticism. A mass meeting was held in San Francisco October 31st, to consider the *Central America* affair, and the principal recommendation was for a competitive route to break down the existing monopoly and bring about improved conditions. A San Francisco journal complains:

"The trouble is that there is no competition on the route. One line has the monopoly, therefore it can make what impositions it pleases upon the public. . . The present Company has an enormously lucrative mail contract. . . Let the contract be divided, and be given to two independent lines. . . If Vanderbilt had not been bought off, he would now have a line through somewhere, in operation." [90]

---

[90] San Francisco *Bulletin*, November 2, 1857. See also the issues of October 21, 23, 24, 1857; November 2, 1857, and December 10, 1857.

This attitude towards the ocean service was a very potent factor in the movement which came to demand overland mail service as the only escape from the exactions on the ocean route.

Chapter III

Pioneer Monthly Mails to the Inter-mountain Region, 1849-1858

The overland route to the Pacific Coast was ever the competitor of the one by ocean. Although in the early years the Government looked upon the land route as impracticable for through postal service, maintaining that the ocean steamer had speed and convenience in its favor, still much emigration continued over land. To the frontiersman of the Mississippi valley the "prairie schooner" was the natural and logical vehicle for transportation. Emigrants from this region who turned their faces westward, naturally used the facilities previously employed by their fathers or by themselves in reaching the then existing frontier. The big Conestoga (Santa Fé) wagons cut the trail to Oregon, and carried the Mormons to Utah. Their dusty-white covers dotted the gold-seekers' trails to California in 1849. But the overland route was long and the journey hard. Broken wagons, discarded equipment, and bleached bones marked the trails; and a trail so marked did not look inviting. There were in this early period, however, some who advocated the overland route for mail, passenger, and express transportation, but they did not meet with encouragement. Therefore during the early fifties, regular government mail service by the overland routes was established to the inter-mountain region only.

But private enterprise was more venturesome. On January 15, 1848, an advertisement in the *California*

Star announced a letter express by land to Independence, Missouri. Letters were to be charged fifty cents and newspapers twelve cents. Agents were appointed in various California towns to receive mail and express matter. An express was sent in April but the gold excitement terminated the service.[91] Another enterprise was begun when some Saint Louis men, inspired by the great migration to California of 1849, undertook to establish an overland mail and passenger line. A single trip with one hundred twenty passengers was made, but as the difficulties encountered were greater than anticipated, a second journey was not undertaken.[92] Toward the close of 1849 the "Great Salt Lake Carrying Company" was organized by S. Roundy, J. M. Grant, and others, at Salt Lake City. Its object was to freight goods from the Missouri River, and to convey passengers to the gold regions. The through fare for passengers to Sutter's Fort was $300, and goods were carried at the rate of $250 per ton.[93]

Heretofore, under Mexican rule, California had depended for mail service upon the irregular arrival of supply vessels and couriers, and the convenience of the commandants. The United States military authorities improved upon this by the establishment of a regular service between their posts, which was open to the public; and by sending occasional messengers to Washington City. April 17, 1848, the military authorities dispatched "Kit" Carson with the first United States mail ever carried overland from the Pacific to the Atlantic.[94]

---

[91] Bancroft, H. H. *Chronicles of the Builders*, vol. v, 281.
[92] —*Idem*, 293.
[93] Whitney, O. F. *History of Utah*, vol. i, 418.
[94] Bancroft, H. H. *History of California*, vol. vii, 143. Governor Kearny established a semi-monthly government express between San Francisco and San Diego beginning April 19, 1847. It was carried by two soldiers on horse-

PIONEER MAILS TO INTER-MOUNTAIN REGION 55

The act of August 14, 1848, directed the Postmaster-general to establish post offices at San Diego, Monterey, San Francisco, etc., and made the postage rate 12½ cents within the state, and 40 cents to the Atlantic Coast.[95] In accordance with this act William Van Voorlies was appointed agent and arrived in San Francisco on board the *California* on her first trip out, in February, 1849.[96]

Although most of the early overland enterprises were promoted by private companies, at least one rather comprehensive project was proposed and considered in Congress. William Bayard presented a memorial to Congress that was referred to the Committee on Post Offices and Post Roads. He proposed to construct a post road from Fort Smith, Arkansas to San Diego, "to open and grade a road eighteen feet wide; to put twenty men and sixty horses on every thirty miles of the road; to have relays at every ten or fifteen miles, with fifty armed men at each relay through the Apache country for the protection of passengers and travelers; to carry the mail each way in four-horse coaches; to commence the service within six months after date of contract; and at the end of fifteen years, to let the road and bridges revert to the government without charge; provided, the government would pay him annually $750,000; give him the right to use government timber, stone, etc., for the road; exact tolls enough to keep it in

---

back, starting on alternate Mondays, and meeting at Dana's rancho where they exchanged mails. – Bancroft, *Chronicles of the Builders*, vol. v, 281.

[95] U. S. *Statutes at Large*, vol. ix, 320.

[96] Bancroft, *Chronicles of the Builders*, vol. v, 282. With the gold excitement on, it was with difficulty that persons were induced to assume the burdens of the office of postmaster; and, with the prevailing high prices, but meagre mail facilities could be afforded. The miners, however, were willing to pay for efficient service, and express companies soon arose to supply the insufficiency of the government service.

repair; and to have the pre-emption right, at ten cents the acre, of four sections of land along the road for every thirty miles of the road." [97] The committee called upon M. F. Maury for an opinion in reference to the project. He expressed himself (April, 1850) as favoring the project, and considered it feasible. The committee after further deliberation, reported in favor of the proposition March 3, 1851, together with a bill (H. R. no. 492). Nothing, however, seems to have come of the proposition.

Although the government was not ready to launch a big transcontinental mail project, there were intermediate regions that must be supplied. New Mexico already had a considerable population when it was transferred to the United States in 1848. The Mormons began the settlement of the Great Basin in 1847, and the influx of immigrants was rapid. These areas began immediately to call for postal facilities.

INDEPENDENCE TO SALT LAKE CITY

During the first three years following the settlement of Salt Lake valley by the Mormons in 1847, the means of communication with the outside world were entirely of a private nature. The first letters from the region were carried eastward by Ezra Benson in August, 1847.[98] Emigrant trains and occasional private expresses were now the only facilities for mail transportation. In the winter of 1849 the Federal Government established a post office at Salt Lake City and appointed J. L. Heywood postmaster. A bi-monthly mail was authorized between Council Bluffs and the Mormon city, and Almond W. Babbitt was engaged to carry

---

[97] U. S. House. *Reports*, 31st congress, second session, no. 95, 3.
[98] Young, L. E. *The Founding of Utah*, 393.

the mail at his own expense.[99] But such a provision was not very fruitful of results and we find that on March 3, 1849, "it was resolved (in a council of the brethren) that Allen Compton should take charge of a mail for Winter Quarters (Nebraska Territory) on the 20th of March, or as soon thereafter as practicable." [100]

It was in 1850 that the first arrangements were made by the United States Post Office Department to provide postal facilities to Utah. A contract was made with Samuel H. Woodson of Independence, Missouri, for the transportation of the mail from the Missouri River to Salt Lake City, monthly each way, for $19,500 per year.[101] The service was to begin July 1, 1850, and to continue for four years. This pioneer mail followed the "Oregon Trail" up the Platte and through South Pass. There were no mail stations maintained by the contractor at first. One team or set of pack animals was used to make the entire trip, and the time allowed for the service one way was thirty days. Due to various difficulties the trip was seldom made in schedule time. The news of the passage by Congress September 9, 1850, of the bill establishing the Territory of Utah reached Salt Lake City by the eastern mail on October 15, 1850.[102] The mail of November 9th, "had passed through snow from one to three feet deep for seventeen days," and the mail going east on the 22nd of November was preceded for some distance by four men sent out by Brigham Young to break the road.[103]

[99] — *Idem*, 395.
[100] *Early Utah Records*, 50. (MS. in Bancroft Library, University of California.)
[101] Root and Connelley, *The Overland Stage to California*, 1. Little, F. *Mail Service Across the Plains*, 1. (Bancroft MS.)
[102] *Early Utah Records*, 115.
[103] — *Idem*, 116.

In July, 1851, Woodson contracted with Feramorz Little of Salt Lake City, to carry the mail between that city and Fort Laramie on the upper Platte for $8,000 per year.[104] The mails from each end of the line were to meet and be exchanged at this intermediate point on the fifteenth of each month. There was then no settlement between Salt Lake City and Laramie; and Fort Bridger, one hundred ten miles east of Salt Lake City, was the only trading post on the route.[105]

The experience of Mr. Little is typical of that of many carriers during this early period of staging. On his first trip east, he and Mr. Hanks, his assistant, reached Fort Laramie in nine days, but his animals were not fit for the return trip, so he obtained five wild Mexican mules from a rancher near Laramie. These notorious animals made his homeward journey quite exciting:

"Four of the mules were thrown down, bound with lariats, blinded and the harness put on them. By a similar process Mr. Hanks put a saddle on the fifth one. When everything was in readiness Mr. Little got into the wagon and took up the lines and Mr. Hanks mounted his mule. The blinds were removed and a lively performance commenced. . . The saddle mule was guilty of all the antics that a wild Mexican mule is considered capable of performing under such circumstances. Those on the wagon ran, bucked, kicked over the traces, and over the tongue of the wagon and back again. The mail and luggage danced about in a general jumble, and some of the provisions were thrown out. Chances had to be taken, for there was no stopping for anything. Mr. Little managed to keep his seat and

---

[104] — *Idem*, 130.
[105] Little, *Mail Service Across the Plains*, 1.

also to keep the animals in, or near, the road. The animals had things pretty much their own way for seven or eight miles over the Black Hills, when they became somewhat slower and a little more manageable. . . They made a successful day's drive with the new outfit. At night the wild animals were secured with lariats and given such limited opportunities to feed as would insure safety." [106]

Upon the October trip his best mules strayed or were stolen, and for that reason his progress was so impeded that provisions gave out, and he and his companion had to subsist for five days on parched corn.[107]

It is not surprising that under such an insufficient contract the Utah mail was very irregular and rather unreliable during the early fifties. Governor Young of Utah, writing to the Utah delegate in Congress, February 28, 1852, says: "So little confidence have we in the present mail arrangements that we feel considerable dubiety of your receiving this or any other communication from us." [108] Again, in his message to the Utah legislature, December 12, 1853, he complains that the mail "contracts heretofore would never justify extra expense, consequently the contractor's feeble attempts, of course, prove fruitless, and we have been left without a solitary mail for over half a year at a time." [109]

Undoubtedly, the service at all seasons was poor at best, but it was practically suspended during the winter months. This condition resulted despite heroic efforts made by the carriers. In the winter of 1852-3, Little and his Indian companion had great difficulty in reach-

---
[106] — *Idem*, 5.
[107] — *Idem*, 21.
[108] *Incidents in Utah History*, 7. (Bancroft MS.)
[109] Whitney, *History of Utah*, vol. i, 490.

ing Salt Lake City with the November mail from Fort Laramie. They were lost for several days about South Pass, and struggled through the snow for over a month. Unable to reach the valley over the ice of Weber River, they finally left their horses, cached the bulk of the mail, and continued on foot, dragging the letter-mail over the snow of the Wasatch mountains for forty miles to Salt Lake City.[110] The December mail had started eastward and westward from that city but was forced to return because of the snow.[111] When spring opened, the carriage of the letter mail was resumed, but according to the *Deseret News* of June 18, 1853, there were twenty-four heavy bags of mail matter which had been cached en route during the preceding eight months when transit had been impossible because of snow, rain, or high water.

In 1854, W. M. F. Magraw became the new contractor upon the route from Independence to Salt Lake City. The service, as before, was monthly each way, and the contract price was $14,440 per year. The mail was to be carried in four-horse coaches, going through in thirty days.[112] During the first year, Indian difficulties occasioned considerable loss to the contractor. Magraw presented his case and condition to the Committee on Post Offices and Post Roads of the Senate; and Senator Rusk, Chairman of the committee, recommended that, in view of the changed conditions which had brought unexpected losses upon the contractor, the annual compensation be raised to $36,000 for the year

---

[110] *Incidents in Utah History*, 21. Little, *Mail Service Across the Plains*, 23.
[111] *Incidents in Utah History*, 19.
[112] U. S. House. *Executive Documents*, 34th congress, first session, no. 122, 335. (Mail contracts.)

ending August 7, 1855.[113] This accordingly was done by the act of March 3, 1855.[114]

The following year Magraw presented a similar claim and the increased compensation was continued for another year by Congress. In this act for the relief of Magraw, enacted in May, 1856, a sum of $17,750 was voted as full indemnity for the property stolen or destroyed by the Indians, and the contract was to be annulled from and after August 18, 1856; and furthermore, the Postmaster-general was authorized to advertize for a new contract.

Under the advertisement of May 31, 1856, Hiram Kimball, of Utah, was found to be the lowest bidder, and accordingly a contract was entered into with him October 9, 1856. The service was to continue monthly with carriages or wagons, and the compensation was to be $23,000 per annum.[115] Kimball was the agent of the Mormon leaders who had plans for the building up of a great carrying company. Even before this mail contract was obtained these leaders, led by Brigham Young, had planned to establish a great express line from the Missouri River to the Pacific Coast. As early as February, 1856, a meeting was held in the Salt Lake Tabernacle to launch the movement. Speeches were made by several prominent men of the Territory; and Governor Young, at the close of his remarks proffered to take stock, and equip three hundred miles of the route.[116] Inasmuch as Brigham Young had at his back

---

[113] U. S. *Congressional Globe*, 33d congress, second session, appendix, 272.

[114] U. S. *Statutes at Large*, vol. x, 684.

[115] U. S. House. *Executive Documents*, 35th congress, first session, no. 96, 353. (Serial no. 957.)

[116] Hayes *Collection*, (Bancroft Library, University of California). A Los Angeles paper gets this information from the *Deseret News* (Salt Lake City).

an entire community vitally concerned in the enterprise, there was no man or group of men better prepared or situated to undertake the successful establishment of a great express and freighting concern.

With the Kimball contract as an aid the plans materialized rapidly, but the winter of 1856-7 was exceptionally severe and work on the line was halted. Only one mail went east from Salt Lake City. The carriers, Little and Hanks, started eastward December 10, 1856, but did not reach Independence, Missouri, until February 27th.[117] Early in the spring, however, companies were organized with outfitting teams, farming tools, etc., to form settlements at intervals along the line.[118] Such settlements would form sources of supplies as well as stage stations; would protect the route, and insure success of the undertaking. The Mormons had a heavy immigration coming in from abroad at this time, by hand-cart and by ox-team, and these stations and settlements would serve a useful purpose in aiding this migration. In an incredibly short time, stations were built and relays of horses and mules provided along the line.

But the enterprise so promisingly begun was destined to an early and abrupt close. By mid-summer the mail contract was annulled and an army was on its way to Utah.[119] This peculiar episode and the motives that prompted it are not a part of the present story. However, jealousy over the mail contract played a part in precipitating the "Utah War." Magraw, the previous mail contractor on the route from Missouri to Salt Lake

---

[117] Little, *Mail Service Across the Plains.*
[118] Tullidge, *History of Salt Lake City,* 150.
[119] U. S. House. *Executive Documents,* 35th congress, first session, no. 96, 353. The service was performed by Hiram Kimball from February 7 to June 30, 1857.

City, was one of the principal persons petitioning the President to intervene in Utah affairs.[120] The approach of "Johnston's Army" cut off communication with Utah during the fall and winter of 1857-8. When the postal service was resumed, S. B. Miles was the new contractor. He was to carry the mail over the route on pack mules in winter and in coaches in summer for $32,000 per year.[121] Such was the condition of the service in 1858 when the general improvement policy was applied to this route along with all other western mail lines.

CALIFORNIA TO SALT LAKE CITY

The first United States mail between California and Salt Lake City was established in 1851. This route was advertised January 27, 1851, and the thirty-seven bids received ranged from $20,000 for "horseback or two-horse coach service," to $200,000 per year for service with "135 pack animals with 45 men, divided into three parties." One bid was for a four-horse coach with a guard of six men, at $135,000 per year. The lowest bid was accepted and a contract was made in April with Absalom Woodward and George Chorpenning for a monthly service at $14,000 per year;[122] the trip each way was to be made in thirty days. No points were designated at which the route should touch, but it was to go "by the then traveled trail, considered about 910 miles long."[123]

---

[120] Magraw's letter to President Buchanan dated October 3, 1856, is quoted in Whitney, *History of Utah*, vol. i, 574.

[121] U. S. House. *Executive Documents*, 35th congress, first session, no. 96, 353.

[122] U. S. House. *Executive Documents*, 32d congress, first session, no. 56, 398, 399.

[123] Chorpenning, George. *Statement of the Claim of George Chorpenning against the United States*, 2.

Chorpenning and his men left Sacramento May 1, 1851, with the first mail. They had great difficulty in reaching Carson valley, having had to beat down the snow with wooden mauls to open a trail for their animals over the Sierras. For sixteen days and nights they struggled through and camped upon deep snow.[124] Upon reaching Carson valley, Chorpenning staked off in the usual western manner, a quarter section of land and arranged to establish a mail station. The town of Genoa, Nevada, grew-up on this site. Chorpenning and several men continued eastward and reached Salt Lake City June 5th, having been delayed somewhat by snow in the Goose Creek mountains.[125]

Throughout the summer, difficulties were experienced with the Indians; and Woodward, who left Sacramento with the November mail, was killed by them just west of Malad River in northern Utah. The December and January mails from Sacramento were forced to return on account of deep snow, but the February (1852) mail was pushed through by way of the Feather River Pass and reached Salt Lake City in sixty days. The carriers endured frightful sufferings; owing to the fact that their horses were frozen to death in the Goose Creek mountains, they had to go the last two hundred miles to Salt Lake City on foot.[126] Permission was obtained from the special agent in San Francisco to send the March mail down the coast to San Pedro and thence by the Cajon Pass and the Mormon trail to Salt Lake City. During the summer of 1852 the service continued to be performed across northern Nevada by way of the Humboldt River; but

---
[124] — *Idem*, 4.
[125] *Early Utah Records*, 127.
[126] Chorpenning, *Statement*, 7.

as winter approached, arrangements were made with the mail agent at San Francisco to carry the Utah mail via Los Angeles during the winter months. The Carson valley post office was supplied monthly by a carrier on snow-shoes.[127] Fred Bishop and Dritt were the first carriers and they were succeeded by George Pierce and John A. Thompson. The latter, "Snowshoe Thompson," a Norwegian by birth, made himself famous in this section by his feats on snow-shoes during succeeding winters. The shoes used were ten feet long and of the Canadian pattern.[128] He often took one hundred pounds upon the journey between Placerville and Carson, and made the trip in three days to Placerville and the return journey in two days.[129]

With the interruption by bad weather of the mail service east of Salt Lake City, the mail was sent westward to San Pedro, where it was transmitted by steamer to the Atlantic seaboard. This increased the weight of Chorpenning's mail from about one hundred pounds to about five hundred pounds.[130] For this additional service Chorpenning made claim and in 1857 received payment on a pro rata basis.[131]

The causes of the irregularity and interruption of the mail service to Utah had not been explained to the Postmaster-general by the Special Agent at San Francisco and so, upon the grounds of the derangement of the service, the Postmaster-general annulled the contract with Chorpenning, and made one with W. L. Blanchard of California. The new contractor was to receive $50,000 per year, and was to maintain a fortified post

---

[127] — *Idem*, 10.
[128] Bancroft, *History of Nevada*, 226, 227.
[129] Shinn, C. H. *The Story of the Mine*, 20.
[130] Chorpenning, *Statement*, 11.
[131] See note 138, below.

at Carson valley.¹³² Upon learning of this new arrangement in January, 1853, Chorpenning set out for Washington and, after setting forth his case before the new Postmaster-general, was reinstated. A verbal agreement was made that the compensation should be increased to $30,000 per year and permission was given to carry the mails via San Pedro during the winter months.¹³³

During the first three years (1851-4) the Utah-California mail was carried except in winter, by the old emigrant route. This route lay from Sacramento through Folsom, Placerville, along the old road through Strawberry and Hope valleys to Carson valley. From this point it led to the Humboldt, which stream was followed nearly to its source. Leaving the Humboldt the route led northeastward into southern Idaho in the vicinity of the Goose Creek mountains, and thence southeasterly around the north side of Great Salt Lake to Salt Lake City.

In the lettings of 1854, the Utah-California mail route was changed to run from Salt Lake City over the Mormon trail to San Diego.¹³⁴ Chorpenning was again

---

¹³² Chorpenning, *Statement*, Appendix, 8. Ben Holladay was one of the sureties of Blanchard. Blanchard was very much put out by the annulment of his contract and appealed to Congress for damages. The act of March 3, 1855, ordered an investigation to see if the contract had been violated and if so, the Comptroller of the Treasury was to adjust and pay the damages. A total of $22,916 was paid Blanchard under his contract. – U. S. Senate. *Executive Documents*, 41st congress, third session, no. 44.

¹³³ Chorpenning, *Statement*, 13.

¹³⁴ This was in general the route discovered and explored by Jedediah Smith in 1826 and again traversed by him in 1827. J. C. Fremont returned from California by this route in 1844. The Mormons used it much after 1847. Howard Egan made a journey over this trail in the winter of 1849-1850. His diary gives a good description of the route. – Egan, W. M., editor. *Pioneering the West, 1846-1878*, pp. 169-180.

The terminus on this mail route was changed from San Diego to San Pedro, November 13, 1854. – Chorpenning, *Statement*, Appendix, 7.

PIONEER MAILS TO INTER-MOUNTAIN REGION 67

the successful bidder. The mail was to be carried monthly each way, through in twenty-eight days, for a compensation of $12,500 per year.[135] Chorpenning thought it worth while to enter a low bid to insure getting the contract, since he expected that the service would probably be increased to a weekly schedule, the time per trip reduced, and the compensation increased.[136]

The service began July 1, 1854, and was to continue for four years. The mail was carried on horseback or on packmules. During that first summer, Indian difficulties arose and continued at intervals for months. The emigration fell off and expenses on the route increased. Similar difficulties had been encountered by the contractors east of the Rocky Mountains, who appealed to Congress and received increased remuneration by the act of March 3, 1855. Encouraged by their success with Congress, and inasmuch as his difficulties continued, Chorpenning went to Washington and presented his claims in June, 1856. Congress responded with an act for his relief March 3, 1857.[137] It provided that the compensation be increased to $30,000 per year from July 1, 1853, to the termination of the contract in 1858; that the full contract pay be allowed during the suspension of the contract in the spring of 1853; and that the Postmaster-general make an additional allowance on a pro rata basis for the extra service performed prior to 1853.[138] A total of $109,072.95 was allowed and paid under the provisions of this act.

[135] U. S. House. *Executive Documents,* 33d congress, second session, no. 86, 711.
[136] Chorpenning, *Statement,* 15.
[137] U. S. *Statutes at Large,* vol. xi, 521.
[138] Chorpenning, *Statement,* 20. These allowances were made May 25, 1857, and November, 1857. The calculations made by the Postmaster-general

During the four years of the duration of the contract (until July 1, 1858), the mail was carried with fair regularity, and often in less than schedule time. The service was usually performed on horseback,[139] but a wagon was used occasionally. The mail of December, 1857, was taken from Salt Lake City to Los Angeles by wagon in twenty-six days,[140] while on horseback the trip often did not consume more than twenty days.[141]

Wells Fargo and Company, Adams and Company, and other express companies maintained express service on the line during this period (1854-8).[142] There was also much freighting and some emigrant travel over the road. The Mormon "State of Deseret" had included

---

in computing the extra pay to be allowed for carrying the Independence mail during winter months to the Pacific Coast, and for the service to Carson valley, were made with the $12,500 contract price as a basis. Chorpenning contended that $30,000 per year should have been the basis. He continued with his claims before succeeding Postmasters-general and Congresses. In July, 1870, Congress passed a joint resolution directing the Postmaster-general to adjust his claims under the law of March 3, 1857. Upon this claim and upon a subsequent claim for damages because of annulment of Chorpenning's third contract on June 5, 1860, the Postmaster-general awarded him damages to the extent of $443,010.60. However, just as the damages were to be paid, a resolution was passed in Congress deferring settlement and on February 5, 1871, a new resolution was passed repealing the one of July 15th previous. The damages were therefore not paid.

In the criminal case in St. Louis in 1858, evidence was brought out in Chorpenning's favor that tended to show that the claim was not the "barefaced fraud" that it had been heralded as, and that desire for revenge and for extortion had figured in preventing the payment of the damages as allowed by Postmaster-general Creswell in 1870. An extensive review and argument of the case was prepared in 1889, but I have found no award or record of payment upon the claim. However, by the joint resolution of June 29, 1866, Chorpenning, and Woodward's widow were paid $54,545 for property destroyed by the Indians on their route in 1851-6.

[139] Carvalho, S. N. *Incidents of Travel and Adventure in the Far West*, 175.

[140] San Francisco *Bulletin*, January 11, 1858.

[141] —*Idem*, July 31, 1856.

[142] Hayes *Collection* (Bancroft Library) R:47, 360, 363. Advertisements in Los Angeles papers in 1855.

the whole of this route with its terminus upon the Pacific Coast. A colony was planted by these pioneers at San Bernardino [143] in 1851 and considerable trade and intercourse was carried-on over this road.

The route was in general that of the present "Arrowhead Trail" automobile road. From Los Angeles the route led to San Bernardino, through Cajon Pass to the Mohave River, which was followed for fifty miles. From the Mohave River the route lay to the north to Bitter Springs, then turned eastward by Kingston Springs to Las Vegas, Nevada. From this famous resting station a dry stretch of sixty miles was crossed leading to the Muddy Creek. After crossing another "bench" the Virgin River [144] was reached, and this stream was followed to Beaver Dams, Arizona. Leaving the Virgin River the road crossed the "slope" and over a little mountain range to the Santa Clara Creek, which stream was followed to the vicinity of the famous Mountain Meadows. From Mountain Meadows the route led to Cedar City and thence almost due north through the Mormon settlements of Parowan, Beaver, Fillmore, Nephi, Payson, Provo, and Lehi to Salt Lake City.[145]

Before the termination of the contract on this route the policy of extensive increases in the western mail

---

[143] Most of the Mormons left San Bernardino in 1857 when Brigham Young called upon them to return to Salt Lake City because of the "Utah War" possibilities. Some of them subsequently returned to California.

[144] The Virgin is a branch of the Colorado. It was probably named for Thomas Virgin, a member of Jedediah Smith's band of trappers who were on this stream in 1827. Virgin was wounded by the Indians at the mouth of the Virgin River. – Dale, C. D. *The Ashley-Smith Explorations*, p. 188.

[145] W. T. B. Sanford, an old Santa Fe trader, living in Los Angeles in the fifties, gives the itinerary of a trip made over the route in 1855. The San Francisco *Bulletin* of January 22, 1858, gives an account of the route, as taken from a previous number of the Los Angeles *Star*. See also, map accompanying Chorpenning's *Statement*.

lines was inaugurated, and partisans of the "Central Route" via Salt Lake City and across northern Nevada were demanding service upon that more direct route to San Francisco. Accordingly, in 1858 this Los Angeles-to-Salt Lake City route was discontinued and the original route of 1851 was re-established and put upon an improved basis.

INDEPENDENCE TO SANTA FÉ

Following the Mexican War the overland trade from the Missouri River to Santa Fé, New Mexico, which had long been of very considerable importance, was given new impetus. The route "from Independence Missouri via Bent's Fort, to Santa Fé" was created a post route by the act of March 3, 1847,[146] and service was to be established upon it as soon as it could be done from the postal revenues arising therefrom. In 1849 a Mr. Haywood carried the mail between Independence and Santa Fé.[147] Emigrants and travelers usually joined with the mail carrier forming a party for protection. A regular monthly coach service was inaugurated July 1, 1850. The *Missouri Commonwealth* speaks in glowing terms of the undertaking:

"The stages are got up in elegant style and are each arranged to convey eight passengers. The bodies are beautifully painted, and made water-tight, with the view to using them as boats in ferrying the streams. The team consists of six mules to each coach. The mail is guarded by eight men armed as follows: Each man

---

[146] U. S. *Statutes at Large*, vol. ix, 194.

[147] Little Rock *Gazette*, July 26, 1849. Captain Buford left Santa Fe June 6, 1849, "with Mr. Haywood the Mail contractor." (Data furnished by Grant Foreman, Muskogee, Oklahoma.) The writer has been unable to find data upon the first mail contract to Santa Fe in the government documents available to him.

PIONEER MAILS TO INTER-MOUNTAIN REGION 71

has at his side, fastened in the stage, one of Colt's revolving rifles; in a holster below, one of Colt's long revolvers, and in his belt a small Colt's revolver, besides a hunting knife; so that these eight men are ready, in case of attack, to discharge one hundred and thirty-six shots without having to reload. . . From the looks of this escort we have no fears for the safety of the mails. . . Two of their stages will start from here the first of every month." [148]

The route followed was the already well established Santa Fé Trail, probably one of the finest natural roads to be found. Day after day, the wagons rolled across the open prairie country with no guide but the beaten track that lay ahead. From Independence the route lay a little south of west through Council Grove on the west branch of the Neosho River and to the Great Bend of the Arkansas. After following the Arkansas a short distance a "jornada" was crossed and the Cimarron or Lost River reached. A little beyond this the mesa country was entered that marked the western boundary of the plains. Within the one hundred ten miles between Fort Union (in the Moro River valley) and Santa Fé, the towns of Las Vegas, Tecalota, and San Jose, were passed.[149] W. W. H. Davis, United States District Attorney for New Mexico in the early fifties, gives this general description of the road over which he traveled in the mail wagon in 1853:[150]

"The distance from Independence to Santa Fé may be divided into three stages, The first, from the starting

---

[148] Quoted in Inman, *The Santa Fe Trail*, 145, 146.
[149] A detailed itinerary of the Santa Fe trail is given in Chittenden, H. M. *The History of the American Fur Trade of the Far West*, vol. ii, 535-543.
[150] Davis, W. W. H. *El Gringo; or New Mexico and her People*, 16. This book was written mainly from a diary kept by the author during a residence of two and one-half years in New Mexico, 1853-1856.

point to Council Grove, is about a hundred and fifty miles and passes through the country of the Shawnees, Caws, and other friendly Indians, and by the roadside is seen the occasional cabin of a frontier settler. The second stage is from Council Grove to Fort Union, some six hundred miles, which lies across the immense plains of the interior of the continent, and is roamed over by the Comanches, Apaches, Arrapahoes, Cheyenes, Pawnees, Kiowahs, and other Indian tribes, and is the home of immense herds of buffaloes and antelopes. The country is generally level, with an occasional roll, and bare of wood except the few cottonwood trees found along the streams. Throughout all this region, water is scarce. The third stage brings us to Santa Fé through a mountainous and partially settled country covered with a growth of inferior pine timber, and tolerably well watered."

During the early fifties the mail train consisted of from one to three wagons, each drawn by four or six mules. The train on which Davis went to Santa Fé in December, 1853, consisted of three wagons; one for mail, one for baggage and provisions, and one an ambulance for passengers. In addition to a driver for each team there were two outriders to hurry up the lagging animals. All told, the party numbered ten men, all well armed. The eastbound mail which they met on the road consisted of one wagon, in the charge of four men.[151]

Some oats and corn were carried, but the chief source of food for the animals was the grass along the road. At night the mules were tethered with a twenty-foot rope from the wagon and allowed to graze. There were no stations for exchange of animals during the

---
[151]—*Idem*, 15.

PIONEER MAILS TO INTER-MOUNTAIN REGION 73

early years. The fare of $150 included forty pounds of baggage and the meals on the way. At night, passengers slept in the wagons or made their beds under the stars, on the hard ground. The table was a rubber blanket or piece of wagon-cover spread on the ground. With the exception of fresh game, the fare was of very limited variety, but was such as the frontier traveler had become accustomed to.

In 1854 a new four-year contract was entered into with Jacob Hall at a compensation of $10,990. The service was to be in six-mule coaches, monthly each way, through in twenty-five days.[152] Indian difficulties increased and Hall appealed to Congress for protection and for damages for the losses sustained. By the Act of March 3, 1855, Congress increased his pay to $22,000 for the year beginning August 18, 1854.[153] The following year the increased compensation was again allowed by the Act of August 18, 1856, and continued throughout the remainder of the term of his contract. This increase was to be in full payment for losses sustained on account of Indian depredations or other disturbances.[154] The service continued upon this basis until 1858, when it was improved to a semi-monthly schedule. Hall was again the contractor and the compensation was $39,999 per year.[155]

SAN ANTONIO TO SANTA FÉ

There was another monthly mail line operating to Santa Fé in the early fifties, which was of considerable importance to the areas served. Better time was made

---

[152] U. S. House. *Executive Documents*, 33d congress, second session, no. 86, 318.
[153] U. S. *Statutes at Large*, vol. x, 684.
[154] — *Idem*, vol. xi, 95.
[155] U. S. House. *Executive Documents*, 35th congress, second session, vol. xi, no. 109, 426.

upon this line from San Antonio than upon the one from Missouri.[156]

The contract of 1854 provided for monthly service in two-horse coaches, through in twenty-five days. David Wasson contracted for this service April 22, 1854, at a compensation of $16,750,[157] but the contract was transferred to George H. Giddings March 13, 1855.[158] Indian depredations upon this line induced Giddings, along with other western mail contractors, to appeal to Congress for protection and for damages, or for increased compensation. The act of August 18, 1856, increased the annual compensation upon this line to $33,500, dating from August 18, 1855, and continuing to the end of his contract on June 30, 1858.

Edward F. Beale, the famous explorer and champion of the overland route by way of Santa Fe, records in his journal under date of July 7, 1857:

"We were passed on the road this morning by the monthly El Paso mail on its way up, by which I received, forwarded by some of my friends at San Antonio, a box about two feet square, for which the moderate charge of twenty dollars was made! The dangers of this road, however, justified any price for such matters. Scarcely a mile of it but has its story of Indian murder and plunder; in fact from El Paso to San Antonio is but one long battle ground." [159]

In 1858 a general improvement in the western mail lines took place. In October of this year the service on

---

[156] Davis, W. W. H. *El Gringo; or New Mexico and her People*, 272.

[157] U. S. House. *Executive Documents*, 33d congress, second session, no. 86, 714.

[158] U. S. House. *Executive Documents*, 34th congress, first session, no. 122, 400.

[159] Bonsal, S. *Edward Fitzgerald Beale, a pioneer in the Path of Empire, 1822-1903*.

this line was increased to a weekly schedule and was performed with six-mule coaches.[160]

---

[160] U. S. House. *Executive Documents,* 36th congress, first session, no. 86. "Mail route no. 12,851; T. F. Bowler, contractor; $16,250 per year for service from Santa Fe to El Paso."

Chapter IV

The Butterfield Overland Mail; the South in the Ascendency

For two decades before the establishment of the great Butterfield Overland Mail in 1858, there had been considerable agitation throughout the United States for an improved method of communication between the east and west coasts. Asa Whitney and others played a prominent part in the advocacy of a Pacific railroad, but during the forties the scheme gave little promise of immediate realization.

The early fifties saw the Pacific railroad project pushed with increased vigor. In the second session of the 32d Congress, (1852-3) the Senate gave more time and attention to this subject than to any other.[161] In January, 1853, Senator Gwin of California, introduced a bill to authorize the construction of a Pacific railroad. A trunk line was to run from San Francisco by way of Albuquerque and along the Red River. Numerous branches were provided for. In fact the bill was framed to satisfy the demands of all sections. The result was a proposition too extensive to be practicable. It was, as Senator Cass said, "too magnificent"[162] to get the necessary support, and the bill failed. However, the discussions had shown the need of more accurate information on the subject, and so the Army Appropriation bill of March, 1853, was amended to provide for

---

[161] Davis, J. P. *The Union Pacific Railway*, 44.
[162] U. S. *Congressional Globe*, 32d congress, second session, vol. xxvi, 285.

the survey of such routes as the Secretary of War should deem expedient.[163] Five corps of engineers were put into the field and five transcontinental routes were explored.[164]

By 1855 the reports of the explorations were before Congress, and it was evident that there were several practical routes. In January, 1855, Senator Douglas introduced a bill providing for the construction of three railroad lines to the Pacific. It passed the Senate by a close vote,[165] but failed in the House of Representatives. A contest which then ensued dissipated the support of the general proposition. There was a majority in each house of Congress in favor of the general project of a Pacific railroad, but slavery sectionalism had become so strong that the choice of a route was almost impossible. Added to this difficulty was the rivalry among various cities – New Orleans, Memphis, Saint Louis, Chicago – each of which desired to become the eastern terminus of the Pacific railroad.[166]

Even before the Pacific railroad question had become hopelessly involved in sectional controversy, western men had started the agitation for a daily overland mail. The Sacramento *Union* was vigorous in its advocacy of the proposition, other newspapers joined the chorus, and the governor and the legislature of California ex-

---

[163] — *Idem*, Appendix, 352.

[164] Albright, G. L. *Official Explorations for Pacific Railroads.*

[165] Passed the Senate February 19, 1855, by a vote of 24 to 21.

[166] That the organization of Kansas and Nebraska as territories in 1854 was largely the result of a struggle over the terminus and route of the Pacific railway has been shown by F. H. Hodder. See "The Railroad Background of the Kansas-Nebraska Act" in *Mississippi Valley Historical Review*, vol. xii, 3-22. A good brief discussion of the political struggle relating to the railroad question and selection of route is presented by Robert R. Russell in "The Pacific Railway Issue in Politics prior to the Civil War," in *Mississippi Valley Historical Review*, vol. xii, 187-201.

erted their influence in behalf of the movement.[167] Agitation for wagon road construction accompanied the overland mail demand and the movement culminated in a monster petition to Congress signed by 75,000 Californians. During the middle of April, 1856, this giant memorial was bound in two splendid volumes and sent by the steamer to the national capital.[168] Some of the fruits of this labor were seen presently in the Congressional appropriations for Pacific wagon roads. In July, 1856, $50,000 was appropriated for construction of a road from Fort Ridgley, Minnesota Territory, to the South Pass.[169] In the following February a more pretentious measure was enacted. It appropriated $300,000 for construction of a road from Fort Kearny via South Pass to the eastern boundary of California; $200,000 for the road from El Paso, Texas, to Fort Yuma on the Colorado River; and $50,000 for a road from Fort Defiance, New Mexico, to the Colorado River near the mouth of the Mohave.[170]

The people of California were not alone in their interest in overland communication; those in Missouri being almost equally concerned. In February, 1855, the General Assembly of Missouri passed an act incorporating the "Missouri and California Overland Mail and Transportation Company."[171] A capital stock of three million dollars was authorized and the issuance of bonds permitted.

---

[167] Sacramento *Union*, September 18, 1854; January 9, 1855; February 8, 1855.
[168] San Francisco *Bulletin*, April 15, 1856.
[169] U. S. *Statutes at Large*, vol. xi, 27.
[170] — *Idem*, vol. xi, 162.
[171] The data upon this project is obtained from a pamphlet (28 pages) containing the charter, memorial and address of this company. Use of this pamphlet was had through the kindness of Miss Stella M. Drumm of the Missouri Historical Society.

The corporators of the above company met at St. Louis on January 14, 1856, to organize and to prepare for the subscription of stock. A committee was appointed to memorialize Congress and to write a report upon the project and its advantages. Colonel William Gilpin, a western enthusiast who had been with Fremont to Oregon in 1843 and who was to become the first governor of Colorado, prepared these addresses. In his own grandiloquent style he set forth the necessity and desirability of such a means of transportation and communication across the continent as was contemplated by the company. Congress was called upon to grant them "the necessary right of way to construct roads; to donate a reasonable amount of public lands for the same purpose; to give them such military protection as may be necessary; and such compensation for the transportation of the government mails and stores as may be just."[172] The large expenditure for ocean mails was alluded to and an appeal made for consideration of the inland states and of the overland route. Alternate sections of land on each side of the road, a military police to guard the mails and stations, and a ten year mail contract at a compensation not exceeding $300 per mile per annum was asked of Congress.[173] Grand as was the scheme it made slight impression upon Congress. No law was passed in compliance with the company's request and the project seems never to have got beyond the promotion stage.

But in the meantime the struggle for an overland mail went on in Congress. In March, 1855, Senator Benton attached to the General Post Roads bill a clause calling for a mail route between St. Louis and San

---
[172] — *Idem*, 5.
[173] — *Idem*, 15.

THE BUTTERFIELD OVERLAND MAIL

Francisco, "by the mouth of the Huerfano and the Little Salt Lake to Stockton on the San Joaquin." This was the route explored by his son-in-law, Fremont, in 1853. It had also been traversed by Lieutenant Beale and in part by Captain Gunnison a few months before "the Pathfinder" journeyed over it. Benton was convinced that this was to be the route of the Pacific railroad. The overland mail, he said, "will give the Central route a development, a notoriety and a prominence which will protect its character and bear down all opposition. . . The post route and the branches are a skeleton of the future railroad." [174] Senator Weller of California also tried to get an overland mail bill through Congress in 1855, but the time was not yet ripe.

During February, March, and April, 1856, four separate bills were introduced providing for an overland mail to San Francisco.[175] Finally in August, near the close of the session, Senator Weller introduced an amendment to the annual Post Office Appropriation bill providing for a semi-weekly mail service between the Missouri River and San Francisco. The mail was to be carried in four-horse coaches within a nineteen day schedule, and the compensation was not to exceed $500,000 per annum.[176]

The advocates of the amendment asserted that the railroad surveys had given assurance that the overland coach service was practicable; that the appropriations for wagon roads had created a sort of moral obligation

---

[174] Quoted by Curtis Nettels in "The Overland Mail Issue during the Fifties," *Missouri Historical Review*, vol. xviii, 523.

[175] U. S. *Congressional Globe*, 34th congress, first session. On February 14, 1856, Mr. Weller, of California, introduced an overland mail bill. Subsequent bills were presented March 2nd, March 25th, and April 17th, by Messrs. Herbert, Phelps, and Kennett, respectively.

[176] U. S. *Congressional Globe*, 34th congress, first session, Part iii, 2201.

to put coaches upon them; and that since eastern congressmen had adequate means of communication with their constituents, the best possible facilities should be afforded to all. The opponents questioned the practicability of carrying the mail at the price stipulated, and argued, that by the amendment, the legislative branch of government was intruding upon the prerogatives of the executive department. The amendment was adopted by the Senate but rejected in the House, and subsequently was lost in a Conference Committee.[177]

Having so nearly succeeded in August, 1856, the advocates of the overland mail were spurred to vigorous action in the short session beginning in December. Several bills were introduced and referred to the Committee on Post Offices and Post Roads. Under the able chairmanship of Senator Rusk of Texas, the Senate Committee gave full consideration to the proposals, consulted experienced western mail contractors, and earnestly endeavored to frame a bill that would be practicable and acceptable. Finally the bill was framed and again attached in the form of amendments to the annual Post Office Appropriation bill.

Compared with the bill of the preceding session, this one offered higher remuneration and also extended the time for making the trip. The framers intended to permit a fairly liberal contract, as an inducement to responsible bidders; for the government had had considerable experience with contractors who had bid too little and then had come to Congress for an extra allowance. Profiting from the experience with the Pacific railroad bills which had been defeated through sectional conflicts, the framers of this measure left undetermined the route and the eastern terminus.

---
[177] — *Idem*, 2225.

When the bill came up in the Senate on February 27th, it evoked considerable debate. Opponents of the measure pointed to the already heavy expense for the ocean mail to California and strongly advised against a further increase. Mr. Crittenden of Kentucky, argued for the principle that the Post Office Department should be as nearly self-supporting as possible. "Wait until your line can go a little further towards supporting itself. . . It is out of season, out of time, inappropriate, extravagant, exaggerated in the highest degree. . . Here is one route established by sea (to California) at a cost of nearly one million dollars, and then there is a land communication to Salt Lake City from the western part of Missouri and from Salt Lake City to Sacramento. . . You have then, perhaps, $1,300,000 now of annual expense in carrying the mail to California. . . The question is whether you will add to it $600,000 or $300,000 more." [178]

In reply to the economy argument, Senators spoke of the full treasury and prospects of ultimate repayment. Mr. Johnson, of Arkansas, said: "It is almost impossible to tell when we shall ever succeed in obtaining an overland communication through our own territory with the Pacific Ocean. I imagine, however, that there never was a time in our history when this government was so well able to make an effort towards the accomplishment of that object as now. The discussions on the tariff bill yesterday demonstrated the fact that there are millions in the treasury not only for the purpose of making what is certainly a fair and reasonable experiment, but millions that we do not know what to do with." [179]

---

[178] U. S. *Congressional Globe*, 34th congress, third session, Appendix, 313.
[179] — *Idem*, 310.

Supporters of the measure denounced the ocean mail service and the Panama railroad as gigantic monopolies that could be broken only by the establishment of this competitive route. "How can we ever supersede the steamships unless we have a mail across the continent?" asked Senator Gwin of California. "We are entirely at the mercy of a steamship company – a gigantic monopoly." Senator Rusk said: "We have a simple proposition before us – it is whether you will continue a contract for a mail, twice a month, across the Isthmus of Panama at $900,000 a year, or whether you will make an experiment to see whether you can get the mail service performed twice a week through your own territory for $600,000 a year." [180] He was, of course, winking at the fact that this was to be a *letter* mail only and that the ocean service would still continue.

The supporters of the measure had objects in view other than merely the transportation of the mail to California. Senator Weller admitted: "I confess that I not only desire to have this mail route but what I regard as equally important, I desire to have a good emigrant route. I believe, by the establishment of a mail route with little posts every ten miles you will have in fact military posts all along that road. In this way you will give protection to your emigrants. That is what I am after. . . This I regard as vastly important to the future interest of your possession on the Pacific." One cannot advise a family "to go overland at the present time, because of hostile tribes of Indians in the way, and the unprotected condition of the road. But give us the mail route, let us establish little posts at every ten miles and then" the emigration will be

---
[180] — *Idem*, 315.

safe. The argument was also advanced that rapid communication with the Pacific Coast would bind that region to the Union and prevent the possibility of the future establishment of a separate nation beyond the Sierras.[181]

When finally the vote was taken, the Senate registered twenty-four for, and ten against the amendment.[182] The House failed to agree, so a Committee of Conference was named.[183] The Conference Committee recommended the amendments providing for the overland mail line; Congress accepted their report, and, on March 3, 1857, the Post Office Appropriation bill became law. The amendments relating to the overland mail read:

"SEC. 10. And be it further enacted, That the Postmaster-general be, and he is hereby, authorized to contract for the conveyance of the entire letter mail from such point on the Mississippi River as the contractors may select, to San Francisco, in the State of California, for six years, at a cost not exceeding $300,000 per annum for semi-monthly, $450,000 for weekly, or $600,000 for semi-weekly, at the option of the Postmaster-general.

"SEC. 11. And be it further enacted, That the contract shall require the service to be performed with good four-horse coaches or spring wagons, suitable for

---

[181] — *Idem*, pp. 308-312. Mr. Benjamin of Louisiana; Mr. Broadhead of Pennsylvania.

[182] — *Idem*, 321. Those voting "Yea" were: Messrs. Benjamin, Bigler, Collamer, Douglas, Durkee, Fish, Fitch, Fott, Foster, Green, Gwin, Harlan, Houston, Johnson, Jones of Iowa, Nourse, Pratt, Rusk, Seward, Slidell, Stuart, Thomson of New Jersey, Weller, and Wilson.

Those voting "Nay" were: Messrs. Biggs, Clay, Crittenden, Hunter, Jones of Tennessee, Mason, Reid, Thompson of Kentucky, Toombs, and Yulee.

[183] The Conference Committee consisted of Messrs. Gwin, Rusk, and Collamer of the Senate; and Davis, Mace, and Denver of the House.

the conveyance of passengers, as well as the safety and security of the mails.

"SEC. 12. And be it further enacted, That the contractors shall have the right of preemption to three hundred and twenty acres of any land not then disposed of or reserved, at each point necessary for a station, not to be nearer than ten miles from each other; and provided that no mineral land shall thus be preempted.

"SEC. 13. And be it further enacted, That the said service shall be performed within twenty-five days for each trip; and that before entering into such contract, the Postmaster-general shall be satisfied of the ability and disposition of the parties bonafide and in good faith to perform the said contract, and shall require good and sufficient security for the performance of the same; the service to commence within twelve months after signing the contract." [184]

The Post Office Department on the 20th of April, 1857, advertised for bids to perform the overland mail service provided for in the above act. Bidders were to name the starting point on the Mississippi River and the intermediate points proposed to be embraced in the route. Separate proposals were invited for semi-monthly, weekly, and semi-weekly trips. Nine bids were received. Three of these proposed routes from Memphis west through Arizona and New Mexico to Southern California and thence north to San Francisco. One bid by John Butterfield and others, proposed this southern route with Saint Louis as the point of beginning, and in another bid the same parties proposed a forked line from Saint Louis and from Memphis, converging at some point east of Albuquerque. Two bids did not indicate the route, but proposed beginning at

---

[184] U. S. *Statutes at Large*, vol. xi, 190.

Saint Louis and at Gaines's Landing respectively. One proposal named the route via Salt Lake City. Another proposed this route in the main, with a detour north of Salt Lake City by way of Soda Springs, Idaho. Still another proposed a more northern route, from Saint Paul, by way of Fort Ridgely, South Pass, Humboldt River and Noble's Pass to San Francisco.[185]

The law clearly stated that the contractors should select the route, but the Postmaster-general's power to select the contractors gave him in reality the choice of route. Postmaster-general Brown was from Tennessee and was strong in his Southern sympathies. He consulted with other Southern leaders and soon the rumor was out that a southern route was to be chosen. Against such a possibility protests were made during the spring and summer of 1857.[186] But despite these protests and in violation of the stipulation in the law, Brown proceeded to select the following route: "from St. Louis, Missouri, and from Memphis, Tennessee, converging at Little Rock, Arkansas; thence, via Preston, Texas, or as nearly so as may be found advisable, to the best point of crossing the Rio Grande, above El Paso, and not far from Fort Fillmore; thence, along the new road being opened and constructed under the direction of the Secretary of the Interior, to Fort Yuma, California; thence, through the best passes and along the best valleys for safe and expeditious staging, to San Francisco."[187] No bid had been received for this particular route, but all the bidders agreed that their respective bids might be held and considered as applying to it. The Postmaster-general, "looking at the respective bid-

---

[185] Postmaster-general's *Report*, 1857, pp. 987-988. In U. S. Senate. *Executive Documents*, 35th congress, first session, no. 11. (Ser. 921.)

[186] Sacramento *Union*, April 16, 1857; July 3, 1857.

[187] Postmaster-general's *Report*, 1857, p. 990.

ders, both as to the amount proposed and the ability, qualifications, and experience of the bidders to carry out a great mail service like this," [188] ordered that the proposal of John Butterfield, William B. Dinsmore, William G. Fargo, James V. P. Gardner, Marcus L. Kinyon, Alexander Holland, and Hamilton Spencer, for a semi-weekly mail at $600,000 per year be accepted. Accordingly, on September 16, 1857, a six-year contract was entered into with Butterfield and his associates. The service was to begin September 15, 1858.

Much criticism naturally arose from the selection of the southern route. A more northern route was followed by most of the emigration, and many had expected that the route by way of Salt Lake City would be chosen. As an answer to this criticism the Postmaster-general in his Annual Report of December, 1857, set forth the reasons which induced a preference for the route selected. He said that the repeated failures of the mail to and from Salt Lake City to cross the mountains because of deep snow "put that route entirely out of the question." Next he maintained that the Albuquerque route also was too cold to insure certainty and regularity for the service, and especially would not afford the desired safety and comfort for the passengers. The minimum and maximum temperatures recorded by the War Department at Albuquerque since 1849, together with the observations of explorers and travelers, he contended, proved that the climatic conditions on this route were unsatisfactory.

The superiority of the El Paso route, especially for winter travel was then set forth. "The Department supposed Congress to be in search of a route that could

---

[188] — *Idem*, 988.

be found safe, comfortable, and certain during every season of the year, as well for the transportation of the mails as for the accommodation of emigrants and the future location of a railroad to the Pacific." In substantiation of the desirability of the southern course he cited that Captain Marcy, who had explored both routes, and Commissioners Emory and Bartlett, Lieutenant Parke, and A. H. Campbell, at the head of the Pacific Wagon Road Office, Interior Department, who had gone over the two routes in 1853, 1854, and 1855 – all expressed a decided preference for the one via El Paso.[189] Further, the fact was cited that Congress had appropriated $200,000 to be expended in the construction of a wagon road between the Rio Grande and Fort Yuma. Then the Postmaster-general continued:

"As the pioneer route for the first great railroad that may be constructed to the Pacific, the Postmaster-general has bestowed upon it all the labor and examination possible. He contends that since the railroads have not concentrated at one point on the Mississippi, this pioneer mail line should point the way by choosing some point west of that river at which the future railroads might concentrate and from which point the line to the Pacific could be projected. . . Thus it is that we have found *west* of the Mississippi what we could not obtain *on it* – a common concentration of railroads to a single point from which the future railroad may commence, swollen and enlarged in its common stem by the contributions of the railways coming in from nearly every State of the Union."[190]

He also added that this route might serve a valuable purpose in our dealings with Mexico; it would help

---

[189] — *Idem*, 998-1001.
[190] — *Idem*, 1004.

both nations commercially in time of peace, and furnish a highway for United States troops in case of war.

But the arguments so ably presented were not sufficiently convincing for the proponents of a more northern route. They saw in the southern choice a sectional favoritism on the part of the Postmaster-general from Tennessee. The Sacramento *Union*, being in a city entirely missed by this southern route was especially strong in its epithets. It was a "foul wrong," "an outrage upon the majority of the people of the state," "a Panama route by land," "an overland route to Mexico, a military road to Texas, and an immigrant route to Arizona." In the East and North the same general view prevailed. The New York *Press* called it the "horseshoe" and the "ox-bow route," while the Chicago *Tribune* condemned it as "one of the greatest swindles ever perpetrated upon the country by the slave-holders."[191] It was perhaps, as a concession to the disappointed and dissatisfied sections that improved facilities were afforded to northern lines in the ensuing year.[192]

Let us now note briefly the character of the route chosen. It was, roughly speaking, in the form of a semi-circle from Saint Louis to San Francisco, the most southern point reached being about six hundred miles below South Pass. The total distance was nearly twenty-eight hundred miles.[193] The route from Saint Louis was by railroad for one hundred sixty miles directly west to Tipton. From this point the stage followed an almost direct southern course, going by way of Spring-

---

[191] Quoted by Curtis Nettels in *Missouri Historical Review*, vol. xviii, 529.

[192] See below, Chapter V.

[193] G. Bailey, special agent of the Post Office Department, who accompanied the first mail east, gives the total distance as 2795 miles, but says that this distance will presently be somewhat shortened. – Postmaster-general's *Report*, 1858, 743.

field, over the Ozark mountains to Fayetteville, and thence to Fort Smith, Arkansas, where the mail from Memphis was met. The route proceeded through the Choctaw country to the crossing of the Red River at Colbert's Ferry. From here it continued southwest across the almost uninhabited region of northern Texas via Fort Belknap to Fort Chadbourne. Upon leaving Choncho the route led across a barren plain, along the Pecos River, through Guadalupe Passe, and across the rolling table-lands to El Paso. From the Rio Grande to Tucson, three hundred sixty miles of rough, broken country without water except at the stations,[194] the course led on to the Pima Indian villages on the Gila River. It then crossed from the Maricopa Wells through a forty-mile desert, striking the Gila again, which it now followed to Fort Yuma. From Fort Yuma to Carrizo Creek, about one hundred miles, the route was heavy with sand and there was no water in the dry season.[195] Here the route left the old San Diego trail, and turned to the north, crossed the mountains at Warner's Pass and continued northwest to Los Angeles. From Los Angeles the road went north over the San Bernardino Range through San Francisquito Canyon, across the Sierra through Canada de las Uvas north through the central valley of California to Firebaugh, west through Pacheco Pass to Gilroy, and thence north to San Francisco.[196]

---

[194] Postmaster-general's *Report*, 1858, 742. Description of the route is also given by Mr. W. L. Ormsby of the New York *Herald*, in a speech upon his arrival in San Francisco. He was the only passenger on the first stage going west. Report of his speech is given in the San Francisco *Bulletin* and *Alta California*, October 12, 1858.

[195] San Francisco *Bulletin*, December 6, 1858. In the *Bulletin* of April 13, 1859, we read: "The Overland Mail Company have succeeded in sinking several wells on the Colorado desert, in each case finding water at a depth of fifty feet."

[196] A good description of the route is given by a special correspondent of

It was a route that offered many obstacles to staging. To afford water, wells had to be sunk and reservoirs made. Over the longest dry stretches relays of teams had to be provided. However, the contractors went about their task with energy, and when the year was up, equipment was ready, stations were built or in process of building, and the preparations were such as would insure the successful execution of the great undertaking.

On September 15, 1858, the first mail coaches left Saint Louis and San Francisco simultaneously for their long overland journeys. The arrivals of the mail, ahead of schedule time, were occasions of great public rejoicings. In Saint Louis the first mail was escorted through the street to the post office by a long procession led by brass bands. In San Francisco salutes were fired, an immense meeting held and enthusiastic speeches made.[197] A San Francisco paper thus describes the reception of the overland mail:

"At a quarter after four o'clock the coach turned from Market into Montgomery street. The driver blew his horn and cracked his whip; at which the horses, four in number, almost seemed to partake of his enthusiasm, and dashed ahead at a clattering pace, and the dust flew from the glowing wheels. At the same time a shout was raised, that ran with the rapidity of an electric flash along Montgomery street, which throughout its length was crowded by an excited populace. As the coach dashed along through the crowds, the hats of the spectators were whirled in the air and

---

the *Bulletin*, who started east October 22, 1858, and wrote letters back to his paper from various points. These are found in the issues of November 5, 19, 27, 1858.

[197] San Francisco *Bulletin*, October 11, 1858.

the hurrah was repeated from a thousand throats, responsive to which, the driver, the lion of the occasion, doffed his weather-beaten old slouch, and in uncovered dignity, like the victor of an Olympic race, guided his foaming steeds towards the Post Office." [198]

Upon the arrival of the pioneer stage, Mr. Butterfield, elated at the success of the great enterprise, telegraphed the President of the United States: "The overland mail arrived today at St. Louis from San Francisco in twenty-three days and four hours. The stage brought through six passengers." President Buchanan replied:

"I cordially congratulate you upon the result. It is a glorious triumph for civilization and the Union. Settlements will soon follow the course of the road, and the East and West will be bound together by a chain of living Americans which can never be broken." [199]

The schedule time for the route was twenty-five days. The first mail from the East came through in twenty-three days, twenty-three hours. Mr. W. L. Ormsby of the New York *Herald* was the only through passenger. The first trip from the West was made in twenty-four days, eighteen hours, and twenty-six minutes. Mr. G. Bailey, special agent of the Post Office Department, was one of the passengers. He reported in part:

"The various difficulties of the route, the scant supply of water, the long deserts, the inconvenience of keeping up stations hundreds of miles from the points from which their supplies are furnished; all these and the minor obstacles, naturally presented to the success-

---

[198] — *Idem*, October 16, 1858. This was the occasion of the arrival of the second stage.
[199] Quoted in Root and Connelley, *The Overland Stage to California*, 13. Butterfield's telegram is dated Jefferson City, October 9th.

ful management of so long a line of stage communication, have been met and overcome by the energy, the enterprise, and the determination of the contractors."[200]

The following summary of distances and of time made on the first trip eastward, is taken from Mr. Bailey's report:

	MILES	HOURS
San Francisco to Los Angeles	462	80
Los Angeles to Fort Yuma	282	72.20
Fort Yuma to Tucson	280	71.45
Tucson to Franklin	360	82
Franklin to Fort Chadbourne	458	126.30
Fort Chadbourne to Colbert's Ferry	282½	65.25
Colbert's Ferry to Fort Smith	192	38
Fort Smith to Tipton	318	48.55
Tipton to Saint Louis (by railroad)	160	11.40
TOTAL	2795	596.35 [201]

The line was equipped at first with the famous Concord spring wagons, capable of carrying conveniently four passengers and their baggage and five or six hundred pounds of mail matter.[202] Later more commodious coaches were used, which carried six to nine inside and one to ten outside passengers.[203] The team usually consisted of four horses or mules, but upon the more difficult stretches additional animals were attached.[204] Most of the horses were mustangs, "wild as deer, and as active as antelope." They were all shod and branded O. M. (Overland Mail).[205] Stations were maintained at intervals of from eight to twenty-five miles. At first

---

[200] Given in the Postmaster-general's *Report*, 1858, 741.
[201] Postmaster-general's *Report*, 1858, 743.
[202] —*Idem*, 741.
[203] San Francisco *Bulletin*, March 19, 1860; December 3, 1859.
[204] —*Idem*, November 5, 1858; March 19, 1860.
[205] —*Idem*, November 5, 1858.

THE BUTTERFIELD OVERLAND MAIL

there were some drives of forty or fifty miles without change of teams,[206] but these were reduced until the average drive was between ten and fifteen miles.[207] Through the New Mexico and Arizona region the stations were large square enclosures with walls of adobe. During periods of Indian hostility guards of four or five men defended these posts. Supplies of hay, grain, and sometimes even water, often had to be hauled long distances.[208] In Los Angeles a splendid brick depot was maintained, consisting of an office, blacksmith shop, stables, and sheds.[209]

The through passenger traffic was not heavy, but there were usually passengers on every coach. Oftimes, however, way passengers were crowded in, to the inconvenience of the through travelers.[210] The continuous riding day and night for twenty-five days was very tiring, and it was a common custom for passengers to remain over at some intermediate station to rest. However, it was said that the journey very often improved the health of the passenger.[211] At first the through fare was one hundred dollars from San Francisco eastward, and two hundred dollars from Saint Louis or Memphis to the Golden Gate.[212] In January, 1859, the fare eastward was raised to two hundred dollars,[213] but was reduced to one hundred fifty dollars in May.[214] This fare

---

[206] — *Idem*, November 27, 1858.
[207] — *Idem*, March 19, 1860.
[208] — *Idem*, December 14, 1859.
[209] — *Idem*, March 19, 1860.
[210] — *Idem*, November 5, 1858.
[211] — *Idem*, January 7, 1859.
[212] — *Idem*, October 11, 1858, and subsequent dates. Also advertisement of December 1, 1858, reproduced in Dunbar, *A History of Travel*, vol. iv, 1315.
[213] — *Idem*, January 10, 1859.
[214] — *Idem*, May 23, 1859.

did not include meals, which cost from seventy-five cents to one dollar each, varying, of course, according to the distance from settled regions. It did, however, allow each passenger to carry forty pounds of baggage without extra cost. In reply to numerous inquiries, a San Diego newspaper recommended the following equipment for the overland passenger:

"One Sharp's rifle and a hundred cartridges; a Colts navy revolver and two pounds of balls; a knife and sheath; a pair of thick boots and woolen pants; a half dozen pairs of thick woolen socks; six undershirts; three woolen overshirts; a wide-awake hat; a cheap sack coat; a soldier's overcoat; one pair of blankets in summer and two in winter; a piece of India rubber cloth for blankets; a pair of gauntlets, a small bag of needles, pins, a sponge, hair brush, comb, soap, etc., in an oil silk bag; two pairs of thick drawers, and three or four towels." [215]

The overland mail line gradually gained in favor until by 1860 more letters were sent by the Butterfield route than by the ocean steamers.[216] Even in England sealed letter-bags were made up regularly for San Francisco and the English Pacific Coast possessions to go overland in the times intervening between the dates of departure of the Panama line of steamers.[217]

Despite occasional depredations by the Comanche and Apache Indians,[218] the schedule was very success-

---

[215] Hayes *Collection*, Bancroft Library, University of California, "Transcontinental Mails," R. 104, 61. The article has reference to the San Antonio and San Diego Mail, but the route for a considerable distance was the same as that taken by the Butterfield.

[216] San Francisco *Bulletin*, April 27, 1860.

[217] — *Idem*, June 30, 1859. St. Louis correspondence of June 6th.

[218] Articles relative to Indian depredations and the need of Government protection are found in the *Bulletin*, October 19, November 27, December 20, 1858; January 12, February 9, July 23, 1860.

fully maintained and the trips came to be made regularly in from twenty-one to twenty-three days.[219] An overland passenger wrote in the New York *Post*:

"The blast of the stage horn as it rolls through the valleys and over the prairies of the West, cheers and gladdens the heart of the pioneer. As it sounds through the valleys of Santa Clara and San Jose, it sends a thrill of delight to the Californian. He knows that it brings tidings from the hearts and homes he left behind him; it binds him stronger and firmer to his beloved country. So regular is its arrival that the inhabitants know almost the hour and the minute when the welcome sound of the post horn will reach them. The Overland is the most popular institution of the Far West." [220]

There was never serious criticism of the conduct of the service upon this line, but the *route* taken was ever the subject of criticism. Efforts were made, time and again, to get the contract cancelled or the line moved farther north. It was not until the outbreak of the Civil War, however, that this line was removed from the route over which it had operated so regularly and so well.

---

[219] The first four mails west came through in 23, 26, 25, and 26½ days respectively. The average time made during the six months from October, 1859, to April, 1860, was 21 days and 15 hours. This information is from a speech of Senator Latham in the Senate May 30, 1860, obtained from figures compiled by the postmaster of San Francisco.

[220] Quoted in the San Francisco *Bulletin*, June 13, 1859.

Chapter V

Extensive Increases in Mail Lines to the Pacific, 1857-1859; Testing the Routes

Great dissatisfaction arose from the North and the West because of the selection of a southern route for the great overland mail line. Although inclined to southern interests, Postmaster-general Brown [221] was also an exponent of the policy of generous postal extension into the West. He applied a liberal interpretation to the powers of the postal department and set about to do his part in furthering the development of the new region.[222] After holding office but two years Mr. Brown had six lines carrying mail to the Pacific Coast, where but two existed when he assumed his position in the cabinet. During this period, also, the frequency of mail transmission had been increased upon the most improved route from semi-monthly to semi-weekly service.

---

[221] Aaron Vail Brown was born in Virginia in 1795. He graduated at Chapel Hill University (N. C.) in 1814, and removed to Tennessee in 1815. He studied law and became the partner of James K. Polk. From 1831 to 1832 he was in the state legislature of Tennessee. He was elected to Congress in 1839. Upon retiring from Congress in 1845 he became governor of Tennessee. "He was for twenty years one of the most trusted leaders of the Democratic party."-Appleton's *Cyclopaedia of American Biography*, vol. i, 393.

[222] U. S. *Congressional Globe*, 34th congress, third session, Appendix, 306. On February 27, 1857, Senator Douglas, in speaking of the retirement of Postmaster-general Campbell, said: "Sometimes I have thought he did not fully appreciate the country west of the mountains; but I do not know of any one east of the mountains who ever has appreciated it fully; and I have no hope of a great reform in that locality until we have a Postmaster-general residing west of the mountains, who is a western man."

Before taking up the specific lines established by Postmaster-general Brown, let us notice the general policy toward the establishment of postal routes, which in part at least, made possible the extensive increases.

The constitution gives to Congress the power "to establish post offices and post roads." During the period now under discussion, it was the practice for each Congress to pass its post route bill in a very ill-considered fashion. The post route bill was very long and was not printed. It was laid on the table and each member asked to examine it in so far as his own state was concerned.[223] No difficulty was encountered in having additional routes added to the bill.[224] The establishment of a route by Congress did not require the Postmaster-general to put a mail upon it. In this he exercised his own discretion. Ordinarily, in the absence of an express appropriation, service was not begun upon a line until the revenues that would accrue gave promise of approximately supporting the service.

Various overland postal routes to the Pacific had thus been established by law with slight consideration of their merits. Such a situation placed very great power in the hands of the Postmaster-general, and in Aaron V. Brown we have a man who seemed willing to make the most of it.

---

[223] U. S. *Congressional Globe*, 34th congress, first session, part iii, 2119.

[224] U. S. *Congressional Globe*, 32d congress, first session, vol. xxiv, part ii. 1664, 1665. For example: Mr. Stuart of Michigan, "I venture to say that in the history of twenty-five years there has never been an application denied." . . . Mr. Fowler: "The mail routes established by Congress do not of course, require the Postmaster-general to put a mail upon them." Another instance is recorded in U. S. *Congressional Globe*, 34th congress, third session, 1060: Mr. Rusk, "I see no use in reading the amendments of the committee, or the bill." Mr. Stuart, "They need not be read. They relate to nothing but the establishment of post routes." Reading was dispensed with and the bill passed.

INCREASES IN MAIL LINES TO PACIFIC

Let us now consider the lines established or improved during 1857-8, and see the routes followed, the facilities afforded, and the merits of the respective lines.

THE EXTREMELY SOUTHERN ROUTE – SAN ANTONIO TO SAN DIEGO

The postal route bill enacted August 18, 1856, established the route "from San Diego, via El Paso, to San Antonio, Texas." In June, 1857, a contract was entered into with James E. Birch for mail service from San Antonio to San Diego.[225] The service was to commence July 1, 1857, and continue for four years. The price to be paid was $149,800 per annum. The service was to be semi-monthly and the time allowed for making the trip each way was thirty days.[226]

This mail line was put into operation with considerable promptness and energy. The route from San Antonio to El Paso was by no means new, as government and freighting trains were continually passing over it. The San Antonio and Santa Fé monthly mail also followed this route to El Paso. The route from El Paso to Fort Yuma was described in the previous chapter. The section from Fort Yuma to San Diego was the poorest section of the road. As late as October, 1858, the mail and passengers were being carried over this section on muleback, whereas coaches were used upon the rest of the route.[227] Major J. C. Woods, superintendent of this line, made a report to the Post-

---

[225] *Texas Almanac*, 1859, p. 139. Mr. Birch was a citizen of Swansea, Massachusetts. He lost his life in the *Central America* disaster of September 11, 1857.

[226] U. S. House. *Executive Documents*, 35th congress, first session, no. 96, vol. xi, 430.

[227] Dunbar, S. *A History of Travel in America*, vol. iv, 1303. A page advertisement of the company is here reproduced with the date October 1, 1858.

master-general in March, 1858, from which I extract the following:

"From Fort Hudson, in Texas to Tezotol on the Gila, a distance of 1200 miles, nearly the whole route is over an elevated dry country. . . . The mountains are all buttes until we reach the coast range. . . We use a coach all the way from San Antonio to San Diego, sometimes drawn by six, never by less than four mules. . . There is enough wood, water and grass for staging and emigrant needs. . . Along the Gila feed is scarcest, but mesquite beans and grass are found. The country we stage over is a grazing and mineral country rather than an agricultural one. . . At Fort Yuma everything has to be imported. There is considerable importation there of flour, pounded parched corn, jerked beef, and sugar, etc., brought on pack animals from Sonora. Goods are being brought from San Francisco by way of the Gulf of California and steamer up the Colorado River. The route is hot in some parts in summer. It is not very cold in winter, and there is but little snow. . . Our line is already forming the basis of a new state, rich in minerals halfway between Texas and California." [228]

This line was in very regular and successful operation during 1857 and 1858. The schedule time was easily maintained, and the through trips came to be made in from twenty-two to twenty-six days.[229]

The improvement effected upon the road from El

---

[228] Postmaster-general's *Report*, 1858, in U. S. Senate. *Executive Documents*, 35th congress, second session, no. 1, part iv, 744-752.

[229] From the Sacramento *Union*, reprinted in San Francisco *Bulletin*, October 31, 1857. Also, see *Bulletin*, May 27, 1858. Letter from San Diego, dated July 7, 1858, published in the *Bulletin*, July 12, 1858. "It is seldom the mail is out twenty-five days, the average time being twenty-three days."–*Texas Almanac*, 1859.

Paso to Fort Yuma by the Congressional appropriation of $200,000 was an important factor in the reduction of the time schedule.[230]

Southern California and Texas were enthusiastic over this mail line. The sentiment and object is well portrayed in the following extract from the Texas *Almanac* of 1859:

"It is certainly a remarkable fact that not a single failure has yet taken place under this important mail contract. If any proof could be sufficient to satisfy the world of the superior advantages of this route for a railroad to the Pacific, it should be such proof as this. Without scarcely any previous expenditure in opening a road through a vast and almost unexplored region, mail coaches are at this moment carrying the mails and passengers a distance of 1475 miles, with actually greater speed than we have on a majority of the short lines within the limits of our own state. . . We, therefore assume that the establishment of this line must lead to the speedy and rapid settlement of the country throughout the entire distance, giving us within a very few years, a continuous succession of farms, ranches, hotels, military posts, stage offices, etc., from one ocean to the other. There can be no doubt that this is very soon destined to be the great overland inter-

---

[230] Law passed February 17, 1857. From the report of N. H. Hutton, engineer on the road, we extract: "The region traversed by this route lies almost entirely within the 'Gadsden Purchase' . . . The improvements are of two kinds: improvements of surface and reduction of grade, and the increase and improvement of watering places. We may safely estimate the entire saving of time effected by our improvements at five travelling days, in addition there is an increase of over seventy miles along running water; the formation of six new watering places, reducing the greatest distance between camps to 27 miles; a reduction of all grades to a slope easily ascended by teams drawing maximum loads, which for six mules is 4,000 pounds and for ten mules about 6,000 pounds." – "Pacific Wagon Roads" in U. S. House. *Executive Documents*, 35th congress, second session, no. 108, vol. xi, 77-85.

oceanic thoroughfare of the nation, affording not only safer but a quicker and cheaper passage to and from California, over our own territory than can now be had by the present circuitous routes, through the sickly regions of foreign nations. The immense amount of travel will soon make a railroad a measure of necessity, the immediate ocean termini of which will be Galveston and San Diego."

The number of passengers on the line varied, but generally there was one or more. The price for through passage with meals was $200. Each passenger was allowed thirty pounds of baggage exclusive of blankets and arms, and extra baggage was taken at one dollar per pound.[231] Armed guards escorted the stage through the Indian country. The company was said to have in its employ sixty-five men, fifty coaches, and four hundred mules.[232] The line made connection at San Diego with the steamer for San Francisco.

When the great Butterfield line was put into operation in September, 1858, a duplication of service resulted over the route from El Paso to Fort Yuma. The Postmaster-general accordingly discontinued the service between those two points upon the San Antonio and San Diego line in December, 1858. The remaining service – from San Antonio to El Paso and from Fort Yuma to San Diego – was improved to a weekly service.[233] This schedule continued to be maintained while Brown remained in office.

---
[231] Dunbar, *op. cit.*, vol. iv, 1303.
[232] *Texas Almanac*, 1859.
[233] U. S. House. *Executive Documents*, 36th congress, first session, no. 86, vol. xiii, 516. "Route 8076. G. H. Giddings, Contractor. Original service, twice a month in six-mule wagons. Distance 1520 miles. Original price $149,800. Service between El Paso and Fort Yuma discontinued from December 1, 1858, saving 600 miles and $59,139 per annum. Service between

CENTRAL MAIL ROUTE TO CALIFORNIA, VIA SALT LAKE CITY

In an earlier chapter we traced the establishment and early history of the overland mail service to Utah. This service was under two separate contracts — one providing for the line from Independence, Missouri, to Salt Lake City, and the other from California to the Utah capital. These two lines came to be looked upon as forming one through line and as such were greatly improved in 1858, in conformity with the general improvement scheme of the administration.

The contract with S. B. Miles for carrying the mail from Independence to Salt Lake City was in effect in 1858. This contract provided for a monthly mail to be carried in four-horse coaches from April 1st to December 1st, and upon pack mules the remainder of the year. The annual price paid was $32,000. West of Salt Lake City the mail was being carried monthly over the southern route to Los Angeles, and then by boat to San Francisco. The price paid was $30,000 per year. These terms compared unfavorably with those given the San Antonio and San Diego line, and with those of the Butterfield contract. California representatives especially, insisted upon improvement on the central route via Utah. The Postmaster-general agreed to make improvements, and accordingly, new contracts were entered into.[234] Upon the line from Independence to Salt Lake City a contract was made with John M. Hockaday and others for a weekly service in four-mule

---

San Antonio and El Paso, or point of junction with the great overland California mail route, 700 miles, improved to weekly trips at $80,485 per year; also the service between Fort Yuma and San Diego, 220 miles, improved to weekly trips at $25,295 per annum. Additional allowance made, $47,648. Commencement of additional service January 1, 1858."

[234] The Washington correspondent of the San Francisco *Bulletin* writes

wagons or carriages at $190,000 per annum on a twenty-two day schedule. The service was to continue from May 1, 1858, to November, 1860.[235]

George Chorpenning, the pioneer California-Utah mail contractor, again received the contract for the service west of Salt Lake City. While in Washington in the spring of 1858 he offered to carry the mail weekly on a twelve day schedule for $190,000 per year. When the contract was drawn up it provided for semi-monthly service through in twenty days at $34,400 per year. However, a sliding scale[236] was inserted in the contract and before July, 1858, the service was ordered improved to weekly trips on a sixteen day schedule at $130,000 per year.[237]

Thus, by July, 1858, a through overland mail along the central route from Independence, Missouri, to Placerville, California, was in operation upon a thirty-eight day schedule. The eastern division of this through line followed the route of the preceding monthly mail, up the Platte and through South Pass.

April 4, 1858: "Senator Gwin has fully accomplished his great scheme for a thoroughly organized overland mail to California, via Salt Lake City. . . The old contract between Independence and Salt Lake has been declared forfeited; and a new one has been let to John M. Hockaday and James H. Jones, and others, who agree to carry the mail between St. Joseph and Salt Lake in twenty-two days for $190,000 per annum. This service commences the 1st of May. . . Mr. Hockaday is the active, substantial man among the contractors. He is an experienced traveler across the Plains, a man of indomitable energy and perseverance." – *Bulletin*, April 29, 1858.

[235] U. S. House. *Executive Documents*, 35th congress, second session, no. 109, vol. xi, 863.

[236] Chorpenning's *Statement*, 24. The contract provided for semi-monthly service through in 20 days at $34,400; through in 16 days for $30,600 additional; through in 14 days for $45,600 additional; and in 12 days for $60,600 additional; making $95,000 per year for semi-monthly, which would make $190,000 for weekly service.

[237] Chorpenning contends that the Postmaster-general promised to order the service improved to the twelve-day schedule, but this improvement was never ordered. See his *Statement*, prepared in 1889.

West of Salt Lake City the line followed the original route of 1851. This circled to the north of the Great Salt Lake, followed the Humboldt River across northern Nevada, and crossed the Sierras via Carson City.

The route was not well stocked at first, but usually the trip was made within schedule time.[238] The mail from the east often reached Salt Lake City in twenty days, and Placerville in thirty-two. We read in a San Francisco paper of August 10, 1858:

"The mail leaving Salt Lake on the 16th of July had no change of animals for nearly seven hundred miles, but it made the Sink of the Humboldt in twelve days, from whence it is two days journey only to Placerville. The mail which arrived yesterday made the complete trip from St. Louis to Placerville in thirty traveling days. The whole time, including four days lying over, was thirty-four. With relays of animals every fifty miles there would be no difficulty in making the entire trip from Placerville to Salt Lake in seven days, and to the Missouri in twenty days." [239]

A Placerville correspondent writes October 11, 1858:

"It appears that Chorpenning intends to run over the route at a snail's speed until the Department will make him another allowance for shortening the time, when the four hundred miles section now being run with one jaded train, will perhaps, be properly stocked and the great Central route made to compete with the circuitous route from San Francisco through Fort Yuma and El Paso to Memphis."[240]

It is, of course, but fair to notice the difference in the remuneration upon the two routes. We read in the San

---
[238] San Francisco *Bulletin*, August 3, and 19, 1858.
[239] — *Idem*, August 10, 1858.
[240] — *Idem*, October 14, 1858.

Francisco *Bulletin* of November 4, 1858: "The schedule time on the Overland route from Placerville to St. Joseph, Missouri, is thirty-five days, yet the mail has always been carried much within that period, and if it were made pecuniarily worth the while of the contractors, the time could be shortened almost one half." [241]

In October, 1858, Chorpenning set out from Salt Lake City to examine a more direct route, south of Great Salt Lake. Three years before, a Utah pioneer, Howard Egan, had explored a direct route from northern California to Salt Lake City which followed very nearly the fortieth parallel, north latitude. In September, 1855, he retraced his steps and won a wager by riding on mule back from Salt Lake City to Sacramento in ten days. [242] This route came to be known as the Egan trail. Chorpenning found the route practicable and immediately set about moving his mail line to this more direct route. By the middle of December the mail was being carried over this new road, the first mail arriving in San Francisco December 21, 1858. Inasmuch as the distance was shortened considerably, less time was required for the trip. The Sacramento *Union* says: "The contractor is removing his stock and coaches to the new road, building stands, forts, etc. Passengers who came through speak in high terms of the road; and it is believed that soon they will be running from Salt Lake in ten days. It can be run in a week without difficulty." [243]

In his annual report of 1858, the Postmaster-general referred to the Utah route thus:

---

[241] — *Idem*, November 4, 1858.
[242] Egan, W. M., ed. *Pioneering the West, 1846-1878, Major Howard Egan's Diary*, etc., pp. 193-197.
[243] Quoted in the *Bulletin*, December 22, 1858.

INCREASES IN MAIL LINES TO PACIFIC

"The routes between St. Joseph and Salt Lake City and between Salt Lake and Placerville, have been so improved that the trips through from St. Joseph to Placerville and back are performed once a week in thirty-eight days each way. For some months past this service has been performed with remarkable regularity, insomuch as to merit special commendation. It has received from the people of California the warmest applause and called forth public demonstrations of a most enthusiastic character." [244]

As the winter storms approached, great interest was manifested in the question as to the practicability of the route for winter travel. It will be remembered that Chorpenning in 1852 transferred the route of his California-Utah mail from the northern course to the one via Los Angeles because of the snows in the north; also, that the chief argument advanced by Postmaster-general Brown in justification of his choice of the southern route via El Paso for the great overland mail contract of 1857, was the impracticability of the northern route for winter travel. If these arguments were to be disproved, it was rather imperative that the contractors on the Salt Lake route should make good. In December, the Sacramento *Union* expressed its confidence as follows:

"The Sierra Nevada, which at Washington has been considered utterly impassable during winter, on account of the deep snow, has been crossed so far this season without inconvenience even. . . We repeat our confidence that Thompson will keep the road across the summit in good traveling condition through the winter, . . . in convincing the Postmaster-general that he has been imposed upon in reference to the impassa-

---
[244] Postmaster-general's *Report*, 1858, 722.

ble depth of snow which falls upon the snowy mountains." [245]

Severe storms delayed some of the mails but their regularity was rather noticeable than otherwise. A Salt Lake City correspondent writes February 14, 1859: "The eastern mails from St. Joseph, Missouri, are coming in very regularly. Hockaday and Company deserve great credit for the manner in which this route has been conducted, particularly through the winter. Only two or three mails have been out of time, and that arose from causes that no human power could prevent. If the Government will give him an equal chance with some others, you will find he can accomplish as wonderful feats as any of Uncle Sam's pets, whether civil or military. The same may be said of Major Chorpenning, on the route from California to this place. He is always ahead of time. Between the two, with an equal show, the mail can be delivered in San Francisco in shorter time than by any other route." [246]

When unable to get through with coaches, the mail was often transferred to the backs of horses, and in some cases men on snow shoes were employed.[247]

As spring opened, arrangements were completed for improvement on the line.[248] More stock, coaches, and stations were provided, and the road was improved. Considerable passenger traffic was now carried by this

---

[245] Reprinted in the *Bulletin*, December 22, 1858.

[246] In the San Francisco *Bulletin*, March 3, 1859.

[247] Chorpenning's *Statement*, 28. "At such times and places as it was impossible to haul the coaches and make the requisite time, the coaches were abandoned and the mails carried on the backs of animals, and by men on snow shoes. . . The famous Snow-shoe Thompson was one of the men who aided in getting these mails across the Sierra Nevadas during the winter of 1858 and 1859."

[248] Genoa correspondence in San Francisco *Bulletin*, April 27, 1859. Also, Chorpenning's *Statement*, 25.

INCREASES IN MAIL LINES TO PACIFIC

line,[249] and it remained in 1858-9 the great competitor of the Butterfield route.

ROUTE FROM KANSAS CITY TO STOCKTON, CALIFORNIA

Probably the case in which the postal function of the Department was most departed from, was in the establishment of the mail route from Kansas City, Missouri, to Stockton, California, via Santa Fé, New Mexico. Upon this line the carriage of the mail was a very secondary consideration. Here more evidently than in any other case, was the Post Office Department playing the role purely of an advance agent of civilization and precursor of the railroad.

A mail route had been established by act of Congress August 3, 1854, from Neosho, Missouri, to Albuquerque, New Mexico; and from Independence, Missouri, via Albuquerque to Stockton, California, in the following March. These were petty items in the general postal route bills, and as such, went by unnoticed. But in December, 1857, Postmaster-general Brown, upon the "solicitation of citizens interested in that section of the country"[250] advertised for bids upon the routes. In the following May a contract was entered into with Jacob Hall to carry the mail monthly from Kansas City, Missouri, via Santa Fé to Stockton, California, for $79,999. The service was to be performed in a six-mule wagon and sixty days were allowed for the through trip.[251] Service on this line commenced October 1, 1858.[252]

From the eastern terminus to Santa Fé the route was

---

[249] San Francisco *Bulletin*, January 17, June 27, July 9, August 7, 1859.

[250] Postmaster-general's *Report*, 1858, 722, 723.

[251] U. S. House. *Executive Documents*, 35th congress, second session, no. 109, vol. xi, 484.

[252] Postmaster-general's *Report*, 1859, 1412. (Serial no. 1025.)

over the well established Santa Fé trail.[253] From this place to Fort Mohave on the Colorado River the plan was to take the route followed by Lieutenant Beale with his wagon road and camel expedition of 1857. This led from Santa Fé down to Albuquerque, on to Zuni, west to the Little Colorado River, along it for some distance and thence west to Fort Mohave. From this crossing of the Colorado, the route went west across the Mohave desert by Lake Elizabeth to Fort Tejon, and thence up through the central valley of California to Stockton.

From the western end of the Kansas-to-Stockton line service began November 1, 1858. The coach that left Stockton on that day was cheered by an assembled crowd. The Concord wagon was of sufficient size to accommodate eight passengers; six mules comprised the team. "The wagon was filled with blankets, provisions, and camping utensils, while the driver and guard were well equipped with Colt's persuaders and Arkansas toothpicks, said to be convenient articles to have on the road . A mail of some fifty or sixty letters was forwarded." [254]

The mail party followed the central valley of California by way of Fort Miller and the Fresno agency and struck the Butterfield route at Visalia. They reached Fort Tejon on the 10th, where they learned of a recent massacre of emigrants by the Mohave Indians in the region to be traversed. After venturing some distance into the desert, they returned to the Fort and applied for an escort. Here the mail from Kansas City overtook them, and they returned with it, reaching

---

[253] Saint Louis correspondence in the San Francisco *Bulletin*, November 29, 1858.

[254] — *Idem*, November 3, 1858.

Stockton, November 24th.[255] Thus the first through trip was made in fifty-four days.

Hostility of the Mohave Indians continued through the winter and interrupted the service. During the following spring and summer, forces of men were at work upon the road between Santa Fé and the Colorado River,[256] but nevertheless the carriers met with considerable difficulty. However, a second through mail arrived at Stockton, May 29, 1859. It appears that these two were the only through mails that reached Stockton during the nine months of the duration of the contract, while four through mails reached Kansas City.[257]

In connection with the Kansas-to-Stockton route, another route should be considered that was established at the same time, from Neosho, in southwestern Missouri to Albuquerque, New Mexico. A contract was entered into with Thomas F. Bowler for this service. It was to be a monthly service in six-mule wagons and the price allowed was $17,000 per year.[258]

Service commenced upon this route October 15, 1858. A letter from Neosho reports the departure of R. F. Green for Albuquerque:

"An event of this kind created quite a sensation at Neosho and there was an illumination, a supper, speeches from the citizens, and a good time generally. Mr. Green expects to arrive at Albuquerque on the tenth of November. John Britton of Neosho accom-

---
[255] Letter of Bonynge, a member of the mail party, dated Stockton, November 30, 1858; in *Bulletin*, December 1, 1858.
[256] — *Idem*, February 21, June 16, 1859. Quoted from the *Southern Vineyard* (Los Angeles).
[257] Postmaster-general's *Report*, 1859, 1412.
[258] U. S. House. *Executive Documents*, 35th congress, second session, no. 109, 447.

panied the mail party as a guide. It is Mr. Green's intention to follow as near as possible the 35th parallel, after intercepting Lieutenant Beale who is now in the field surveying the route for this line. This information will be exceedingly gratifying to those who have all along contended that the best, most direct and practicable route for the railroad is on the thirty-fifth parallel. A wagon road and the mail coach must precede this location, but there is no doubt that Lieutenant Beale's route, via Albuquerque, will prove the shortest and most practicable, and free from the impediments of snow and cold weather." [259]

From Albuquerque it was intended that the mail should be forwarded on to California over the Kansas and Stockton route. It appears that this route was established "through the intercession of Hon. John S. Phelps, Representative in Congress from the Neosho district, and from the supposition that it would aid in determining the best route for the future Great Pacific Railroad." [260]

Service upon this line also was interrupted by Indian hostilities. Hall reports that he left Neosho, Missouri, for Albuquerque, November 5th with the mail, consisting of four or five pounds of letters and papers. He was attacked by Comanche Indians who wounded him, took him prisoner, and destroyed the mail. He did not escape until February and reached St. Louis March 11, 1859.[261] Here then, also, Indian hostility practically prohibited the execution of the mail contract.

---

[259] Letter of the Saint Louis correspondent of the San Francisco *Bulletin*, appearing November 19, 1858.

[260] — *Idem*, November 19, 1858.

[261] Given in an affidavit to be forwarded to the Postmaster-general. – Saint Louis correspondence of March 14, 1859, in the *Bulletin*, April 7, 1859.

THE ROUTE VIA TEHUANTEPEC

The route via Tehuantepec had long been advocated as the quickest and the best route to our Pacific Coast possessions. It remained for Postmaster-general Brown to put mail and traffic across the isthmus. On June 8, 1858, he contracted with the Louisiana Tehuantepec Company on the following terms:

To convey mails from New Orleans, by Minatitlan, Suchil, Ventosa and Acapulco, to San Francisco, twice a month and back, in safe and substantial steamers between New Orleans and Minatitlan; in safe and substantial river steamers between Minatitlan and Suchil, and in post coaches or good covered spring wagons between Suchil and the Pacific; the residue of the route to San Francisco in steamers; the pay to be at the rate of $286,000 per annum.[262]

The trip was to be made in fifteen days. But a single year's service was contracted for, as Brown believed that one year's trial would test the route and would stimulate competition for future lettings of the contract for the ocean mail.

Service began upon the route the latter part of October, 1858. Fifteen Concord coaches had been sent from New York the first of the month and a similar number were ready for shipment.[263] One hundred American horses and mules were sent from New Orleans to the isthmus. A force of men was set at work making and repairing the road, and all arrangements were rushed to completion.

The first mail left New Orleans October 27th, reached Minatitlan on the 30th and arrived at Tehuantepec and Ventosa November 2nd. The mail and pas-

---
[262] Postmaster-general's *Report*, 1858, p. 718.
[263] New York correspondence in the *Bulletin*, November 1, 1858.

sengers were taken up by the Panama steamer and arrived at San Francisco November 14th. In San Francisco, the newspapers especially, were delighted with the achievement. The editor of the *Bulletin* writes:

"The completion of the Tehuantepec route and the reception over it of the mails and passengers from New Orleans in eighteen days, is the great feature of the news today. Had no delay occurred we should have received our New Orleans correspondence in fifteen days. . . It is undoubtedly the shortest route; . . . One improvement follows so closely on the heels of another that we have hardly time to express our satisfaction when something new occurs. Scarcely have our people ceased rejoicing at the success of the great Overland Mail communication, before they are called to exult over the enterprise of the Louisiana Tehuantepec Company in bringing the mails in eighteen days from New Orleans." [264]

Passengers coming over the route spoke rather highly of it. The scenery over the isthmus and the healthfulness of the climate were emphasized and contrasted with those features upon the Panama route.[265]

Throughout the winter and the following spring, the mail from New Orleans continued to arrive regularly; usually making the trip in from fifteen to eighteen days, and thus bringing news dated five to eight days later than that carried in the Panama mail.[266] The news by the overland mails also was antedated by that of the Tehuantepec route. The splendid accomplishment of

---
[264] San Francisco *Bulletin*, November 15, 1858.
[265] — *Idem*, December 3, 1858; December 15, 1858; February 2, 1859.
[266] — *Idem*, December 6, 1858.

the company seemed to present this as the favorite route for the transmission of the United States mail.

By the end of the year 1858 the extension of postal routes to the Pacific Coast had reached its high-water mark. Postmaster-general Brown could well say in his annual report of December that the postal system was then extended over the whole country from one ocean to the other, and that the excess of expenditures over revenue could now be regarded as the maximum that would be required for some time to come.[267] Six lines were now in operation:

1st. The Central Route, from Independence, Missouri, to Placerville, California, via Salt Lake City, weekly.

2nd. Kansas City, Missouri, to Stockton, California, via Santa Fé, monthly.

3rd. The Butterfield Route, from St. Louis to San Francisco, via El Paso, Texas, semi-weekly.

4th. San Antonio, Texas, to San Diego, California, semi-monthly.

5th. New Orleans to San Francisco, via Tehuantepec, semi-monthly.

6th. New York to San Francisco, via Panama, semi-monthly.

Of these six lines, four had been put in operation during Brown's brief term of office. No wonder that the West was enthusiastic over the accomplishments of the Postmaster-general. Mass meetings passed resolutions[268] commending his policy, and the newspapers of Missouri and California praised him unreservedly.

---

[267] Postmaster-general's *Report*, 1858, 723.

[268] Mass meeting in San Francisco, October 11, 1858. See *Bulletin*, October 12, 1858.

The Saint Louis *Republican* says: "Governor Brown has done more for the mail service in Missouri and the West in his brief period of office, than any one of his predecessors for a whole term." [269] Senator Gwin, of California, said in the Senate in June, 1858, "We are indebted to nobody as much as we are to him [Brown] for the establishment of these routes to California." [270]

But there was one note of discord in the hymn of praise to Brown. It was charged that he had unduly favored the South and southern routes. When the great overland mail bill passed Congress in the spring of 1857, it was generally expected that the regular emigrant route by way of Salt Lake City would be chosen. We have already seen how the southern route by way of El Paso was selected by the Postmaster-general. Again, a semi-monthly route was established from San Antonio to San Diego in the summer of 1857, while the route by Salt Lake City continued on a monthly basis. The Tehuantepec route also was characterized as a southern route, inasmuch as it benefited primarily the New Orleans region.

Among the overland lines the principal rivalry was between the "Central" and the "Butterfield" routes. In the summer of 1858 the contracts for these routes provided for thirty-eight and twenty-five day schedules, respectively. The contract prices for the two lines showed a similar discrepancy. Friends of the Central route tried to get its schedule improved. A joint resolution was introduced in Congress authorizing and directing the Postmaster-general to increase the speed from thirty-eight to thirty days, with a pro rata increase in compensation. It passed the House by a large ma-

---

[269] St. Louis *Republican*, September 16, 1858.
[270] U. S. *Congressional Globe*, 35th congress, first session, part iii, 3004.

jority, but met some opposition in the Senate. Some Senators did not believe that the land routes could equal the water routes in any case. Senator Gwin asserted that the mail route chosen by the Postmaster-general "is an exclusively southern route. . . It is believed not only by the people on this side but on the other side of the mountains that the route named in this resolution is a better one, and one certainly where all the emigration, I may say, has gone to California." [271]

Senator Toombs of Georgia, replied: "The Butterfield route was not selected as a southern route or a northern route, but as a United States route, upon the cheapest, best, and nearest way of getting the mails through." Senator Broderick, of California, would give up other routes but wanted the Central retained. "Give us this route and that across Tehuantepec, and I think the people of California will be satisfied." [272]

The resolution passed Congress, but was vetoed by the President, who said that the Postmaster-general already had discretionary power to order the improvement if it were desirable,[273] and also that the contractors had offered to make the improvement at less than a pro rata increase. The Washington correspondent of the San Francisco *Bulletin* writes of the President's action:

"It is said that the President refused to sign the bill because the projected route was likely to demonstrate the feasibility of a Central Railroad to the Pacific. . . It is quite evident that in this, as in other matters the President is guided by the filibuster faction who will support no other but the extreme Southern route." [274]

---
[271] — *Idem*, 3002. Debate in Congress, June 12, 1858.
[272] — *Idem*, 3003. Debate, June 12, 1858.
[273] U. S. House. *Executive Documents*, 35th congress, second session, no. 28. (Veto message of President Buchanan.) vol. v, 1, 2.
[274] Letter of June 19, 1858. *Bulletin*, July 14, 1858.

With the Butterfield line in successful operation in October, 1858, the rivalry was transferred from the halls of Congress to the western prairies. In the San Francisco *Bulletin* of October 14, 1858, we read:

"Since the late successful trip over the Southern Route, everybody's attention seems to be directed to the roads across the Plains; and a spirited rivalry has already begun to manifest itself between the advocates of the Southern and the friends of the Central routes. The Sacramento *Union*, which for the last six years has persistently hammered away on the wagon-road topic, is in high dudgeon at the alleged favoritism that has been exhibited by the Postmaster-general towards the Los Angeles route; while the San Francisco *Herald* thinks it the height of ill manners for us to question the *means* adopted by the Department for getting the mail through. . . We are pleased to note the rivalry springing up between the two routes. There is nothing like competition to put life and spirit into a business. . . Let the rivalry progress. The livelier it gets the better."

From a Salt Lake City correspondent we read: "The contractors are ready and anxious to carry the mails from St. Louis to San Francisco *tri-weekly*, in less time than the Southern route, for the same compensation which that gets for carrying it semi-weekly." [275]

As the time for the delivery of the President's message drew near, considerable interest was manifested in the merits of the various routes. From Sacramento we read: "It is thought that the President's message will be received by the Salt Lake route somewhat in advance of the Butterfield line, and bets to that effect are easily

---

[275] Dated, Salt Lake City, January 10, 1859, in the San Francisco *Bulletin*, January 24, 1859.

attainable. . . . It is even possible that the Tehuantepec route will beat both the stage routes." [276]

Arrangements were made upon both of the big stage routes to have a special express carry the message with the best possible speed. By some sort of jugglery at Washington a fair test was prevented. A Saint Louis Correspondent offers an explanation:

"The management of the Washington part of the business of sending the message was intrusted to A. R. Corbin, a lobby agent in that city, whose services were called into requisition during the process of the engineering the overland mail bill through Congress. He got the necessary copies. Butterfield saw about getting the fast express put through. Hockaday and Company, the Salt Lake mail contractors, are heavy sufferers by some piece of jugglery. These gentlemen long ago made application for a package of the message and documents to be forwarded by a similar express through Utah to San Francisco, desiring to make a test of speed to the Pacific with the Butterfield express. Additional horses were purchased, sent out on the road and disposed along at the stations, so as to form perfect and regular relays. A promise was obtained from Washington that the documents would be forthcoming, and a messenger came down from St. Joseph to St. Louis to await their coming, but strange to say, the President refused them a copy of his message, (so I learn from Washington) and Hockaday's agent instead of getting a fair start with Pardee, (Butterfield's express agent) is still in this city with no prospect of obtaining the document until it appears in our city papers. The enterprise will necessarily be abandoned, although the mail contractors incurred an expense of $8,000 to con-

---

[276] — *Idem*, December 24, 1858.

summate it in proper style. As Mr. Corbin is in the interest of the Southern route, he may explain why and how the Northern mail line was deprived of its design of making a trial of speed with the other." [277]

The Butterfield line was the first to bring the President's message to San Francisco, arriving December 26th. On the 28th the message arrived on the mail steamer, and it reached Placerville by the Central route on January 1, 1859. The lateness of the date on the Central route was due to the delay in procuring the message at the eastern terminus. This line, however, brought the message through from Saint Joseph in seventeen days, and would have arrived first at the western terminus had it had an even start with the Butterfield line.[278]

---

[277] — *Idem*, January 3, 1859.
[278] — *Idem*, January 4, 1859.

Chapter VI

Should the Postal Service be a Pioneering Agency or a Business Undertaking? Reform and Conflict 1859-1860

The postal system was founded, and for many years was conducted, upon the principle that it should be self-supporting. However, in the fifties there were many Congressmen who did not subscribe to this doctrine. They did not look upon the Post Office Department as a mere business undertaking which must needs be self-supporting. To them the postal service, especially in its western lines, was and should be, primarily a pioneer of civilization; marking the trails and keeping them open to travel, encouraging settlement, and acting as the precursor of the railroad.

When the great overland mail bill, which resulted in the establishment of the Butterfield line, was being debated in Congress in March, 1857, the two positions were well presented. The question, however, was by no means settled and it continued in subsequent Congresses to be actively debated. Collamer, senator from Vermont, and former Postmaster-general, was spokesman for the time-honored policy. "The principle has been," he said, "that the Department should pay its own expenses, except that, when there was a change in the rates of postage, an appropriation was made to meet the temporary loss which would result from that change for a year or two. At the time I had the honor of undergoing the drudgery of this department the postages paid its expenses. That was in 1849 and 1850." [279]

Mr. Toombs of Georgia added: "In other states a route must pay a certain proportion of its cost or is discontinued. In this sense California has been most favored. If I go to California I must pay my passage. If I send a messenger I pay for him. If I send a message make me pay for that. This is the rule to which we should adhere." Mr. Weller of California replied that there were routes in every state that were not self-supporting. Senator Seward approved the wider field for postal activity. He once said: "I regard the inland postal system as a great instrumentality for maintaining, preserving and extending this Union." [280] Mr. Maynard protested against the doctrine that the post office should be self-supporting:

"It may have been proper in the early period of the Government when the country was comparatively small and the Treasury empty and burdened with debt, but our condition is entirely changed. . . If we act on that principle we must then stop every mail route where the service on it does not pay expenses. Millions are spent on the army and navy, why not some on this department which does so much good for the people? This Department is not merely the means of communication and correspondence but is the great means of our civilization. . . We are a migratory people. Our brothers, our neighbors, our children go away from us and the means of communication with them by letter and newspapers is one of the strongest ties that binds us together as a homogeneous people." [281]

---

[279] Speech in the debate on the Overland Mail bill, 1857. U. S. *Congressional Globe*, 34th congress, third session, Appendix.

[280] U. S. *Congressional Globe*, 35th congress, first session, 2889.

[281] — *Idem*, 2419, 2420.

In criticism of the use of the postal system as a pioneering and civilizing agency, Senator Toombs of Georgia, one of the chief exponents of economy, remarked in 1859: "The present Postmaster-general totes civilization in his mail bags, and lets it out all over the Indian country going to the Pacific Ocean. . . . He says he has civilized two-thirds of the continent by his mail service." [282] Although the exponents of retrenchment and reform seemed to be dominant in the Senate, their arguments were met by some of the western senators who advocated increased mail facilities. Senator Gwin, of California, argued thus:

"I hope nobody will take spasms when I say that I am in favor of all the routes and always have been, and always intend to stand up for them. I look upon this policy of extending routes across the continent and establishing connections with the various sections of the Union over this uninhabited country, as one of the most important policies ever adopted by this Government. I have been in favor of all of them from the first; and I will go so far as to say, notwithstanding I expect to be looked upon almost as a monster, that I am in favor of another route from St. Paul to Puget Sound; and I will put it on this bill or any other, if I can do it. . . . By keeping up these routes you will people all that section of country. . . . There is a spirit of destruction and pulling down prevalent here, in regard to all appropriations." [283]

Some criticism of the extensive increases in western mail lines had been expressed in the first session of the thirty-fifth Congress (1857-8), and as the postal deficit mounted, the movement for reform gained momentum.

---
[282] U. S. *Congressional Globe*, 35th congress, second session, 1456.
[283] — *Idem*, 1504.

When the Post Route bill was taken up in the second session, an attempt was made to tack-on a postal reform program in the form of amendments. Senator Yulee of Florida, chairman of the Committee on Post Offices and Post Roads, reported the bill from his committee February 24, 1859, with the desired amendments attached. He indicated that the Department anticipated a saving of about six and one half million dollars if the proposed amendments were adopted. The principal reforms proposed by the committee were for the abolition of the franking privilege, the substitution of "Star Bids" in the letting of contracts, and the increase of the postage on letters from three to five cents.[284] After extended debate the Senate passed the bill, February 25th, with the amendments substantially as reported by the Committee. Upon reaching the House it received a very cold reception and was not considered by that body until the final day of the session, and then failed of passage.[285]

In the meantime the annual Post Office Appropriation bill had come up for final consideration. As the bill came from the House it carried no unusual provisions, but upon being considered in the Senate the reform advocates succeeded in attaching to it also, the postal reform program for abolishing the franking privilege and raising the postage rates. The Senate also passed one amendment reducing the service on the Butterfield route to weekly trips; and another increasing that on the Central route to weekly trips upon a twenty-five day schedule. Senator Rice, of Minnesota, also succeeded in getting an amendment accepted providing for a mail service on the route from Saint Paul,

---
[284] — *Idem*, 1292.
[285] — *Idem*, 1677.

Minnesota, to Seattle, Washington. This last amendment drew from Senator Hunter of Virginia the comment: "It seems that our experiments in the way of economy are likely to result very unfortunately. Instead of reducing the service – we are likely to end with one more mail route than we had before, and to have increased service on another." [286]

The bill passed the Senate March 1, 1859; but with its provision for abolishing the franking privilege and raising the rate of postage, it could expect little favor in the House. Time and again the Senate had voted to abolish franking, only to have the measure meet with a decided negative in the popular body. Senator Brown, of Mississippi, had aptly expressed the situation in the previous session: "Who dreams that the House of Representatives is going, in this sort of way to give up this privilege? Why, sir, it is half their stock in trade. You would bankrupt the political fortunes of at least half of them, as they think, by abolishing the franking privilege." [287]

When the measure was returned to the House a very effective method of combatting the Senate amendments was devised. Mr. Grow objected to the bill's being taken up, saying that the Senate had added an amendment raising the postage, and that the Senate had no right to originate a bill for raising revenue. The House passed a resolution, March 3rd, returning the measure to the Senate since section thirteen was in the nature of a revenue bill. The Senate replied that it was competent to judge of its own action.[288] Finally, in an attempt to save the appropriation bill a conference com-

---
[286] — *Idem*, 1510.
[287] U. S. *Congressional Globe*, 35th congress, first session, 2889.
[288] U. S. *Congressional Globe*, 35th congress, second session, 1674.

mittee was appointed.²⁸⁹ It reported a bill which was substantially the original House bill. This was passed by the House but failed in the Senate in the last hour of the session.

The failure of the annual appropriation bill brought considerable embarrassment upon the Post Office Department,²⁹⁰ and stimulated a thorough investigation of the conduct of the Department. Another event of rather far-reaching consequence occurred about the same time. Postmaster-general Brown died March 8, 1859. He was replaced by Judge Joseph Holt of Kentucky, late Commissioner of Patents.

It was evident almost at once that the management had changed hands. Mr. Holt's views regarding the purpose and duty of the Post Office Department were quite in contrast with those of Brown. The new Postmaster-general looked upon the post office as a business concern that should be conducted upon business principles and be made self-supporting, if possible. Such a policy, if applied strictly, would be fatal to Trans-mississippi lines. But even when applied with moderation it had a profound effect upon the service.

Upon assuming office Joseph Holt found the following lines to the Pacific Coast in operation: ²⁹¹

	ANNUAL COST	ANNUAL RECEIPTS
From New York and New Orleans via Panama to San Francisco, semi-monthly,	$738,250	299,972.61

---

²⁸⁹ — *Idem*, 1677.

²⁹⁰ The Post Office Department was deprived of the use of its own revenue. The President refused to convene a special session of Congress. Statements evidencing the indebtedness of the Department to contractors and agents were issued. In putting these on the market some had to submit to heavy discount.

²⁹¹ Postmaster-general's *Report*, 1859, p. 1408, in U. S. Senate. *Executive Documents*, 36th congress, first session, no. 2, (Serial no. 1025).

From New Orleans to San Francisco via Tehuantepec, semi-monthly,	250,000	5,276.00
From San Antonio via El Paso to San Diego, semi-monthly (weekly from San Antonio to El Paso and Fort Yuma)	196,448	601.00
From St. Louis and Memphis, via El Paso to San Francisco, semi-weekly,	600,000	27,229.94
From Kansas City, Missouri, to Stockton, California, monthly,	79,999	1,255.00
From St. Joseph, Missouri, via Utah City, to Placerville, weekly,	320,000	5,412.03

The gross annual disbursements for these six routes were thus $2,184,697 and the receipts from them but $339,747.34, showing a loss to the department of $1,844,949.66.

To the Postmaster-general this table was an indictment against the Department, and he set about to correct what he considered abuses. The San Antonio and San Diego mail was reduced from a weekly to semi-monthly service, July 1, 1859, and the compensation reduced from $196,000 to $120,000. The service on the central route from Independence to Placerville, via Salt Lake City, was similarly reduced to semi-monthly trips, producing a saving of $115,000 to the Department. The Kansas City to Stockton route was discontinued. The Tehuantepec line, having been contracted for for but a single year's service, was dispensed with when the Postmaster-general refused to renew the contract. An effort was made to curtail the service upon the Butterfield route, but the contract had been so drawn that he was unable to alter the service. The contract for the ocean mail via Panama expired September 30, 1859, whereupon the Postmaster-general contracted for nine months' service with Cornelius Vanderbilt at the rate of $351,000 per year. Thus the annual expenditure upon the mail service to the Pacific Coast was reduced by $908,687.[292]

It was evidently with a feeling of satisfaction in duty performed that the Postmaster-general presented his first annual report. It exposed glaringly, the deficits upon the various lines and indicated his steps in the direction of retrenchment and reform. He attached to his report a rather full exposition of his views upon the problems presented:

"For a series of years the government has been occupied in advancing certain great national objects in the direction of our Pacific possessions, the entire burden of which has been imposed upon this department, though its connection with these objects is exceedingly slight and only incidental. . . It has been openly avowed by the friends of the policy which maintained these routes, that they were intended as the pioneers of civilization, as the means of rapid and regular communication between remote military posts and the government, and most especially as an instrumentality for promoting the settlement of our frontiers, and thus appreciating the value of the national domain. . .[293]

"The transportation and delivery of the mail with the utmost dispatch and security are the true and only mission of this department; in accomplishing this, it discharges its whole duty to the country. . . There are those who maintain that the adjustment of the mail service should be made subservient, if not subordinate to the interests of commerce and travel, and that the rapid and cheap conveyance of passengers and the support of railroad, steamship and stage companies, should as carefully be looked to and as anxiously provided for by

---
[292] — *Idem*, pp. 1411-1415.
[293] — *Idem*, 1426.

the department as the transportation of the mails. This is a fatal fallacy whose bitter fruits may now be seen in the enormous sums paid to these companies for mails, some of which are so light as scarcely to yield a revenue sufficient to defray the expense of carrying them on horseback. Four-horse coaches are thus run upon border and unfrequented routes, and steamboat lines are subsidized at an outlay which would afford postal accommodations to entire states." [294]

The transportation of the mails overland before the completion of a railroad was considered impracticable by the Postmaster-general because of their bulk. As dispatched semi-monthly they averaged ten tons. This amount he considered to be too large for overland transmission even when divided into semi-weekly allotments. The overland routes had been demonstrated as available for a light mail and could be used in case of foreign war or such emergency, and now there was no further necessity for their extensive employment. He believed that the law of March 3, 1845, announced the proper principle in reference to mail contracts when it provided that contracts were to be tendered to "the bidder tendering sufficient guarantees for faithful performance, without other reference to the mode of such transportation than may be necessary to provide for due celerity, certainty, and security of such transportation." Inasmuch as this law was still in force, Holt announced that hereafter only "Star Bids," [295] in conformity with the above law, would be invited.

---

[294] — *Idem*, 1402.

[295] In the Post Office Department files the lines upon which the service was performed with "celerity, certainty, and security," with no reference to the mode of conveyance, were marked with a star, hence the term "Star Bids."

The interposition of Congress in the way of legislative contracts was decried by the Postmaster-general:

"This department cannot much longer occupy its present equivocal position. If not allowed to return to the principles on which it was conducted in its earlier and better days – the days alike of its independence, its efficiency, and its renown – borne down by pressure of the existing course of legislation, it must ultimately become an established burden on the national revenues. The first step which would probably follow thereafter would be for Congress, in creating and adjusting the principal post routes, to declare what should be the compensation of the contractors. This would open an almost illimitable field for mercenary intrigue and spoliation. An approach to the inauguration of this system has already been made, and the results are before the country. Since 1853, Congress has interposed and made extra allowances to contractors amounting to $649,161.22 beyond what the department regarded them as entitled to receive under their contracts, and beyond what it was believed the postal service demanded or justified." [296]

Thus, during the summer of 1859, while Congress was not in session, momentous changes had taken place in the postal affairs. Not only had overland service to the Pacific Coast been curtailed or reduced, but in practically every state local lines had received similar treatment. Naturally, the localities affected were quick to protest, and when they received no encouragement from the Post Office Department, they turned their appeals to their representatives in Congress.

The House of Representatives did not turn a deaf ear. When the annual Post Office Appropriation bill

---
[296] Postmaster-general's *Report*, 1859, 1429.

was reported in the House it carried the following provision:

"The Postmaster-general is hereby directed to restore the inland service on all the routes under contract on the 4th of March, 1859, unless the same have expired by their own limitation; and where the service has been actually performed by the contractor, notwithstanding such discontinuance, the Postmaster-general shall pay the contractors, as if no change had been ordered." [297]

Champions of Holt and of retrenchment appeared, but they were in the minority in the lower house. Washburne, of Illinois, said: "In my district the service has been literally slaughtered. Every cabin which dots the prairies has felt the effects of this action of the Post Office Department." [298] Colfax said the proviso was added to prevent contractors coming in for damages that would exceed ultimately the amount saved by the Postmaster-general's retrenchment. The bill passed the House with the above proviso on May 17, 1860.

In the Senate the proviso found fewer supporters. The Democratic Party had a majority in this body and hence the Administration had better support here than it received from the House, where the recently-formed Republican Party had a plurality.[299] The Finance Committee, to whom the bill was referred, recommended striking out the House proviso for the restoration of the curtailed service. The proposition was

---

[297] U. S. *Congressional Globe*, 36th congress, first session, 2113

[298] —*Idem*, 2115.

[299] Rhodes, J. F. *History of the United States since the Compromise of 1850*, vol. ii, 417. The Senate was composed of thirty-eight Democrats, twenty-five Republicans, and two Americans. The House was composed of 109 Republicans, 88 administration Democrats, 13 anti-Lecompton Democrats, and 27 Americans.

debated May 26th. A letter from the Postmaster-general, justifying his action, was read. Senator Pearce of Maryland, spoke of him as a man of unquestioned integrity, and decided administrative talent: "Mr. Holt, with every disposition to grant all the service properly demanded, has firmness enough to endeavor to protect the Government from ruinous extravagance." [300] Senator Yulee, of Florida, was decidedly against a wholesale restoration of the discontinued service. "It proposes," he said, "to reinstate it all, to pay for service done without authority, and to lay the foundation for claims for damages which never will end, and the amount of which we cannot now contemplate. . . If Congress does not sustain the action of the Department now, we must bid farewell for the future to any attempt at reform by the administration in the Department." [301]

The overland lines and the extended service were not without their champions. Among these, Senator Gwin of California was especially prominent. He retorted:

"You begrudge the expense of transporting our letters to and from the Pacific Coast. . . You knew these plains and mountains, covered with perpetual snows existed when you so eagerly sought possessions on the Pacific Coast. After you got these possessions did you not intend to communicate with them for postal, military, commercial, and social purposes? Did you not intend to make us one people, part and parcel of you? Did the statesman who shaped that policy count the cost of conveying letters to these distant possessions, when they risked war and engaged in war to get them at the cost of tens of millions?" [302]

---

[300] U. S. *Congressional Globe*, 36th congress, first session, 2374.
[301] — *Idem*, 2393.
[302] — *Idem*, 2529.

The bill passed the Senate June 1st, but it had been so amended as to strike out the House proviso for restoring the discontinued postal service. The House refused to concur with the Senate amendments, and as the Senate further insisted upon them, a Conference Committee was appointed. This committee reported June 9th, that after three meetings it had been unable to agree. It was accordingly dismissed and a new committee appointed. Three days later this second Conference Committee reported disagreement and the House managers recommended giving up the demand for restoration of service on the routes from Neosho to Albuquerque and from Kansas to Stockton, since almost every one agreed that these were unnecessary. Amendments incorporating these changes were passed by the House, with the hope that the Senate would concur in the revised measure, but it was to no avail. The Senate, on June 20th, notified the House of its disagreement and called for another Conference Committee. Two days later this third Conference Committee reported its disagreement and asked to be discharged. On June 25th the Senate asked for another Conference Committee. This fourth committee reported its inability to reconcile the opposing views of the two houses. The House at last receded from its position and the Senate view prevailed. A wholesale restoration was not ordered.

Chapter VII

Mail Service to the Pike's Peak Region 1858-1860

While the through mail lines to California were being improved and the routes tested, and while Congress was debating the question of postal policy, a new need for postal extension arose in the inter-mountain region. The discovery of gold by W. Green Russell at the present site of Denver, Colorado, in the summer of 1858 was a signal for the usual stampede. The advance column of the Pike's Peakers reached the diggings in the fall of 1858, but the main army advanced the following spring. No sooner had these argonauts pitched their tents at the mouth of Cherry Creek than there arose a demand for means of communication with their relatives and friends in "the States." The little embryo towns of Auraria and Denver on the South Platte were in the no-man's-land triangle between the two famous highways to the West – the Santa Fé and the Oregon trails. Meagre as were the mail facilities on these two routes, the embryo Denver was not so located as to enjoy them. Two hundred miles of waste land separated the Colorado pioneers from their nearest post office at Fort Laramie on the North Platte. This stretch must be spanned and a link created to connect them with home and friends.

Jim Saunders, a trader who had been in the country before the miners came for gold, agreed to establish an express line to Fort Laramie.[303] He was to receive

---

[303] *Reminiscences of General William Larimer and of his son William*

fifty cents for letters and twenty-five cents for newspapers. William H. H. Larimer, one of the Colorado pioneers of 1858, writes of this first express:

"He [Saunders] got his list and on November 23, 1858, started with his squaw in a little wagon drawn by four Indian ponies for his two hundred mile journey. . . . No mail has ever arrived in Denver that was more anxiously awaited than that which he brought on his first trip. . . . Saunders returned on January 8th, but with nothing for father or me." [304]

In the second number (May 7, 1859) of the pioneer newspaper of Colorado we read:

"Occasionally an express is sent for what mail matter may be there [at Fort Laramie] but it is attended with heavy cost and long delay. . . . Three days ago the Laramie mail came in, bringing we learn 1500 letters and a great number of papers which were delivered to their proper owners upon payment of fifty cents for each letter and ten cents for each paper. This is a heavy tax, yet we were glad to get them at any price." [305]

The Saunders Express was short lived. It was replaced in the early spring of 1859 by one of the most remarkable institutions established in early Colorado — the "Leavenworth and Pike's Peak Express."

During the winter of 1858-9 William H. Russell and John S. Jones were in Washington, D. C. They conceived the daring scheme of running a stage-coach express to the Pike's Peak region. Alexander Majors, the experienced western freighter, refused to join in the enterprise. Reports were yet rather vague and in-

---

H. H. Larimer, *two of the founders of Denver City*, p. 136. Saunders was a native of Pennsylvania and was with the Indians on the North Platte when the gold excitement occurred.

[304] — *Idem*, 135.
[305] *Rocky Mountain News*, May 7, 1859.

definite. The value of the discoveries had not been proved. It was rather certain that there would be a heavy emigration to the Rocky Mountains in the spring of 1859, but the resources of the country and the permanency of the settlement were problematical indeed. Despite these facts Russell and his associates launched into the enterprise as though no doubt was entertained as to the ultimate realization of their highest hopes. Kentucky mules and Concord coaches sufficient to stock the line were quickly purchased with notes payable in ninety days.[306] When the notes became due Jones and Russell were unable to redeem them and the great freighting firm of Russell, Majors and Waddell came to the rescue and took over the line.[307] Of this great firm Horace Greeley wrote while on his way to Denver in 1859:

"Russell, Majors and Waddell's transportation establishment is the great feature of Leavenworth. Such acres of wagons! such pyramids of extra axletrees! such herds of oxen! such regiments of drivers and other employes! No one who does not see can realize how vast a business this is, nor how immense are its outlays as well as its income. I presume this great firm has at this hour two millions of dollars invested in stock, mainly oxen, mules and wagons. (They last year employed six thousand teamsters, and worked 45,000 oxen)."[308]

The first coaches left in pairs for security and mutual aid. Among the pioneer express party were Beverly D. Williams, superintendent of the line, and Dr. J. M.

---

[306] Mr. Root says there were about 800 mules and over 50 coaches. He saw the coaches landed on the levee and says they were the first Concord coaches brought to Kansas. – Root and Connelley, *The Overland Stage to California*, pp. 153, 154.
[307] Majors, A. *Seventy Years on the Frontier*, p. 165.
[308] Greeley, Horace. *An Overland Journey*, p. 47.

Fox, agent for Denver. Stations were located and stock distributed along the line.

The first arrival at Denver of the "L. & P. P. Ex. Co." coaches occurred on May 7, 1859. These coaches had taken nineteen days in transit, but the time would soon be reduced to six or seven days. Great was the delight of the pioneers of "Pike's Peak." Instead of news from one to three months old, brought at monthly intervals, they could now enjoy weekly communication and feast on news fresh from the States – but seven days old! The arrival of this first express was the occasion for the publication of the first "Extra" (two columns) ever published by a newspaper in Colorado.[309]

This "Extra" gives the following information obtained from Mr. Williams, relative to the route:

"Stations are established at intervals of 25 miles after leaving Junction City, 172 miles out, to this place . . . The road after passing Ft. Riley, follows an entirely new route, all the way, keeping along the divide between the Republican and Solomon's forks of the Kansas River, crossing the heads of the tributaries of the latter fork for some distance, then bearing a little northward, crossing the heads of Prairie Dog, Sappa and Cranmer creeks, tributaries of the Republican, and striking the river near the mouth of Rock Creek, between longitude 101 and 102 degrees; it then follows the south side of the Republican to a point near the source, thence striking due west it crosses the heads of Beaver, Bijou and Kiowa creeks, tributaries of the Platte, passing through a beautiful pine country for sixty miles, and striking Cherry Creek twenty miles above its mouth. The whole length of the road is 687 miles by odometer measurement, but it will probably

---

[309] *Rocky Mountain News*, "Extra," May 9, 1859.

be shortened 75 miles by cut-offs in various places – one very considerable one at this end, terminating the road directly at the mouth of Cherry Creek. The road throughout its whole length is good when broken and traveled, but the coaches that have just arrived made the first track over it."

Horace Greeley writes from Station 18 on June 2, 1859: "Off the five weeks old track to Pike's Peak, all is dreary solitude and silence." On the next day the editor wrote:

"The road from Leavenworth to Denver had to be taken some 50 miles north of its due course to obtain even such a passage [described as bad] through the American Desert." [310]

The first return coach from Denver reached Leavenworth on May 20th, having been ten days upon the prairie. The Leavenworth *Tribune* reported: "It brings $700 in shot and scale gold and four passengers." The issue of the following day records: "There was a celebration here today in honor of the arrival of the first Overland Express. It passed off with great eclat. The procession was composed of military, firemen, and civilians. . . A thousand persons participated in the affair." [311] Frank Root, for years an express messenger, writes of the return of the first coach to Leavenworth: "A large and anxious crowd gathered in front of the Planter's Hotel, eager to learn everything. . . The express vehicle bore a decoration which read: 'The gold mountains of Kansas send greetings to her commercial metropolis.' A coach dispatched a short distance out to escort it into the city bore a banner labeled 'Leavenworth hears the echo from her mineral moun-

---

[310] Greeley, Horace. *An Overland Journey*, p. 104.
[311] Quoted in Larimer, *Reminiscences*, etc., p. 173.

tains and sends it on the wings of lightning to a listening world.' " [312]

The coaches now began to arrive at weekly intervals. But the express route was hardly established before a transfer was effected which led to an abandonment of the Republican River route in favor of the one along the emigrant trail up the Platte. The last coach over this pioneer route (reaching Denver June 6) carried a very distinguished passenger in the person of the famous editor of the New York *Tribune*. Horace Greeley's report upon the newly discovered gold fields of the Rocky Mountains was to have a very important effect in stabilizing affairs.[313] It did much to counteract the decided reaction that had already set in against the country and that was carrying all before it with the condemning cry of "Pike's Peak Humbug."

In May, 1859, Jones, Russell and Company purchased from Hockaday and Liggett the contract for mail transportation from Missouri to Salt Lake City. Hockaday and Liggett had found themselves in a precarious financial condition. The reduction of their service to a semi-monthly basis by Postmaster-general Holt, carrying as it did a reduction in the compensation from $190,000 to $130,000, was sufficient to force them to sell at a sacrifice.[314] Their contract was assigned May 11, 1859, to Jones, Russell and Company for a

---

[312] Root and Connelley, *The Overland Stage to California*, p. 154.

[313] Greeley, Horace. *An Overland Journey*, p. 146.

[314] U. S. *Congressional Globe*, 36th congress, second session, p. 573. The contractors were ruined by the curtailment. The Washington correspondent of the San Francisco *Bulletin* says, in speaking of this case: "It is really pitiable to contemplate the financial ruin which the order of curtailment in this case has occasioned to the parties. . . . Hockaday's mental faculties have been seriously affected by his pecuniary misfortunes and Liggett's fortune is lost." – *Bulletin*, July 17, 1860. A bill for their relief was passed in Congress during the spring of 1860, but it was vetoed by the President. A similar bill

MAIL SERVICE TO PIKE'S PEAK REGION 151

bonus of $50,000. Their property connected with the route was to be appraised, which resulted in a payment of $94,000 additional.[315] Mr. Majors says: "Messrs. Hockaday and Liggett had a few stages, light, cheap vehicles, and but a few mules and no stations along the route. They traveled the same team for several hundred miles before changing, stopping every few hours and turning them loose to graze." [316]

Since the Utah mail was to be carried on the Platte route the new contractors found it advantageous to transfer their express line from the Republican to the Platte route in order that the two lines might be run jointly. The transfer of stock and supplies to the Platte route was effected in June and by August the coaches were running semi-weekly on a seven-day schedule. This service was maintained during the summer, but as winter approached it was reduced to a weekly schedule, and was conducted on that basis throughout the winter.[317]

During the year 1859 the "L. & P. P. Ex." was one of the most important and influential institutions of Colorado. Its weekly or semi-weekly budget of news was eagerly awaited not only by the pioneers of Colorado but also by their fellow citizens in "the States." Passenger transportation was one of its chief sources of revenue. This service was especially appreciated by

---

was passed the next year and the President finally allowed it to become a law without his signature. This measure provided for $40,000 to reimburse them for damages sustained by reason of the curtailment. This amount is considered less than the actual loss sustained.

[315] U. S. *Congressional Globe*, 36th congress, second session, p. 573. From President Buchanan's message vetoing a bill for the relief of Hockaday and Liggett.

[316] Majors, A. *Seventy Years on the Frontier*, p. 165.

[317] *Rocky Mountain News*, June 11, 18, 1859; Aug. 20, 27, 1859; Sept. 3, 1859.

business men who could now cross "the Plains" in one week instead of consuming four to six, as was required by other means of conveyance. During the spring and summer, there was heavy passenger and express traffic to Denver. The returning coaches ran with lighter loads but usually a consignment of the shining dust was carried by the eastbound coach.

The location of the terminus of the express line had a very significant influence in determining the fate of town companies at the mouth of Cherry Creek. In the spring of 1859 Auraria and Denver were the chief competitors. Auraria, on the west bank of the creek, had been founded first, and was larger than the settlement on the opposite bank. However, the newer town company had advantages to offset its drawbacks. William Larimer, the chief leader in the Denver Town Company, was an experienced town promoter. Before leaving Leavenworth he had discussed with his neighbor, William H. Russell, the question of town companies and stage lines and the inter-dependence of these two institutions. When the Denver Town Company was organized, Russell was given an original share in it.[318] Two days after the arrival of the first express Larimer writes to his son John:

"Russell's train changes the whole face of matters here. They are locating in Denver City. Denver is all O. K. Since writing the above the Denver City Company met and donated nine original interests to the Leavenworth and Pike's Peak Express Company. That company consists of ten persons. William H. Russell now holds one original share in Denver City, so you see we are now all right, if not before. . . This is fine; their monied influence will make this *now*

---

[318] Larimer, *Reminiscences*, p. 106.

the certain point. Will and I are delighted with this move. Judge Smith only wanted to give 1,000 shares but we preferred the way we passed it as we have them now fully committed to help along the town, procure capital and hasten the railroad. I shall sleep soundly tonight." [319]

The regular advertisement run in the *Rocky Mountain News* of 1859 gives the following information:

"Each stage is capable of carrying eight passengers with comfort and ease. Passage through to Leavenworth $100, board included. . . Special attention is given to the comfort of ladies traveling in the coaches. . . Our drivers are sober, discreet and experienced men. The teams are the choice of 800 mules." [320]

Stations were established at intervals of ten or fifteen miles along the route, and fresh teams were ever ready to keep the coach going both night and day. Passengers took rest and sleep as best they could to the accompaniment of the swaying and creeking of the coach and the chuckling of the wheels.

William N. Byers, who made a trip to the States and back in the summer of 1859, has this to say:

"A tribute of praise is due the Leavenworth and Pike's Peak Express Company for the very superior accommodations they offer to travelers over their route.

"On our recent journey from the States, we found their stations along the South Platte fitted up in the best style possible. Several new stations have also been made below the crossing, in addition to the old Salt Lake mail company's stations. Houses have been erected, wells dug, and the conveniences of life are rapidly being gathered around points along a distance of

---
[319] — *Idem*, p. 174.
[320] *Rocky Mountain News*, August 20th and subsequently.

hundreds of miles, where two months ago there was not a fixed habitation. Passengers by this line get their regular meals, on a table and smoking hot." [321]

The arrival and the departure of the coach was an occasion of importance. The departure of the express was compared to that of a steamer from San Francisco:

"The four-mule coach is driven up to Bradford's corner, and the crowd assembles; packages are stored away by the careful employees of the company and lastly parting drinks are taken by the passengers and their friends, hands shaken, seats taken and the coach is off, to make the passage of the prairie ocean in seven days. The crowd now disperse feeling that an event has occurred." [322]

The arrival of the express was an even greater event. The schedule was maintained with remarkable regularity. S. T. Sopris writes:

"When the hour of its arrival approached a crowd would assemble at the office, corner of 'F' and McGaa streets (Fifteenth and Market) and it was seldom there was a wait of more than a few minutes before the four 'spanking bays' would appear in sight, coming down from Larimer street, and with screeching of the brakes pull up in front of the company office." [323]

An hour or more were now consumed while the mail was being changed. In the meantime the expectant crowd grew larger and the waiting line often extended around the block. Much time was consumed in delivering the mail since the carriage charge was usually paid in dust which had to be carefully weighed out.

---

[321] — *Idem*, August 13, 1859.

[322] — *Idem*, April 11, 1860.

[323] Sopris, S. T. *First Stage Coach*, p. 2. MS. in possession of the State Historical and Natural History Society of Colorado.

Men with money would often buy a front position in the line from some person whose time had a smaller commercial equivalent.

The express charge for carriage of letters was twenty-five cents, and ten cents was collected upon newspapers. This was in addition to the regular United States postage, which was three cents on half ounce letters. The government was very slow in providing Colorado with mail facilities. For a time during the summer of 1859 it was thought that the government service had been established, but the people were doomed to disappointment. The express company failed to receive the anticipated mail contract and was forced to continue private charges for the services performed.[324] But in the spring of 1860 Congress was moved to action. A Denver newspaper reported in May that B. D. Williams, "Delegate from Jefferson Territory" had procured, with the assistance of Colfax, Craig, and others, the passage through the House of an appropriation for immediate mail service to Denver. The paper's appreciation was thus expressed: "All honor and praise is due Mr. Williams for his tireless efforts in behalf of the people of Jefferson."[325] It was not, however, until August, 1860, that the first regular United States mail was received.[326]

---

[324] *Rocky Mountain News*, July 9, 1859.

[325] —*Idem*, May 2, 1860. "Jefferson Territory" was the spontaneous government that arose in the Rocky Mountains as the forerunner of Colorado. It had no legal existence, but never-the-less had a governor, a legislature, and a delegate to Congress. A copy of the "Laws of Jefferson Territory" is in the library of the State Historical and Natural History Society of Colorado. Delegate Williams who had come to Denver in 1859 as the superintendent of the "L. & P. P. Ex." line served at Washington without pay. He did not receive official recognition by Congress but exerted some influence upon matters pertaining to the people whose representative he was.

[326] *Rocky Mountain News*, August 22, 1860.

Postage was not necessarily prepaid upon the letters sent in 1859. This situation tempted some patrons to take letters that they had received and read, mark them "opened by mistake," and demand a refund of postage at the window of the express office. William H. H. Larimer, who was a clerk in the office in 1859, says that these "mistakes" became too common and that they were sometimes forced to question applicants as to whom they expected mail from. In case of doubt the letter would be opened at the customer's request and a few lines read to make sure. Young Larimer cites one instance. He started reading. The letter commenced: "Your wife has been raising hell ever since you left. . ." The man interrupted: "Hold on, I think that is my letter," took it, paid for it, and disappeared.[327]

The rates on express matter other than letters was correspondingly high. The *Rocky Mountain News* once complained that they were compelled to pay $30.10 on a bundle of paper weighing forty-three pounds. In 1861 the express rates to Denver ranged from 20c to 40c per pound depending upon the size of the shipment.[328]

In February, 1860, the legislature of Kansas granted a charter to the "Central Overland California and Pike's Peak Express Company." This newly formed corporation absorbed the "L. & P. P. Ex.," which had been operating its line to Denver during the preceding year, and thus also obtained the United States mail contract for service to Utah. Soon the George Chorpenning contract for service upon the route from Salt Lake City to Placerville, California, was annulled for alleged

---

[327] Larimer, *Reminiscences*, p. 177.
[328] *Rocky Mountain News*, January 2, 1861.

failures [329] and a new contract made with William H. Russell for a semi-monthly "star" service.[330] This gave the "C. O. C. & P. P. Ex. Co." control of the entire mail service over the central route to the Pacific Coast. The directors of this company were A. Majors, John S. Jones, Wm. B. Waddell, B. C. Card, W. S. Grant, J. S. Simpson, and W. H. Russell. Russell was chosen president, and B. F. Ficklin, general road agent. The Leavenworth *Times* of February 13, 1860, speaks thus of the directors of this organization:

"These great mariners of the plains represent an executive ability, a comprehensive knowledge of the wants and necessities incident to overland trade and travel, a fearless independence, a profuse liberality, a faith in western resources and capabilities which will make their names conspicuous in the growth and progress of an almost illimitable region of which it may be truly said –

'The elements of Empire here are plastic yet and warm
The chaos of a mighty world is rounding into form.' " [331]

The meagre amounts of gold found in the Pike's Peak country in 1858 were slight justification for the great rush of 1859. But fortunately for the immigrants

---

[329] Chorpenning, G. *Statement*, p. 33. (Pamphlet, Bancroft Library, University of California.) "May 11, 1860, Postmaster-general Holt ordered my contract annulled on the ground that the service was not performed in accordance with the terms of the contract. . . When my contract was annulled my coaches were running over the road weekly and carrying such of the mails as were given me. The department gave me no notice of dissatisfaction with the service, as was the regular custom. . . My contract was annulled upon charges I have proved false and unfounded."

[330] U. S. House. *Executive Documents*, 36th congress, second session, no. 73, vol. x, 347. "Route no. 12801, from Salt Lake City to Placerville, California, 768 miles, and back twice a month, $33,000 per year. Contractor, W. H. Russell."

[331] Quoted in the *Rocky Mountain News*, February 29, 1860.

and the country, quartz gold in large paying quantities was discovered on the branches of Clear Creek in May, 1859.[332] The news spread rapidly and as the prospectors scattered over the mountains important new discoveries were made in every direction. Denver grew because she was well situated to become a distributing point for the mountain mining towns. The earliest mail service to the mining camps was by private expresses. Presently regular coach service was established for the transportation of mail, passengers, and express. In March, 1860, two tri-weekly lines of stages were running regularly from Denver to the mining region about present Central City.[333] Other express service connected Denver with Boulder to the north, and Colorado City to the south. In the meantime gold had been discovered in South Park, the Upper Arkansas, and on the Blue River. In June, 1860, tri-weekly stages were running into these camps and crossing the continental divide to Breckenridge, Utah Territory.[334]

The Post Office Department was urged to provide mail facilities to these newly formed towns in the Rocky Mountains. In response to the requests, on April 7, 1860, bids were called for weekly service from Julesburg to Denver and from Denver to Boulder, Colorado City, Breckenridge, and Missouri City. The service was to begin July 1st if practicable. On July 4, 1860, the *Rocky Mountain News* published a letter received from Schuyler Colfax giving the following information regarding the mail contracts for the ensuing year:

---

[332]—*Idem*, May 28, 1859. The first important discovery was made by John H. Gregory of Georgia on May 6, 1859, at the site of present Central City.

[333] *Rocky Mountain News*, March 28, 1860. One line went by way of Golden City and the other by Mount Vernon canyon.

[334]—*Idem*, June 27, 1860.

"Denver to Colorado City weekly, H. G. Weibling for $2,360; Denver to Boulder, Nebraska Territory [335] weekly, M. G. Smith at $894; Denver to Breckenridge Utah Territory weekly, Thomas Bridge, $2,495; Denver to Missouri City weekly, H. G. Weibling, $1,030."

By August the contractors were all on the ground and had their respective lines in operation.[336] The regular mail stages were incapable of carrying the heavy traffic to the mines and local stage companies supplied the demand. During the summer of 1860 two and three daily stages were required to provide the transportation facilities to some of the more active mining camps.[337] In the fall of this year the "C. O. C. & P. P. Ex. Co." extended its stage lines to Central City in present Gilpin County. Competition between rival express lines became so keen that it was declared to be cheaper to ride the stage than to stay at home.[338]

Although the "C. O. C. & P. P. Ex. Co." was running tri-weekly coaches from the Missouri River to Denver in the summer of 1860, these were for passengers and express service only. Its government contract provided for but semi-monthly mail service upon the Platte River route to Salt Lake City, and this did not apply to Denver at all. The region that became Colorado had no United States mail service until August, 1860, and then but a weekly schedule was provided. The contract for service from Julesburg to Denver was awarded to E. F. Bruce of Saint Joseph, and temporary

---

[335] The region that in 1861 was organized into Colorado Territory comprised portions of four organized territories in 1860 – Kansas, Nebraska, Utah, and New Mexico. A "Territory of Jefferson" performed some of the functions of government in the region in 1859 and 1860, but its jurisdiction had but slight recognition.

[336] *Rocky Mountain News*, August 22, 1860.

[337] —*Idem*, June 20, 1860.

[338] —*Idem*, October 23, 1860.

arrangements were made with the "C. O. C. & P. P. Ex. Co." for carrying this weekly mail.[339] It seems that Bruce did not qualify, for on August 29, 1860, a contract was made with E. S. Alvord of the Western Stage Company for a weekly mail service from Fort Kearny to Denver. This service continued to June 30, 1861.[340] The Western Stage Company also had a stage line from Omaha westward to Fort Kearny. This now gave them a through line to the Denver region. The first coach on this route left Denver for Omaha September 20, 1860.[341] Hinckley's Express Company of "Jefferson Territory" established a special express messenger service to the States in connection with the Western Stage Company in the fall of 1860.

The Western Stage Company in its United States mail bags naturally carried a large part of the mail matter for the region served. For over a year the "C. O. C. & P. P. Ex. Co." had had a monopoly upon the mail and express carriage to the Pike's Peak region and the establishment of the United States mail service now cut materially into their revenues. In an effort to save to themselves some of this business they cut their express charges on letters from twenty-five cents to ten cents, and on newspapers from ten to five cents. Since their coaches ran tri-weekly they were thus able to maintain a fair express business.[342] Their passenger fare was also reduced from $100 to $75 for passage from Saint Joseph to Denver. From July to August they had carried $136,000, in gold dust by express.[343] But

---

[339] — *Idem*, July 4, 1860; August 22, 1860.

[340] U. S. House. *Executive Documents*, 37th congress, second session, pp. 137, 198. (Serial 1139.)

[341] *Rocky Mountain News*, September 20, 1860.

[342] — *Idem*, September 26, 1860. These express charges were in addition to the regular government postage.

[343] — *Idem*, August 8, 1860.

MAIL SERVICE TO PIKE'S PEAK REGION 161

this company was carrying a heavy burden. They were in 1860 conducting the Pony Express without government subsidy, and were suffering a financial loss thereby. True, they had a mail contract for the line from Saint Joseph, Missouri, to Placerville, California, but it was only a semi-monthly service and the remuneration was small. These contractors were holding-on with the hope of procuring the daily mail contract on the central route. They could see that such a service was soon to be established and were staking their all to win it. Meanwhile financial embarrassment threatened them.[344] Employees did not always get their pay promptly and one of them transformed the company's name into "Clean Out of Cash and Poor Pay."[345] But the company continued service and received the praise of its beneficiaries. The *Rocky Mountain News* in an editorial of December 19, 1860, gave a short review of the company's history and paid tribute as follows:

"This old pioneer line which made its advent in Denver on the 8th day of May, 1859, still continues the even tenor of its way, winning popularity and steadily growing in public favor. . . it stands today, probably, the best fitted, best stocked and best managed route of the same magnitude in the world. . . In months the arrivals at Denver do not vary two hours from the regular time. Stock on the route is fed with grain, costing from six to ten cents per pound as freely as if on the prairies of Illinois, with oats at fifteen cents per bushel.

"Unlike the Butterfield route, with its subsidy from the government of $600,000 per year, for carrying the mails, this colossal enterprise has been built up and is

---
[344] San Francisco *Bulletin*, October 19, 22, 1860.
[345] Root and Connelley, *Overland Stage to California*, p. 584.

wholly sustained by individual enterprise. The benefits that have accrued to this country from its establishment would be hard to estimate and can hardly be overrated. It is doubtful whether we would at any time prior to July last have been favored with any kind of mail facilities had it not established and maintained its line for many months, with actual heavy loss. Its projector and President, William H. Russell, well deserved the name of 'Napoleon of the West.' "

Chapter VIII

The Pony Express, Demonstrator of the Central Route

Much has been written of the famous Pony Express, but most accounts have stressed the romantic and spectacular side, failing to show the motives which actuated its founders, or to portray its relationship to the other problems of overland communication and westward expansion. The Pony Express was not an end in itself, but a means to an end. There had been previous suggestions for the establishment of a fast overland express,[346] and an attempt was made in Congress in 1855 to provide such a service,[347] but these first efforts did not succeed. With the establishment of the overland stage lines a rivalry had arisen between the Butterfield and

---

[346] Senator Gwin had ridden overland to the Capital in the fall of 1854. He was accompanied part of the distance by B. F. Ficklin, then General Superintendent of the freighting firm of Russell, Majors, and Waddell. Upon this journey the scheme for a fast overland express was discussed. Gwin, in his *Memoirs*, 120, (Manuscript in Bancroft Library, University of California), speaks of B. F. Ficklin as the man "who originated the scheme [of the Pony Express] and carried it into operation." In a speech given in Stockton, California, upon his return to California (reported in the San Francisco *Bulletin*, August 31, 1860) Senator Gwin speaks of the Pony Express as "fostered and nurtured by his [Gwin's] labor."

Mr. Morehead in his *Narrative* in Connelley's *Doniphan Expedition*, 614, says that he and Mr. Rupe returned in January, 1858, from taking supplies to the army enroute to Utah. They had left Fort Bridger December 26, 1857, and Russell had had them continue on to Washington. Morehead says: "With Secretary Floyd the question of the feasibility of a pony express across the continent was presented by Mr. Russell, and fully discussed. Captain Rupe's views were called for, and he expressed the opinion that it was entirely practicable at all seasons on this route, all the way to California."

[347] Representative McDougall of California introduced a bill in February, 1855, providing for a daily overland mail to California. It was defeated

the "Central" routes, and with the assembling of the thirty-sixth Congress in December, 1859, everything pointed in the direction of a general revision of the overland service.[348] Partisans of the Central route were active but they met with considerable opposition. It was with the idea of demonstrating the practicability of the Central route for year-round travel and to secure an enlarged mail contract that the Pony Express scheme was conceived.[349]

During the winter of 1859-60, while Mr. William H. Russell was in Washington, he discussed the over-

---

March 2, 1855. The next day Senator Gwin proposed a scheme for a weekly express to be carried within fourteen days at a compensation not to exceed $6,000 per trip. This measure also was defeated. – U. S. *Congressional Globe*, 33d congress, second session, 1117.

[348] See below, Chapter IX.

[349] The Washington correspondent of the San Francisco *Bulletin* wrote of the project of Russell, Majors, and Waddell, January 30, 1860: "Their object in establishing this express is not so much to make money at present, as it is to prove by actual experiment the superiority of the Salt Lake route."

The *Rocky Mountain News* of May 23, 1860, makes the following comment upon the establishment of the Pony Express: "The Express Company deserve great credit for concentrating public attention on the Central route, and it is hoped that their enterprise will *shame* Congress into legislation in favor of the opening of a daily or tri-weekly mail route to Denver, Utah, and California. The southern route is backed up by the entire South."

H. H. Bancroft, in his *History of Nevada*, 228, says that the object of the founders was never distinctively made known. However, he says that Walter Crowinsheld of Nevada who assisted to re-stock the road after the Pah Ute outbreak of 1860, was of the opinion that the line was established with a view to obtaining the mail contract when the feasibility of the route was demonstrated. Bancroft goes on to say that Russell, Majors, and Waddell made no effort in that direction. This is hardly true. Russell was lobbying in Congress, and the Butterfield company was moved to the Central route in 1861 only after a working arrangement had been made with Russell, Majors, and Waddell.

The close relation of the Pony Express to the mail contract is shown in a letter from W. H. Russell, dated New York, September 27, 1860. (Published in the San Francisco *Bulletin* of October 16, 1860.) In this letter he says that his company's mail contract expires November 30th, and that they cannot continue the Pony Express unless their mail contract is renewed. "A mail contract alone would justify us to continue the Pony. . . We have how-

WILLIAM H. RUSSELL
the founder of the Pony Express

THE PONY EXPRESS 169

land mail question with Senator Gwin of California. The Senator contended that it was necessary to demonstrate the feasibility of the Central route before he would be able to get from Congress the desired contract. He appealed to Russell to launch a swift overland express and agreed to obtain from Congress a subsidy to reimburse the firm for the undertaking.[350] The plan appealed to Russell and he agreed to put through the enterprise. The following dispatch is the first definite notice we have found regarding the Pony Express:

WASHINGTON, January 27, 1860.
To JOHN W. RUSSELL: Have determined to establish a Pony Express to Sacramento, California, commencing the 3rd of April. Time ten days.
WM. H. RUSSELL.[351]

Upon coming west Russell presented the plan to his partners, Majors and Waddell. The venture did not appear to them as a practical business proposition but they were finally induced to agree to the scheme in order to make good the pledge of Russell to Gwin that their firm would establish and operate a Pony Express.

Upon deciding to establish a Pony Express, the actual preparations were pushed with vigor. A Saint Louis news letter of February 6, 1860, announced that the "horse express" would begin operations April 3rd, and that "horses and riders are now being placed on the line ready for this new enterprise in this fast age."[352]

Russell, Majors and Waddell were operating the

---

ever attained our principal object, that of practically demonstrating that the route is feasible and practical, and with a good mail contract, and in that way only, the Express can be sustained."
See also Majors, *Seventy Years on the Frontier*, 167.
[350] Majors, *Seventy Years on the Frontier*, 182.
[351] *Rocky Mountain News*, February 15, 1860.
[352] Printed in the San Francisco *Bulletin*, February 29, 1860.

semi-monthly mail line from the Missouri River via Salt Lake City to Placerville, California, and were thus in a position to make speedy preparations for launching the Pony Express. Many stations were already established from the eastern terminus to Salt Lake City, but beyond that point more extensive preparations had to be made.[353]

Mr. Russell assumed managerial charge of the eastern division of the line which lay between Saint Joseph and Salt Lake City; B. F. Ficklin was stationed at Salt Lake City; and W. W. Finney at San Francisco.[354] Horses were purchased and distributed along the line. The best riders obtainable were employed. Stock tenders repaired to their respective stations with the relay and extra animals.[355] Within about two months after the plan was decided upon, everything was in readiness for launching the initial express. On March 17, 1860, the following advertisement appeared in the San Francisco *Bulletin*:

"PONY EXPRESS – NINE DAYS FROM SAN FRANCISCO TO NEW YORK. The Central Overland Pony Express Co. will start their Letter Express from San Francisco to New York and intermediate points on Tuesday, the 3rd day of April next, and upon every Tuesday thereafter, at 4 o'clock P.M. Letters will be received at San Francisco until 2¾ o'clock P.M. each day of departure. Office – Alta Telegraph Office, Montgomery St. Telegraphic Dispatches will be received at Carson City until 6 o'clock P.M. every Wednesday. Schedule time from San Francisco to

---

[353] Majors, *Seventy Years on the Frontier*, 182. Mr. Majors says the firm was then operating a daily mail. This is a mistake. The service was but semi-monthly at this time.
[354] Bradley, G. *The Story of the Pony Express*, 23.
[355] San Francisco *Bulletin*, March 30, 1860.

New York: For Telegraphic Dispatches, 9 days; for Letters, 13 days. Letters will be charged between San Francisco and Salt Lake City, $3 per half ounce and under, and at that rate according to weight. To all points *beyond* Salt Lake City, $5 per half ounce and under, and at that rate according to weight. Telegraphic dispatches will be subject to the same charges as letters. All letters must be enclosed in stamped envelopes. Wm. W. Finney, Agent Central Overland Pony Express Co."

The appointed day was looked forward to with great expectancy. Californians were highly elated. Was it possible that they were to be brought so close to their friends beyond the mountains and plains? True to plans, on the 3rd of April all was in readiness for a simultaneous start from the two ends of the line. In San Francisco a "clean-limbed, hardy little nankeen-colored pony" [356] stood waiting for his precious letter bags which were to be sped across the continent. The little fellow looked all unawares of his famous future. Two little flags adorned his head-stall, and from the pommel of his saddle hung a bag lettered "Overland Pony Express." This pony had but a short run to the boat which was to carry the express to Sacramento. Here began the real Pony Express. Harry Roff, mounted on a spirited half-breed broncho, started eastward, covering the first twenty miles, including one change, in fifty-nine minutes. At Placerville he connected with "Boston" who took the route to Friday's Station, crossing the eastern summit of the Sierra Nevadas. Sam Hamilton next fell into line and pursued his way by Carson City to Fort Churchill. The run to this point, 185 miles, was made in fifteen hours and

---

[356] — *Idem*, April 3, 1860.

twenty minutes, and included the crossing of the Sierra Nevadas through thirty feet of snow.[357] Robert H. Haslam ("Pony Bob"), Jay G. Kelly, H. Richardson, and George Thatcher followed each other on the route to Salt Lake City.[358]

A large crowd assembled at Saint Joseph to witness the launching of the Pony Express. The Hannibal and Saint Joseph train was due in the early afternoon but the minutes dragged into hours before the eastern mail arrived. Then as darkness was settling down upon the little town the roar of a cannon from the express office announced the arrival of the train and the inauguration of the Pony Express. Lots had been cast among the men employed to ride the express to determine who should take the first ride. Number one fell to a young sailor lad, "Billy" Richardson.[359] The bright bay mare was ready, he leaped into the saddle and dashed away to the ferry. From the west bank of the "Big Muddy" he careered into the darkness, carrying his light but precious burden to the Kansas station forty miles away.

The arrangements were so well planned and executed that the express was carried through in excellent time, as per schedule. The receptions of the ponies along the route and at the opposite ends of the line were very enthusiastic. The approach of the west-bound Pony Express was telegraphed ahead from Genoa, Nevada, and expectant crowds gathered to receive the first ar-

[357] This was possible because pack trains of mules and horses to the Washoe mines kept the trail open.

[358] This statement of rides and riders is based upon Majors, *Seventy Years on the Frontier*, 176.

[359] There has been much dispute as to who was the first rider from Saint Joseph. The many claims put forth are duly considered by Louise Platt Hauck in her article, "The Pony Express Celebration," in the *Missouri Historical Review*, vol. xvii, 437. She seems to have settled the dispute in favor of Johnson William Richardson.

rival. In Sacramento, J Street was lined its entire length for hours before the fleet messenger arrived.[360]

The reception in San Francisco is graphically given in the *Bulletin*:

"It took seventy-five ponies to make the trip from Missouri to California in 10½ days, but the last one – the little fellow who came down in the Sacramento boat this morning had the vicarious glory of them all. Upon him an enthusiastic crowd were disposed to shower all their compliments. He was the veritable Hippagriff who shoved a continent behind his hoofs so easily; who snuffed up sandy plains, sent lakes and mountains, prairies and forests, whizzing behind him, like one great river rushing eastward. . .

"The boat waited for the Pony Express at Sacramento until 5 o'clock, yesterday afternoon. The instant it arrived it came on board, and the *Antelope* put on all steam to accomplish an early trip. Meanwhile at the theatres it had been announced that on the landing of the boat there would be ceremonies of reception, music, jollification and some speeches. . . The California Band traveled up and down the streets waking all the echoes, fetching out the boys, and making the night melodious. Bonfires were kindled here and there on the Plaza and on the wharves. . . The organized turn-out reached the foot of Broadway at midnight. With waltzes and Yankee Doodle, the airs of all the nations and several improvised black-oak dances, the spirits were maintained until near one o'clock when the *Antelope* came steaming down, wheeled, threw out her hawsers, was made fast and the glorified pony walked ashore.

"The crowd cheered till their throats were sore; the

---

[360] Letter from Sacramento in the San Francisco *Bulletin*, April 16, 1860.

Band played as if they would crack their cheeks, . . . the boys stirred up their bonfires and the speech makers studied their points. The procession reformed, opened right and left, and the pony, a bright bay . . . paced gaily up to his stand. The line closed again, the Band went ahead, the firemen followed with their machines, the center of attraction, the Hippagriff, came next, and citizens fell in behind. There was one lady on the ground. As the pony trotted into line, she tore the ribbons from her bonnet and tied them around his neck. All moved up to the Pony Express office. While the twenty-five letters that were brought were being distributed, the speechmakers were proceeding to uncork the bottles of their eloquence. Their friends said 'hear hear,' but the boys would leave it to the pony. He considered a moment, eyed the ribbon around his neck, looked a bit sleepy, thought of his oats, and uttered a loud *neigh*. So the speeches were corked down again, the speech-makers tied comforters around their throats, the Dashaways cheered hoarsely, the rag-tag-and-bob-tail took something warm, the morning papers went to press, the crowd to bed and the Pony to his stable. . . Long live the Pony!" [361]

The following, taken from the Way-bill of the Pony Express shows the time made on this first notable trip to San Francisco: Left Saint Joseph at 6:30 p.m. on the 3rd of April; arrived at Salt Lake City, 6:30 p.m. on the 9th; at Carson City, 2:30 p.m. on the 12th; at Placerville, 2:00 p.m. on the 13th; Sacramento, 5:30 p.m. on the 13th; San Francisco, 1:00 a.m. on the 14th.[362]

The route taken by the Pony Express was that traversed by the then existing overland mail via Salt Lake

---

[361] — *Idem*, April 14, 1860.
[362] — *Idem*, April 14, 1860.

City, and was that in general followed by the Mormon pioneers in 1847 and the California Argonauts of 1849. From Saint Joseph, it lay a little south of west until it struck the old overland military road at Kennekuk, forty-four miles out. Thence it diverged a little northwesterly across the Kickapoo Indian reservation via Granada, Log Chain, Seneca, Marysville, and Hollenberg; up the Little Blue valley to Rock Creek, Big Sandy, Liberty Farm, and over to Thirty-two-mile Creek; thence across the divide and over the prairie and sand-hills to the Platte River. The route then led westward up the valley to Fort Kearny. For two hundred miles west of Fort Kearny the road followed along the Platte River via Plum Creek, Midway, Cottonwood Springs, O'Fallon's Bluffs, Alkali, Beauvais Ranch, and Diamond Springs to old Julesburg. Here the South Fork was forded, and the route followed up the Lodge Pole Creek, across the Thirty-mile Ridge, and along it to Mud Springs; thence to Court-house Rock, past Chimney Rock and Scotts Bluffs, and on to Fort Laramie; thence over the foot-hills at the eastern base of the Rocky Mountains, via South Pass, to Fort Bridger, and on to Salt Lake City.[363] From Salt Lake City westward the Chorpenning mail route of 1859 was followed. This lay south of Great Salt Lake, to Camp Floyd, thence to Deep Creek, Ruby Valley, Smith's Creek, Fort Churchill and Carson City. From here it went by Genoa, over the Sierra Nevadas to the south of Lake Tahoe, down the western slope of the Sierras to Placerville, and thence to Sacramento. From this point the express was taken by boat to San Francisco.

---

[363] Description of the route follows that given by Root and Connelley, *The Overland Stage to California*, 113.

Along this route, stations were established at intervals averaging about fifteen miles each.[364] Stationhouses were built of logs, stone, or adobe, according to the material most available in the section. Some of these houses, in the areas where Indians were hostile, were regular little fortresses. Those stations rebuilt after the Indian difficulties in Nevada in the summer of 1860, were constructed of stone or adobe and were sixty feet square with walls eight to ten feet high.[365] Usually, two men were maintained at each station to care for the stock and to keep all in readiness for the arrival of the riders.

The horses employed were the best obtainable. A large part were half-breed California mustangs, famous for speed, endurance, and dependability.[366] They were fed and housed with the greatest care, for they must measure up to the severest tests. Ten, fifteen, or twenty-five miles, each must cover with scarcely a breathing-spell; and it took good mettle to endure the strain.

The riders were the pick of the frontier. They were young men, selected for their nerve, light weight, and general fitness. They were armed, but generally depended upon the fleetness of their ponies for safety from Indian attacks. The life of the rider was exciting and his work often dangerous. It was no fit position for a tender-foot or a coward. Over the level prairies and through the mountain fastnesses the rider must know the path or make it. Hostile Indians might lie in ambush, but he must not hesitate.[367] Day and night,

---

[364] *Buffalo Bill's Life Story*, 45.

[365] *Territorial Enterprise* (Nevada), August 4, 1860.

[366] Majors, *op. cit.*, 175.

[367] J. G. Kelley tells of riding the Pony Express during the Indian difficulties in Nevada in 1860. He had to ride through a forest of quaking asp trees where the preceding rider had been shot. "A trail had been cut through these

in sunshine or storm, the precious burden must go on. If a rider galloped into a station and found that his "relief" had been killed or disabled, then he must do double service.[368] In the two minutes allowed for the

little trees, just wide enough to allow horse and rider to pass. As the road was crooked and the branches came together from either side, just above my head when mounted, it was impossible to see ahead more than ten or fifteen yards, and it was two miles through the forest. I expected to have trouble, and prepared for it by dropping my bridle reins on the neck of the horse, put my Sharp's rifle at full cock, kept both spurs into the flanks, and he went through that forest like a 'streak of greased lightning.' At the top of the hill I dismounted to rest my horse, and looking back, saw the bushes moving several places. As there were no cattle or game in that vicinity, I knew the movements must be caused by Indians, and was more positive of it when, after firing several shots at the spot where I saw the bushes moving, all agitation ceased." — Visscher, *The Pony Express*, 41.

Howard R. Egan, one of the Pony Express riders, writes:

"The express rider at Shell Creek was too sick to undertake the ride, and I volunteered to take his place. The ride at that time was from Shell to Butte, . . . I started just at dark and made pretty good time, but being careful to not overdo the pony, but give him frequent breathing spells, at which times I would let him go on the walk, and was doing so when I was about in the middle of Egan Canyon and, just before turning a sharp point ahead of me, I could see the next turn of that, and on the side of the hill towards me the light of a fire was shining. . . In going very carefully along and keeping a sharp lookout for a sentinel, I reached the point where I could see the camp. They were on both sides of the road and about in the center of the bend. Well, I had to make up my mind very quickly as to what I should do. Should I turn back and go north to another canyon about six or eight miles, where there might be another party of Indians, if they had planned to catch the express rider? I could not wait long, as their dogs might scent me and give the alarm.

"Well, I soon decided to go straight, so, taking my pistol in my hand, I rode on as close as I dared, then striking in the spurs and giving an awful yell, a few jumps of the pony brought me to about the middle of the camp, when my gun began to talk, though pointed up in the air, and my yells accompanied each shot. I got a glimpse of several Indians who were doing their best to make themselves scarce, not knowing but there might be a large party of whites after them. When I made the next turn, I was out in the little valley at the head of Egan Canyon and had two trails that I could take to finish. I chose the shortest but the roughest and got home all right. . .

"Later I got it from some friendly Indians that there had been a trap set to catch an express rider for the purpose of seeing what he carried to make him travel so fast." – Egan, W. M., ed. *Pioneering the West, 1846-1878*, 226.

[368] On one occasion when Howard R. Egan was riding out from Salt Lake

transfer of rider and mail pouch from the foam-flecked horse to the fresh and eager pony, he stretched his weary muscles and then was off on the road again. "Buffalo Bill" covered one such double-stretch when he rode continuously for 320 miles in 21 hours and 40 minutes.[369]

Mark Twain's description of the passing of the Pony Express is famous:

"Here he comes! Every neck is stretched further, and every eye strained wider. Away across the endless

City he had a rather long continuous ride. His brother-in-law, who rode the route immediately to the west, had a sweetheart in the city whom he wished very much to see. They arranged that instead of meeting as usual, they should pass each other and continue on the others route. The lover thus reached Salt Lake City and had the night to see his lady and rest. But to young Egan the fates were less kind. Upon reaching the end of his double route the eastbound pony was met and he had immediately to begin the return ride. This gave him a continuous ride of 330 miles, perhaps the longest ride made on the Pony Express.

On another occasion Egan rode from Salt Lake City to Fort Crittenden, a distance of fifty miles, then started at sundown for Rush Valley in a very heavy snow storm, and the snow knee deep to his horse. He says: "I could see no road, so that as soon as darkness came on, I had to depend entirely on the wind. It was striking on my right cheek, so I kept it there, but, unfortunately for me, the wind changed and led me off my course, and instead of going westward I went southward and rode all night on a high trot, and arrived at the place I had left at sundown the evening before with both myself and horse very tired. Now the only thing to do was to jump on to the horse I had rode the evening before and proceed on twenty-five miles further. Then, instead of having a night's rest at my home station, I was riding all night, in consequence of which I met the 'Pony' from Sacramento and was compelled to start immediately on my eastward trip to Salt Lake City. This made my continuous ride 150 miles besides all night in deep snow." – Egan, Wm. M., ed. *Pioneering the West, 1846-1878*, 281.

[369] *Buffalo Bill's Life Story*, 47. Many famous riders might be mentioned and rides enumerated if space would permit. This romantic and spectacular side of the Pony Express has been given rather full consideration at the hands of others. See Majors, *Seventy Years on the Frontier*; Root and Connelley, *The Overland Stage to California*; Bradley, *The Story of the Pony Express*; Visscher, *A Thrilling and Truthful History of the Pony Express*; Egan, *Pioneering the West*; Mary Pack, *The Romance of the Pony Express* (Pamphlet issued by the Union Pacific Railroad). Root and Connelley give a list of the known riders on page 131 of their book.

dead level of the prairie a black speck appears against the sky and it is plain that it moves. Well, I should think so. In a second or two it becomes a horse and rider, rising and falling, rising and falling — sweeping towards us, nearer and nearer — growing more and more distinct, more and more sharply defined — nearer and still nearer, and the flutter of the hoofs come faintly to the ear — another instant, a whoop and a hurrah from our upper deck, a wave of the rider's hand, but no reply, a man and a horse burst past our excited faces, and go winging away like a belated fragment of a storm!" [370]

At the beginning each rider rode a distance of thirty to fifty miles, using three horses. But soon the run was extended until each man rode from seventy-five to one hundred miles.[371] A round trip over this run was made twice a week, for which the riders received a salary of $50 to $150 per month.[372]

The riders did not dress uniformly, but the usual costume was a buckskin hunting shirt, cloth trousers, tucked into high boots, and a jockey cap or slouch hat.[373] A complete buckskin suit with the hair on the outside to shed the rain was provided for stormy weather.[374] But the rider out from Saint Joseph was an exception to the general rule, and was profusely equipped. This description is from one of the riders: [375]

"We always rode out of town with silver mounted trappings decorating both man and horse and regular

---

[370] Mark Twain, *Roughing It*, 54.
[371] *Buffalo Bill's Life Story*, 45. Also, Hayes *Collection* (Bancroft Library), *Southern California Local History*, viii, 223.
[372] Majors, *op. cit.*, 175. Also, Bradley, *The Story of the Pony Express*, 26.
[373] *History of Buchanan County and Saint Joseph, Missouri*, 92.
[374] Hayes *Collection* (Bancroft Library), R. 50: 223.
[375] J. H. Keetley, in a letter dated Salt Lake City, August 21, 1907. Given in Visscher, *The Thrilling and Truthful Story of the Pony Express*, 33.

uniforms with plated horn, pistol, scabbard, and belt, etc., and gay flower-worked leggings and plated jingling spurs resembling, for all the world, a fantastic circus rider. This was all changed, however, as soon as we got on to the boat. We had a room in which to change and to leave the trappings in until our return."

The mail was carried in four small leather bags called *cantinas*, about six by twelve inches in size, which were sewed to a square "macheir" which was put over the saddle in such a way that one letter bag was in front and one behind each leg of the rider.[376] Three of the bags were for through mail and one for way mail. This latter contained a way-bill or time card, on which each station keeper put a record of the arrival and departure of the mail.[377] The same macheir (*mochila*) was transferred from pony to pony and from rider to rider until it reached the opposite end of the line. The letters, before being placed in the pockets, were wrapped in oiled silk to preserve them from moisture. The maximum weight for any mail was twenty pounds, but this weight was rarely reached.[378] The charges at the beginning were five dollars for each half ounce or fraction thereof, but it was gradually reduced to one dollar per half ounce. Each letter had in addition, to pay the regular ten cent government postage.

It is difficult to determine the total or the average amount of mail carried by the Pony Express. This conveyance was employed with some misgivings at first, but gained in popularity as it proved its efficiency and as the rates were reduced. An average of forty-one letters to San Francisco addresses were brought to the

---

[376] — *Idem*, 33.
[377] *History of Buchanan County and Saint Joseph, Missouri*, 92.
[378] — *Idem*, 92.

Pacific Coast between November, 1860, and April, 1861. From April, 1861, to July, 1861, the average was sixty-four; and from that date to the withdrawal of the Pony Express, in October, 1861, the average was ninety.[379] Californians seemed to employ the Pony Express more extensively than did their friends in the East. As early as April 21, 1860, two hundred five letters were sent east by a single express.[380] A Saint Louis correspondent writes May 10, 1860: "California letter writers have more than half covered the cost of several trips, and if as many letters were sent from this end of the line westward, the express would now pay."[381] Mr. Frank Root, who was chief clerk in the Atchison, Kansas, post office, says that during the last six or seven weeks before the enterprise was abandoned, an average of 350 letters was brought in each trip from the Pacific Coast.[382]

Before the Pony Express was in operation two months, there was a grave danger that it would have to be abandoned. It was interrupted by the Washoe Indian War in Nevada. During the latter part of May, 1860, several stations in Nevada were burned and the stock driven off by the Indians.[383] The departure of the Pony Express of May 31st from San Francisco was postponed on account of the Indian difficulties.[384] W.

---

[379] The San Francisco *Bulletin* usually printed the names of those residing in San Francisco to whom Pony Express letters were addressed. From 26 such lists appearing between November 1, 1860, and April 1, 1861, I find an average of 41 letters received. Twelve lists between April and July 1, 1861, give an average of 64; and seventeen lists between July 1st and November 5, 1861, give an average of 90 letters.

[380] San Francisco *Bulletin*, April 21, 1860.

[381] —*Idem*, May 10, 1860.

[382] Root and Connelley, *op. cit.*, 117.

[383] San Francisco *Bulletin*, May 26, 1860; June 2, 1860.

[384] —*Idem*, May 31, 1860.

W. Finney, general agent of the Pony Express, appealed for men and money to enable him to reopen the route. Volunteers came forward and subscriptions were raised. Colonel Hays and Captain Steward with volunteers and some regulars pursued the hostile Indians towards Pyramid Lake.[385] On June 9th, twenty picked men left Carson City with the Pony Express for Salt Lake City, and the difficulties were soon cleared up and the stations rebuilt and restocked. The four delayed expresses from the East were brought into San Francisco June 25th.[386] This was the only interruption of any moment during the nineteen months that the Pony Express was in operation. It is estimated that this trouble and delay necessitated an expenditure by the Pony Express Company of upwards of $75,000.[387]

After this Indian interruption, the Pony Express was placed upon a semi-weekly schedule.[388] It continued upon that basis during the remainder of its existence.

The time consumed in making the overland trips by the Pony Express was usually a little greater than that announced by the schedule. But by the aid of the telegraph at each end of the line good time was made in the transmission of messages. The best time was that made in carrying the news of Lincoln's election. This express left Fort Kearny November 8th, and arrived at Fort Churchill the morning of the 14th, making the trip in precisely six days.[389] This special express passed the regular ones that had left Saint Louis November 2nd and November 6th.

---

[385] — *Idem*, May 28, 1860; June 9, 1860.

[386] — *Idem*, June 25, 1860.

[387] Root and Connelley, *op. cit.*, 122.

[388] San Francisco *Bulletin*, January 24, 1860. Advertisements of the Pony Express company, July 3, 1860, and subsequently.

[389] — *Idem*, November 14, 1860.

FACSIMILE OF THE PONY EXPRESS LETTER
which carried the news of Abraham Lincoln's election

THE PONY EXPRESS

As winter approached the experiment was watched with great interest. Was the Central route to be practicable for year-round travel? In November, 1860, it was announced that after December 1st the schedule time would be extended to fifteen days between Saint Joseph and San Francisco, and to eleven days between telegraph stations.[390] This extended schedule, according to Mr. Russell, was to continue until May 1st, unless, in the meantime, Congress should order the regular mail service on the route improved from a semi-monthly to a semi-weekly basis.[391]

An editorial in the San Francisco *Bulletin* draws attention to the importance of the Pony Express experiment as follows:[392]

"A few weeks are to perhaps settle the fact whether the first Daily Overland Mail, telegraph, and railroad shall enter California by the shortest and most central route, or be compelled by the inclemency of winters on that route to seek a passage-way by making a long circuit through a milder climate."

Though the schedule was extended for the winter months the Pony Express was not able to equal the schedule time. The telegraph extended to Fort Churchill from the west and to Fort Kearny from the east end. As the news for the papers was telegraphed to and from these points the length of time taken between these stations by the pony was of considerable interest and the data as to time made is available. The average for twenty-two midwinter trips between these points was 13.8 days. One trip was missed entirely.

---

[390] Saint Louis correspondence November 14th, in the *Bulletin*, November 27, 1860.

[391] Mr. Russell's announcement in a New York paper of November 20, found in the *Bulletin*, December 8, 1860.

[392] — *Idem*, December 29, 1860.

Upon four trips sixteen days were consumed in making the distance between the telegraph termini, and upon one, seventeen days were taken.[393] Upon February 5th the news by the southern Butterfield Overland mail telegraphed from Los Angeles to San Francisco, was of three days' later date than that by the last Pony Express.[394] This was the occasion of great rejoicing in Los Angeles.[395] The missing express was not sent through because of the snow blockade on the railroad east of Saint Joseph. However, the next pony brought

---

[393] The following data were gathered from the San Francisco *Bulletin* and *Alta California*, December, 1860, to April, 1861. The Pony Express made the following time during the one winter it was in operation:

Left Fort Kearny	Arrived at Fort Churchill	Time between telegraph stations
Dec. 3	Dec. 14	11 days
" 7	" 18	11 "
" 10	" 22	12 "
" 14	" 27	13 "
" 18	" 29	11 "
" 21	Jan. 2	12 "
" 24	" 6	13 "
" 28	" 11	14 "
" 31	" 14	14 "
Jan. 4	" 20	16 "
" 7	" 23	16 "
" 11	" 27	16 "
" 14	" 30	16 "
" 22	Feb. 8	17 "
" 26	" 11	16 "
" 29	" 11	13 "
Feb. 2	" 15	13 "
" 5	" 18	13 "
" 12	" 25	13 "
" 16	Mar. 2	14 "
" 20	" 5	13 "
" 25	" 10	13 "

[394] *Alta California*, February 5, 1861.

[395] California *Star*, February 9, 1861. The Butterfield schedule time between telegraph stations was fifteen days, and this could have been improved. – *Alta California*, February 5, 1861.

THE PONY EXPRESS

news of one day's later date than that by the southern mail,[396] and thereafter was able to maintain its primacy.

As spring and summer came, the Pony Express made decided improvement. During April and May an average of about nine days only was taken to make the trip which, during the winter, had required from twelve to sixteen days.[397] During the summer the telegraph was pushed forward from both ends and the transmission of news and messages was accordingly expedited.[398] The Pony Express continued until the through wire was in operation. However, as the telegraph neared completion, interest waned in the Pony Express, except for that portion lying between the approaching termini of the telegraph line. When the telegraph line was completed on October 24, 1861,[399] the Pony Express came to a close. The pony was fast, but he could not compete with the lightning.

As indicated above, the Pony Express was begun as an individual undertaking without government subsidy, but with the expectation of subsequent favorable consideration at the hands of Congress. In the spring of 1860, when the enterprise was launched, the Overland

---

[396] —*Idem*, February 9, 1861.

[397] The successive trips between Fort Kearny and Fort Churchill (the telegraph termini) from April 1st to June 1, 1861, were made in the following number of days respectively: 10, 10, 9, 9, 9, 9, 8, 9, 9, 9, 8, 8, 8, 8, 10.

[398] July 15, 1861, the easternmost telegraph station from the Pacific Coast side was fifty miles east of Fort Churchill. The station was successively moved as follows: August 2nd, 100 miles east of Fort Churchill; August 9th, 50 miles farther; August 19th, 40 miles farther; September 6th, 35 miles more; September 27th, 25 miles more. This station at Ruby Valley, 250 miles east of Fort Churchill, continued the easternmost transmitting station until the line was completed.

From the eastern side the westernmost telegraph stations were located as follows: August 9th, 50 miles west of Fort Kearny; August 27th, 60 miles farther west; September 14th, 55 miles more; October 8th, 368 miles additional.

[399] See San Francisco *Bulletin*, October 25, 1861.

Mail service question received extended consideration in Congress, but the conflict of competing interests prevented the final passage of any Congressional laws upon the subject at that session. As it became evident that such would probably be the outcome, an effort was made to subsidize the Pony Express alone. Senator Latham of California, introduced a bill into the Senate June 1, 1860,[400] directing the Postmaster-general to contract with the Central Overland California and Pike's Peak Express Company for carrying not more than fifty letters weekly for the Government for $2,000 per month, or $3,000 if carried semi-weekly, for a space of two years. Also the company was to be given the right to pre-empt quarter-sections of land at twenty mile intervals along the route.[401] This bill was reported back from the committee on Post Offices and Post Roads with amendments by Senator Gwin on June 14th, but was never heard of again.

Notwithstanding the failures in Congress the projectors of the enterprise did not lose heart, but continued to operate the express despite the lack of governmental aid.[402] The California legislature, on February 6, 1861, called upon Congress to aid the Pony Express.[403]

During the Congressional short session of 1860-1, ad-

---

[400] U. S. *Congressional Globe*, 36th congress, first session, part iii, 2519.

[401] The provisions of the bill are taken from a letter of the Washington correspondent of the San Francisco *Bulletin*, dated June 5, 1860, and appearing in the *Bulletin* of June 26, 1860. The bill is not given in full in the *Congressional Globe* nor in the *Reports of Committees*.

[402] The Washington correspondent of the San Francisco *Bulletin* writes June 19, 1860: "Even if its [the Pony Express] proprietors fail to get legislation now they know it will be for want of time, and they will be encouraged to hold on, expecting Congress to do something for them next winter." – S. F. *Bulletin*, July 13, 1860.

[403] *Alta California*, February 7, 1861.

vocates of the Central route renewed their efforts for an adequately subsidized mail service on their favorite line. They at last succeeded and the law of March 2, 1861, provided for a daily overland mail on the Central route and a semi-weekly Pony Express, the compensation for the joint undertaking to be $1,000,000 per annum. The section of the law referring to the Pony Express reads:[404]

"They [the contractors] shall also, be required during the continuance of their contract, or until the completion of the overland telegraph, to run a pony express semi-weekly at a schedule time of ten days eight months and twelve days four months, carrying for the Government free of charge, five pounds of mail matter, with the liberty of charging the public for transportation of letters by said express not exceeding one dollar per half ounce."

The original projectors of the Pony Express did not receive the mail contract. Instead, the law provided that the Butterfield Overland Mail line be moved to the Central route. However, a working arrangement was made whereby Russell, Majors, and Waddell operated the Pony Express and the daily mail coach service from the Missouri River to Salt Lake City, and the Overland Mail Company operated that portion of the line west of Salt Lake City.[405]

At first, while the express was a private enterprise, the rates charged were $5.00 per half ounce or fraction thereof. In August, 1860, and thereafter, one-fourth ounce letters were accepted at $2.50 each.[406] These rates continued during the first year. In April, 1861,

---
[404] U. S. *Statutes at Large*, xii, 206.
[405] Saint Louis correspondence in *Bulletin*, April 4, 1861.
[406] — *Idem*, August 14, 1860.

the charges were reduced to $2.00 per half ounce,[407] and on July 1st, in conformity with the law, half ounce letters were carried for $1.00.

The Pony Express was inaugurated as an advertiser and demonstrator of the Central route, rather than as an immediate money making scheme. When the daily mail was established on this route in July, 1861, this first object was attained. As a financial undertaking the project did not succeed. Alexander Majors, one of the original projectors of the enterprise, says that "the business transacted over this line was not sufficient to pay one-tenth of the expenses, to say nothing about the amount of capital invested." [408] Although this is no doubt an exaggeration, it is nevertheless true that the Pony Express brought considerable financial embarrassment upon its projectors.

From the standpoint of the nation the Pony Express was eminently successful. It demonstrated the practicability of the Central route and marked the path for the first trans-continental railroad. By shortening the distance between the Atlantic and the Pacific coasts it helped to unite the Pacific Coast and the Rocky Mountain region to the Union during that first ominous year

---

[407] San Francisco *Bulletin*, April 15, 1861; April 20, 1861.

[408] Majors, *Seventy Years on the Frontier*, p. 185. Bradley, in his *Story of the Pony Express*, p. 174, calculates the expenditures and receipts as follows:

Equipping the line	$100,000
Maintenance, $30,000 per month	480,000
Nevada Indian War	75,000
Miscellaneous	45,000
Total	$700,000

Receipts about $500,000, leaving a net loss of $200,000.

Root and Connelley say (p. 118): "The enthusiastic projector of the pony sank at least $100,000 and the partners who lent aid to the enterprise also lost their fortunes."

of Civil War. It showed the conquest of the West in one of its most spectacular phases, and is an act in the great Western drama that will always be recalled and reenacted as one of our precious heritages.

# Chapter IX

The Fight for a Daily Mail on the Central Route, 1859-1861[409]

In chapter V we noted the competition between the central and southern mail routes and the distinct advantage of the latter in schedule, remuneration, and frequency of trips. In chapter VIII attention was called to the fact that the Pony Express was launched by the contractors on the Central route with a view to receiving an improved mail contract. The position taken by champions of the Central route is well presented by an editorial in the San Francisco *Bulletin* on January 31, 1860:

"The route of the great Overland mail [Butterfield] certainly ought to be shortened. It is now several hundred miles longer than the Salt Lake route, and for that reason can never become an immigrant road; nor will it ever be availed of in time of war for the passage of troops between the two oceans. The energy and enterprise which have brought us the mails overland from St. Louis to San Francisco in from 18 to 24 days, if expended upon as short and available route as can be found, would give us the mails regularly in sixteen days. It was a stupid blunder if nothing worse, on the part of the Administration, which compelled the contractors to take the circuitous route from St. Louis via Memphis and El Paso to San Francisco. Butterfield and Company from the beginning, like shrewd business

---

[409] The preceding chapter covers the same period as does this one, but it was thought advisable to treat the Pony Express as a separate topic.

men, would have much preferred to take the most direct, available route between the great centers of population on the Pacific and in the Mississippi valley. But sectional purposes prevailed over right and reason. The Administration was desirous of carrying the route in such direction as should benefit Southern interests, in the idea that the future Pacific Railroad would be sure to follow the track of the mail coaches. . .

"For ourselves, we believe that a route which should traverse or connect with the Pike's Peak and Salt Lake regions would prove itself on all accounts the most advantageous. The Salt Lake route is the one almost always chosen by overland immigrants, because of its shortness and its abundance of feed and water for stock. . . Let the Salt Lake route be as well stocked as the Memphis now is, supplied as liberally with stations, and no difficulty would be experienced in making good time over it at all seasons. Indeed, we doubt much whether the snows there would prove as serious a barrier to the mail coach as the mud of Southwestern Missouri and Arkansas is during the winter, and the overpowering heat of the Southern desert during the summer. . .

"We see that the Department has advertised for new proposals to carry the mails between Placerville and Salt Lake, the former contractor having failed.[410] We hope that the service will not be re-let. The time is

---

[410] This imminent failure of Chorpenning was noted by the San Francisco *Bulletin* of the October 13th previous. It was reported that Senator Broderick had induced Jones to keep up the service. "The line in the meantime became indebted to Jones to the amount of $30,000 to secure which the latter recently attached the stock. Jones, it appears, ran the mail on the western division of the route – that is, between Placerville and Gravelly Ford on the Humboldt. The eastern division is in the hands of Howard Egan and other Mormons to whom also the line is indebted for some six months service."

Howard R. Egan writes: "Father [Howard Egan] was George Chorpen-

auspicious for the consolidation, of the Salt Lake and Butterfield interests. Let Congress provide for such a result."

The railroad convention, meeting in San Francisco in September, 1859, adopted a resolution in favor of a daily mail upon the central route with a twenty-day schedule.[411] The editor of the *Rocky Mountain News* of newly-founded Denver, contended in his issue of January 25, 1860, that the mail could better be carried over a central route through Denver, South Park, and Camp Floyd than over the "barren Southern route."

By the beginning of the year 1860, it seemed that there was somewhat of a change in the attitude toward the overland mails. The Saint Louis correspondent of the San Francisco *Bulletin* writes February 13th:

"Horace Greeley, ever since his return from the Pacific, has advocated the entire abandonment of the ocean service and the organization of a daily route overland. The prominent newspapers of the country are now recommending the same thing. Members of Congress, Washington advices say, have simultaneously fallen into the idea. Butterfield and Company have all along behaved so well with their route, that people whatsoever their preferences and prejudices, are now compelled to admit that a daily Overland mail is

---

ning's agent or partner, when he had the contract to carry the mail from Salt Lake to California . . . as the time came that money failed to come to pay off the men or other expenses, Father was forced to dig up and use every resource to keep the Mail going, expecting every day to receive the money that he had been told by letter from the boss had been sent by a trusty agent by way of California. . . Chorpenning had written that he would soon have another payment from the government and for Father to keep the mails running as long as possible, but after a few months there came a change of contractors." – Egan, W. M., ed. *Pioneering the West*, 211-213.

[411] San Francisco *Bulletin*, September 26, 1859.

just the thing for California. In support of this the *Bulletin's* late feat of publishing the President's message in the brief space of fifteen days from St. Louis has been quoted far and wide." [412]

Several bills were early introduced, looking to the improvement of overland lines. A Washington correspondent well describes the situation in Congress:

"There will be a vigorous contest over this Overland mail system. It is one of the most difficult questions before Congress, on account of the rival interests of contractors, the sectional prejudices of Congress, the different political influences controlling the House from that backing the Senate and the Administration, and the really vast expense involved in establishing anything like an efficient system such as the times demand." [413]

March 13, 1860, the Overland Mail bill (H. R. no. 304) was considered in the House of Representatives.[414] Mr. Colfax, chairman of the committee on Post Offices and Post Roads, explained that it was a simple bill inviting proposals for carrying the entire mail between the Atlantic and Pacific states on a single line. The committee was of the opinion that the entire mails could be carried overland in twenty days, for less than a million dollars a year. The bill did not bind the department to accept any of the bids. The call would be for bids to carry the mail daily in twenty days; also for bids for tri-weekly and for bi-weekly service.

The Senate considered this House Overland Mail bill as too indefinite, and too much inclined to result

---

[412] — *Idem*, March 6, 1860.

[413] Washington correspondence of March 30th, in the *Bulletin*, April 14, 1860.

[414] U. S. *Congressional Globe*, 36th congress, first session, part ii, 1131.

in delay. Accordingly, substitutes were proposed. The Senate committee on Post Offices and Post Roads gave much attention to the bill, but with the various interests to satisfy, the committee was unable to agree upon a plan at once practicable and acceptable. Senator Rice, of Minnesota, and others from the far north wanted a northern route. Southerners were for the Butterfield route, or for the New Orleans, San Antonio and El Paso route, or both; and the Central route via Salt Lake City had numerous supporters. As the opposition of the retrenchment advocates and others imperiled the three route project, Senator Gwin decided to introduce a separate bill providing for improved service upon the Central route alone. But Senator Rice objected because the northern route was dropped, and Senator Benjamin of Louisiana and others objected because the Southern route was dropped. The result was that Gwin's bill (S. no. 394) was dropped and never brought up again.[415]

Senator Gwin succeeded in getting the Overland Mail bill considered in the Senate May 24th,[416] but found himself in somewhat of a dilemma. This bill was a Republican measure, having been framed by leaders of this new party as a bid for California support. If their bill were enacted this accomplishment would be used as political capital against Gwin in the coming fall elections. The other democratic senator from California, Mr. Latham, was also anxious to get some credit for the passage of a bill so important to his state. The republican measure must be supplanted by substitutes of their own. Gwin's substitute provided for a semi-weekly mail from Saint Joseph to Placerville, to cost

---
[415] — *Idem*, 1647-1649.
[416] — *Idem*, 2338.

not over $462,000 and to be performed in twenty days; another line, to run from Saint Paul via Saint Cloud and from Superior, Wisconsin, via Crow Wing, to the Dalles in Oregon, twice weekly, and to cost not over $200,000; and the Butterfield route to be transferred from Memphis and Fort Smith to the route between San Antonio and El Paso, at no additional cost.

The famous Hale bill was now proposed as a substitute for that proposed by Gwin from the committee on Post Offices and Post Roads. Senator Hale said of the overland mail service:

"It has haunted me wherever I have been for weeks. . . In conjunction with some friends who felt an interest in the matter, and who made me their organ — for I knew but very little about it — a bill was prepared and put into my hands with a suggestion that that would meet the views of a great many gentlemen who were interested, and probably a majority of this House." [417]

The people of California strongly advocated Hale's bill. It proposed a tri-weekly mail on the Central route for not to exceed $600,000 for the first year, and then to be daily thereafter for not over $200,000 additional. The northern route was provided for as in Gwin's bill. It provided that that part of the Butterfield route between Saint Louis and Memphis and El Paso be discontinued, and the balance increased to tri-weekly, and that the Postmaster-general contract for tri-weekly mail service in ten days' time between New Orleans and El Paso for not over $300,000. Contractors on these routes were to have the privilege of forwarding printed matter semi-monthly on a thirty day schedule. Both the Gwin and the Hale measures pro-

---

[417] U. S. *Congressional Globe*, 36th congress, first session, 1648.

vided that the cost of the service be paid from the general treasury.[418]

Upon May 30th the bills were debated. Some Senators thought the Butterfield contract was the only thing that stood in the way of a thorough re-organization of the overland service. It would be better, they said, to give the contractors a year's pay and get rid of them. Others answered that the Butterfield was the most sucessful of all the western lines, and should not be interfered with. Certain Senators were for abolishing the ocean service entirely, while others considered it indispensable.[419] In both the regular and the evening sessions of June 19th, the conflict continued. But it was a fight between sections and conflicting interests, and they were not reconciled. The next day the Overland Mail bill was debated for the last time and no agreement was reached.

In the meantime a rather important provision was incorporated in the Post Office Appropriation act approved June 15, 1860. Section four of this law provided that the compensation for ocean mail service should be limited to the postage upon the mail carried.[420] The evident intention of the authors of this section was to force all the mail overland, but its significance evidently did not attract Congress, for this section was not debated in either House. However, the Postmaster-general soon saw its import, and immediately approached the steamship people relative to the renewal of the ocean service. He was met with a flat refusal. So much of the first class mail was going overland that it was not profitable to the steamship people

---

[418] — *Idem*, 2338, 2339.
[419] — *Idem*, 3146, 3147.
[420] — *Idem*, Appendix, 480.

to transport the heavy matter (much of which was franked) for the postage merely. Holt informed Senator Yulee, chairman of the committee on Post Offices and Post Roads, of this situation in a letter dated June 20th, and recommended legislation. He contended that "the bulk of the California mails renders it impossible at any reasonable cost to send them by any other than the ocean route." [421]

Senator Yulee proposed an amendment to the Post Route bill June 22nd, authorizing a contract for ocean mail service to California at a cost not to exceed $400,000 per annum, and an amendment providing for a ten-cent letter postage to California for all mail from the states east of the Rocky Mountains.

Here now was an opportunity for the proponents of the overland service to engraft their program upon the Post Route bill. Accordingly, Senator Wilson proposed a substitute for Yulee's amendment relative to the ocean mail. Wilson's substitute was almost identical with the Hale bill that had been swamped two days before. But since alteration of the Butterfield contract had met with such stubborn opposition from Senators from the Southwestern States, Wilson proposed to leave that line undisturbed.

Senator Hale, in speaking against Yulee's proposal expressed his opposition to the ocean service. He called attention to the fact that Senator Gwin had for the past three months been urging action upon the overland mail question, lest in the end the government would be forced again into the arms of those interests. "We here do not know all the influences that are operating upon us; but I am satisfied myself that there has been, in some way or other – I do not know how, and

---

[421] — *Idem*, 3232.

do not undertake to say, but I think I have felt it, though I have not seen it – an influence operating in that direction to retard legislation in this body upon this subject, with the very hope and expectation that we should find ourselves where we now are – forced almost, as a necessity, to take up this contract with steam vessels." [422]

Senator Lane, of Oregon, spoke against the steam mail service, and Gwin hoped that Wilson's amendment would be adopted. Senator Green, of Missouri, thought it was not wise to undertake to carry the whole of the mail overland.

On the last day of the session (June 25) the Senate again took up the Post Route bill. Yulee presented the bill with amendments which he said he hoped steered clear of all objections. It provided for a daily mail on the Central route, a weekly mail on the northern route, and a temporary ocean mail contract. This measure passed the Senate and reached the House during the last hour of the session. Mr. Sherman objected: "There are ninety-nine amendments to that bill, and I will never consent that we shall, at this hour of the session, undertake to consider them. . . The Senate has had this bill before them for months, and now, when they bring it to us in the last hour of the session, I am not willing to consider it." [423] Colfax pleaded for the bill, though not defending the Senate, but to no avail. The motion to suspend the rules and take up the amendments failed to get a two-thirds vote and hence the measure was lost.[424]

The disappointment over the defeat of the overland

---

[422] — *Idem*, 3233.

[423] — *Idem*, 3302.

[424] — *Idem*, 3302. The vote upon the question of the suspension of the rules was 94 yeas, 55 nays.

mail legislation was very keen, especially in California. An endeavor was made to place responsibility for the defeat of Hale's bill, the measure which had held out most to California in the way of improved mail facilities. A considerable proportion of the press blamed Gwin for its defeat. It was contended that as a powerful member of the majority party in the Senate, and member of the Post Office and Post Routes committee, he had not done all possible to secure its passage.[425]

Senator Gwin had up to this time consistently worked for the overland mail service. He had perhaps, done more than any other man in Congress in the way of obtaining mail facilities for the Pacific Coast. It is true that Gwin did not work for Hale's bill, but for his own, which provided smaller facilities. Here, as ever, the motive prompting the act is difficult to ascertain. We cannot believe that he was against the overland service, though he possibly was doing his utmost to have the improved service come as his own gift. The Washington correspondent of the San Francisco *Bulletin* offers the following explanation:

"Mr. Gwin was persuaded by the Administration to contribute to the defeat of Hale's bill with the most positive assurance that after the adjournment of Congress the Department would immediately put up the service via Salt Lake, to semi-weekly trips in twenty days time between St. Joseph and Placerville. This, you see, would accomplish two ends: 1st, it would prevent the Republicans from getting any credit from the legislation proposed by Mr. Hale and supported by every Senator on his side the chamber; and 2nd, it would secure Dr. Gwin the sole credit of having ob-

---

[425] San Francisco *Bulletin*, July 17, 1860.

tained the service via the Central route, and thus secure him needed capital to aid in his re-election." [426]

If this explanation, coming from the opposition press, is not entirely true, it is somewhat supported by Gwin's statement to President Buchanan after the adjournment of Congress. In a letter urging the making of a contract with Russell, Majors and Waddell for a tri-weekly mail service on the Central route for $900,000 per year, Senator Gwin says: "I was induced to believe from conversations with you and the Postmaster General, that if the public necessities required it you would have the mails – letters as well as printed matter – carried overland, if Congress failed to legislate further on the subject. That necessity has arisen." [427] In this letter the contract with Russell, Majors and Waddell is recommended for acceptance. These contractors on the Central route had offered to carry the entire mail overland from Saint Joseph to Folsom three times a week within twenty-five days, for $900,000 per annum, and after the first year, six times a week for the same compensation. [428] Their conduct of the Pony Express and their general ability is referred to. Gwin was undoubtedly working hard for the Central route. It is very probable that he had promised the contractors on this line, when they established the Pony Express that they could depend upon a government mail contract over that route. Gwin possibly believed that the failure of the general overland mail bill, coupled with the prevention of an ocean mail contract through limitation of compensation to postage received,

---

[426] Washington correspondence dated July 2d, in *Bulletin*, July 21, 1860.

[427] Gwin's letter to Buchanan, published in the *Bulletin*, July 28, 1860.

[428] — *Idem*, July 28, 1860. The terms are also given in the St. Louis correspondence of July 6th, published in the *Bulletin*, July 21, 1860.

would together best insure the desired contract upon the Central route.[429]

Whether the Postmaster-general had promised in the event of such an emergency, to give the desired contract, it is difficult to say, but it is clear what happened. The Postmaster-general's hostility and distrust of the overland service prevailed, and the emergency was met with a temporary contract for ocean service, rather than for improvement upon the central overland route.

Reference has been made to the law limiting compensation upon the ocean mail to postages received. Steamship companies refused to carry the mails upon those terms. Commodore Vanderbilt explained that previously, about ninety per centum of the receipts came from the letters, which constituted but two per centum of the weight. There was a larger and larger per centum of the letter mail going overland, and he "declined performing 98 per cent. of the California postal service for about $300,000, while others receive $1,000,000 for performing the remaining two per cent."[430]

After considerable difficulty arrangements were made with Vanderbilt for a tri-monthly mail via Panama. The compensation was to be for the postages, but the distinct promise was made that the President

---

[429] The *Bulletin* of September 6, 1860, explains: "Gwin never openly opposed Hale's bill; he strangled it by treachery. . . A direct vote would surely pass the bill, so he prevented it. . . His arrangement with the Administration was that no Overland bill should pass, and that then the Post Office Department should, without legislation, give him a tri-weekly mail via Salt Lake City, the credit of which he should take to himself, after his colleague had failed, and after the Republicans had been robbed of the capital that they expected to make out of the passage of Hale's bill."

[430] Letter of Commodore Vanderbilt to the Public, published in the *Bulletin*, July 24, 1860.

would recommend to the next Congress that additional compensation be given. In pursuance of this promise, $350,000 was appropriated at the next session for the tri-monthly service.[431]

There was but little alteration in the Overland Mail service during 1860. Upon the central route a "star" in lieu of the pre-existing coach service was established from Salt Lake City to Placerville upon the sixth of June. This reduced the expenditure $47,000. Those portions of the line between Placerville and Carson City, and between Saint Joseph and Fort Kearny were improved to weekly service at an increased cost of $24,381.[432] This was necessitated, the Postmaster-general explained, by the increasing population in the vicinity of the Pike's Peak and the Washoe mines. A contract was made for weekly mail service from Fort Kearny, one hundred ten miles east of Julesburg on the Salt Lake route, to Denver, a distance of four hundred miles, in six and one-half days.[433]

The Butterfield route remained unchanged. The San Antonio and San Diego route was modified by discontinuing the line from San Diego to Fort Yuma, making a saving of $28,695. Between El Paso and Camp Stockton a "star" was substituted for the coach service, and the semi-monthly improved to a weekly mail with a reduction of the expenditure of $12,579. The service was improved to weekly between San Antonio and Camp Stockton, thus completing a weekly

---

[431] U. S. *Congressional Globe*, 36th congress, second session, Appendix, 335. Post Office Appropriation Act, approved March 2, 1861.

[432] Postmaster-general's *Report*, 1860, 435. In U. S. Senate. *Executive Documents*, 36th congress, second session, no. 1, part iii, 435. (Serial no. 1080.)

[433] —*Idem*, 441.

service from New Orleans to San Francisco. As thus modified, the retrenchment upon this line amounted to a saving of $101,000 over the cost in 1859.[434]

In conformity with a law passed June 21, 1860, the Postmaster-general contracted with the California Stage Company for daily service in stages between Sacramento, California, and Portland, Oregon. The schedule time was seven days from April 1st to December 1st, and twelve days the remainder of the year. The price paid was $90,000 per annum and the service began September 15, 1860.[435]

The Postmaster-general expressed the belief, in his annual report of December, 1860, that the experience of the past year had fully vindicated his retrenchment policy, and that the financial condition of the department was improving as fast as the legislation of Congress would permit.[436] In reference to a bill before Congress for a daily overland mail on the Central route, he said: "The enterprise in its practical operation would no doubt result in a complete failure, owing to the character of the road, the rigors of the winter and the bulk and weight of the mail." It would be a "lavish outlay that would prove beneficial only to the contractors." But Congress did not entirely concur, and the supporters of the daily mail were spurred to greater efforts by remembering how nearly they succeeded at the previous session.

---

[434] — *Idem*, 437.
[435] — *Idem*, 436.
[436] — *Idem*, 436. The receipts and expenditures upon the routes to the Pacific were given as follows:

	Cost	Receipts
From N. Y. to S. F. via Panama	$350,000	$170,825.40
Overland via El Paso, etc.	600,000	119,766.76
Saint Joseph to Salt Lake City	125,000	4,305.64
Salt Lake City to Placerville	83,241	978.50
San Antonio to Camp Stockton	70,000	593.41

The annual post route bill was taken up in the Senate, February 2, 1861. Section 18 provided for a daily overland mail on the Central route for not over $800,000. Senator Hale said he was for a daily overland mail as he had been the year before, but that he was for dispensing with the Butterfield route since it was too much to have both. The bill was again considered February 18th.[437] Senator Gwin wanted a conference committee and contended that a contractor could not be obtained if the price were limited to $800,000. Senator Latham, of California, feared failure and so recommended an agreement with the House.

In the meantime the Senate committee on Post Offices and Post Roads was considering a proposition to consolidate the Central route line with the Butterfield, terminate the latter, and have but one route across the country.[438] On February 23rd, Senator Gwin said he believed they could get a daily overland mail performed for $1,000,000. If they could not get a daily stage, he was for a tri-weekly, and for a tri-weekly Pony Express. "I know perfectly well the mails can be carried cheaper over the Central route than any other, because it is the shortest and best."[439] Finally the bill passed the Senate without amendment on February 26th, but it was with the understanding that it would be corrected and improved by amendments to the Post Office Appropriation bill.

According to this Post Route law,[440] a daily mail service was to be established upon the Central route for not over $800,000. The letter and newspaper mail was

---

[437] U. S. *Congressional Globe*, 36th congress, second session, part i, 986.
[438] — *Idem*, 1109.
[439] — *Idem*, 1128.
[440] — *Idem*, Appendix, 325, 326. (Laws of the United States.)

to be carried through in twenty days, and the pamphlet, magazine and periodical and public document mail in thirty-five days; the latter class to be sent by water if desired by the contractor at his own expense. The law provided for extending the mail contract on route no. 8076 in Texas, so as to connect with the Butterfield and furnish semi-weekly connection with New Orleans, provided it could be done at an additional expense not exceeding $80,000 per annum. It provided that the cost of these mail connections with the Pacific Coast should be charged to the general treasury instead of against the Post Office Department. It also provided for a ten-cent postage rate on letters between any state east of the Rocky Mountains and any state or territory on the Pacific Coast.

The Finance committee of the Senate reported the Post Office Appropriation bill to the Senate with amendments, February 27th. The next day Senator Wilson offered an amendment which was almost identical with the provision finally enacted. It provided for transferring the Butterfield line to the Central route and making it a daily, on a twenty to twenty-three day schedule; and for the conduct of a pony express semi-weekly until the completion of the overland telegraph. The compensation to be allowed was $1,150,000.

Senator Gwin favored reducing the amount to $1,000,000 and giving the contractors on the Central route a right to bid for the contract rather than giving it outright to the Butterfield contractors. He did not think it fair to these men who had started the Pony Express, to be put off to give place to the Butterfield people."[441] He also favored the continuance of the ocean

---

[441] U. S. *Congressional Globe*, 36th congress, second session, part ii, 1271.

service, which he considered a cheap and a good service.

Senator Latham, of California, said that he understood that the Butterfield Company had agreed to take the stock of the Central Overland California and Pike's Peak Express Company on the Central route, at an appraised price.[442] Senator Douglas spoke in favor of Wilson's amendment. It was voted upon and carried by a vote of twenty-one to nineteen. Gwin now proposed an amendment to reduce compensation from $1,150,000 to $1,000,000. Latham was opposed. There was some debate as to whether the contract would be taken at the smaller sum. Gwin absolutely assured the Senate that it would. Senator Douglas remarked: "It is refreshing to hear the Senator from California (Gwin) and the Senator from New Hampshire (Hale) advocating economy. It is one of the bright signs of the time."[443] The amendment was agreed to.

The Post Office Appropriation bill became law March 2, 1861. The sections providing for the daily overland mail follow:

"SEC. 9. And be it further enacted, That in lieu of the daily service on the central route provided by the act entitled 'An act for the establishment of post routes' approved February 27th, 1861, the Postmaster-general is hereby directed to discontinue the mail service on route number 12578, from St. Louis and Memphis to San Francisco, California, and to modify the contract on said route subject to the same terms and conditions only as hereinafter provided, said discontinuance to take effect on or before July 1, 1861. The

---

[442] — *Idem*, 1275.
[443] — *Idem*, 1277.

contractors on said route shall be required to transport the entire letter mail six times a week on the Central route, said letter mail to be carried through in twenty day's time, eight months in the year, and in twenty-three days the remaining four months of the year, from some point on the Missouri River connected with the East, to Placerville, California, and also to deliver the entire mails tri-weekly to Denver City, and Great Salt Lake City; said contractors shall be required to carry the residue of all the mail matter in a period not exceeding thirty-five days, with the privilege of sending the latter semi-monthly from New York to San Francisco in twenty-five days by sea, and the public documents in thirty-five days. They shall also be required, during the continuance of their contract, or until the completion of the overland telegraph, to run a pony express semi-weekly at a schedule time of ten days eight months and twelve days four months, carrying for the Government free of charge, five pounds of mail matter with the liberty of charging the public for transportation of letters by said express not exceeding one dollar per half ounce. For the above service said contractors shall receive the sum of one million dollars per annum; the contract for such service to be thus modified before the 25th day of March next, and expire July 1, 1864."[444]

The remaining sections of the law provided that the Butterfield route contractors should be given their pay during the time required to change to the Central route and be given two month's pay on their existing contract as liquidated damages for the change of route. They also provided that if these contractors declined to accept the above modification of their contract, then the

---

[444] U. S. *Statutes at Large*, vol. xii, 206.

contract was to be annulled and advertisement made for service in conformity with the above law.

The plan for the transfer of the Butterfield line to the Central route was a rather happy solution of a vexed problem. As indicated above, when the law of 1857 providing for the great overland mail, was passed, it was expected by many that the Central route would be chosen. During the past three years considerable dissatisfaction with this southern route had been expressed, and various attempts had been made to abrogate the contract or transfer its operation to a more northern line. But since it was a legislative contract in which the usual proviso permitting the Postmaster-general to alter the contract was omitted, the line was found to be rather beyond reach.[445]

But by the first of March, 1861, a new situation had arisen. Seven states had passed secession ordinances and a southern confederacy had been formed. Reports began to come to Congress of depredations upon, and interferences with, the Butterfield mail service through Texas.[446] These developments perhaps helped Congress to decide upon the features embodied in the above law, but the Civil War was not responsible for the establishment of the daily overland mail on the Central route. As noted above, Hale's bill in 1860 provided for such a daily service. The defeat of all overland mail legislation during the first session only stimulated greater effort in the next.

---

[445] Postmaster-general Holt, in 1859, wanted to reduce the service upon this route, but upon submitting the question to the Attorney-general was informed that the contract was unique and that he did not have the power to alter it.

[446] U. S. *Congressional Globe*, 36th congress, second session, 1112. Gwin said in the Senate, February 22d: "We have just received notice that the Butterfield route is cut up by the roots. . . It is stopped in all its stages through the state of Texas."

The feature of this legislation of March 2, 1861, that was affected, if not produced by secession and its probable consequences, was the provision for the transfer of the Butterfield line to the Central route. Had it not been for the secession development, a semi-weekly southern line to the Pacific Coast would undoubtedly have accompanied the daily service on the more direct route at the north.

The Butterfield Company accepted the terms embodied in the above law, and the Postmaster-general, on March 12, 1861, ordered a modification in its original contract in compliance with this Act of March 2d.[447]

---

[447] Postmaster-general's *Report*, 1861, 560. In U. S. Senate. *Executive Documents*, 37th congress, second session, no. 1, part iii, 560. (Serial no. 1119.)

Chapter X

The Million Dollar Mail in Operation
1861-1862

When the Butterfield mail company was given its million dollar contract and was moved northward, provision was made to continue the local service on the former route. A contract was made with the Overland Mail Company for tri-weekly service between Los Angeles and, Monterey, California at $40,000 per annum.[448] The southwestern states were to be served by the line from San Antonio to Camp Stockton, Texas, and its extension westward via Tucson to Los Angeles, California. This extended line commenced operation April 1st, but with the development of the Civil War it was found impossible to continue the service.[449]

The law did not designate the route, but required that Denver and Salt Lake City should be provided with a tri-weekly service. It was assumed that the main line would pass through these cities if a practicable and direct route were available.

When the overland mail bill was passed, March 2, 1861, an arrangement had been made between the Butterfield company and the "C. O. C. & P. P. Ex. Co." whereby the latter was to operate the daily mail and Pony Express upon the division of the line east of Salt

---

[448] U. S. House. *Executive Documents*, 37th congress, second session, no. 137, vol. xi, p. 551. (Serial 1139.)

[449] The eastern portion of this line was curtailed June 30, 1861, and the portion from El Paso to San Diego and Los Angeles was made a weekly at $125,000 per year. This latter part of the line was discontinued August 2, 1861.– U. S. House. *Executive Documents*, 37th congress, second session, no. 55, vol. v, p. 4.

Lake City. At a meeting of the stockholders of the "C. O. C. & P. P. Ex. Co." on April 26, 1861, the Board of Directors was reorganized by the election of Bela M. Hughes as president.[450] Preparations were now made for the inauguration of the improved service, and the new president together with the retiring president, Mr. Russell, set out for an inspection of the line. One of the important matters for decision was the question of route to be followed by the daily mail. Ever since the inauguration of mail service to Salt Lake City the contractors had taken the route along the Platte River, by way of its north Fork, and through South Pass. This was the emigrant trail and a good road, but it was not a direct route. Then also, Denver now was to be supplied. This infant metropolis lay two hundred miles to the south of the upper bend of the North Platte and a little south of the meridian of Salt Lake City. If a direct route could be found westward from Denver it would dispense with the necessity of a branch line to that city and at the same time would shorten the distance to Salt Lake City by about two hundred miles. The pioneers of Colorado,[451] as well as the contractors, were naturally very anxious that the daily mail line traverse their newly-formed territory. However, the front range of the Rockies loomed up as a rather formidable wall. Could a gateway be found through it or a practical pass over it? Upon the answer much de-

---

[450] *Rocky Mountain News* (Denver), May 8, 1861. The Saint Joseph *Gazette* says of General Bela M. Hughes: "No better man could be found to preside over the affairs of an enterprise of this magnitude. His enterprise and high character pointed to him as the man for the post. The whole board is well and widely known throughout the West."

[451] Colorado Territory had been organized by Congress on Feb. 28, 1861. It was formed from portions of Kansas, Nebraska, Utah, and New Mexico, and comprised most of the "Territory of Jefferson" projected two years before.

pended. The mail company favored a route via the Cherokee Trail and Bridger's Pass. This would offer a shorter road than the South Pass route, but would still be round about. John S. Jones, one of the directors of the "C. O. C. & P. P. Ex. Co.," was in Denver in April, 1861, and in behalf of his company made a definite proposition to the settlers. The mail company would run its main line via Denver if the citizens there would agree to build the stations from that point to Fort Bridger and would bridge the North Platte and Green rivers. Since there was no road on a more direct line westward his company was not willing to take the risk of opening a road and building stations through unknown country. The *Rocky Mountain News* took the proposition very seriously:

"There are but two alternatives. One to give him [Jones] satisfactory assurances that the stations will be supplied hence by way of the Cherokee Trail; the other to permit the line to remain where it now is. By the former we will receive a daily mail, in 4½ to 5 days from the Missouri River, and in ten days from California, a daily Pony Express each way, the great bulk of the overland travel and trade, and the telegraph line before next winter, and eventually the great Interoceanic Railway. By the latter we lose all except perhaps the Railway, and will receive but a tri-weekly mail, a branch telegraph line, provided we give the stock subscription asked by the Telegraph Company. Certainly our business men and property owners cannot long hesitate in making their choice." [452]

It was explained by this newspaper that there should be hundreds willing to provide mail stations because of the abundance of work that would be offered by the

---

[452] *Rocky Mountain News*, April 18, 1861.

mail company. The company would pay the men for keeping the stock, buy all the produce they could raise, and give each station keeper 160 acres of the mail company preemption claim. Little towns would spring up around many of the stations and thus reward the pioneer settler. A bridge across the North Platte and a ferry at Green River would require small outlays and would bring excellent returns in the form of tolls. But the people of Denver and especially those in the mining camps immediately westward were desirous of having the line run up Clear Creek in a more direct course toward Salt Lake City. They refused to believe that no practicable pass existed in this direction.

Interest now centered in an attempt to discover a route over the "Snowy Range." The various towns immediately affected, subscribed men and money for an exploring expedition and the party under Captain E. L. Berthoud assembled at Empire City on the 6th of May. B. M. Hughes and W. H. Russell, arrived in Denver May 6, 1861. Their object was to determine the route for the daily overland mail. Russell, especially, was well and favorably known there. The *Rocky Mountain News* in speaking of his arrival said: "The people of Pike's Peak will extend him a warmer welcome than to any other man who has ever visited us." Toward the end of the month a grand complimentary ball was given him at Golden, where he and the newly-arrived Governor Gilpin shared honors. The stay of President Hughes was rather short, while Russell remained for a month in the region. On May 8th the old scout and guide, James Bridger,[453] arrived

---

[453] The *Rocky Mountain News* of May 8, 1861, says of him: "This well-known pioneer came to this country forty years ago (1822) with Henry's expedition, and afterwards with Sublette, and was of Weaver's party when

at Denver to assist in laying out the route and stations northwestward over the Cherokee Trail. But the enthusiasm for a more direct route was such that Hughes and Russell directed him, together with Captain Emory and Tim Goodell,[454] to join the Berthoud party and seek a practicable route across the range.

The discovery of Berthoud Pass was an important event in the history of Colorado and was at the time hailed as a solution of the route question for the overland mail. The exploring party seeking a pass consisted of nine men, including Captain Berthoud and James Bridger. They followed up Clear Creek to a point two miles east of the last forks of the stream and established "Camp Bridger." On May 11th they climbed the range to the north of camp but were unable to reach the summit. The next day Emory and Bridger turned toward Tarryall in South Park to explore in that direction. Upon this day Captain Berthoud went up the north fork of Clear Creek and upon climbing northward to the summit discovered the pass that now bears his name.[455] Several days were spent in making reconnoissances of the range and blazing a pack trail to the new pass. They then descended the western slope

they came on to Salt Lake in that winter, supposing it certainly to be the Gulf of California or the Pacific Ocean. The captain says they found gold everywhere in this country in those days but thought it unworthy of their notice to mine for it as beaver (then worth $8. per pound) was the best paying gold they wanted to mine for in the creeks and rivers." See J. C. Alter's *James Bridger* for a good account of the old frontiersman's life.

[454] Tim Goodell was a well-known mountaineer and guide. He and James Baker had been guides for Capt. Marcy in the difficult winter expedition (1857-58) from Fort Bridger to New Mexico. Goodell was located at the mouth of Thompson's Creek about fifty miles north of Denver in the spring of 1861. – *Rocky Mountain News*, March 20, 1861.

[455] One of the principal scenic highways of Colorado now crosses the range at Berthoud Pass. The present road is a beautiful boulevard. The pass has an elevation of 11,330 feet.

along Frazier River (called by them, "Moses Creek," in honor of a member of their party) to the Colorado River, and after continuing as far as Hot Sulphur Springs, retraced their trail to Golden.[456]

News of the discovery of Berthoud Pass and a practical route over the range was quickly carried to Denver, and W. H. Russell took a coach to Empire City, from which point he examined the proposed route. Russell was convinced that the route was feasible and in accordance with this view made investments in city lots and mining claims at Idaho Springs.[457] He now hurried to the States by a special coach which made a new record of three days and twenty-one hours from Denver to Leavenworth.[458] Upon his arrival, a meeting of the Board of Directors of the mail company was held and it was decided to "dispatch Major Bridger and E. L. Berthoud immediately to review, locate, and mark out this proposed new road from Denver to Great Salt Lake City." [459]

On July 6th the Berthoud-Bridger expedition left Denver for Salt Lake City. From Hot Sulphur Springs they turned northwestward to the headwaters of Yampa River and followed the stream to near the mouth of Little Snake River. Here they turned southwest to the White and followed it to the Green. After ferrying Green River they went up the Uinta, crossed the Wasatch range, descended Provo River to Provo, and thence continued to Salt Lake City.[460] Upon the return

---

[456] The story of the exploring expedition is given in the report of E. L. Berthoud, printed in the *Rocky Mountain News*, June 4, 1861.

[457] *Rocky Mountain News*, June 10, 1861.

[458] — *Idem*, June 21, 1861. From the Leavenworth *Conservative* of June 11th.

[459] *Rocky Mountain News*, June 19, 1861.

[460] — *Idem*, August 19, 1861. Berthoud's report from Salt Lake City dated August 4, 1861.

journey distances were measured and some improvements in route made. Berthoud reported that "beyond a shadow of doubt a good wagon road of easy, practicable grade . . . can be quickly and cheaply built to Provo." He gave the distance as 426⅝ miles and the estimated cost of a first class road $100,000.[461]

In the meantime the first of July had arrived and the daily overland mail had to be inaugurated. Stations had not been built on the Cherokee Trail and the Berthoud Pass route was not yet fully explored. The mail company therefore, had no choice but to inaugurate the service upon the old emigrant and stage route via South Pass. In so doing Denver was left off the main line and was supplied by a tri-weekly branch from Julesburg.[462]

The first coach of the daily overland mail left Saint Joseph July 1st, and reached San Francisco upon the evening of the 18th. No such demonstration greeted its arrival as had honored the first mail on the Butterfield route or the initial Pony Express. As a news carrier it was being anticipated by the Pony Express that was running semi-weekly over the same route.

Fear was entertained as to the treatment the Indians would give the daily mail, especially in view of the fact that so many of the regular troops had been withdrawn from the service on the Plains. But Senator Latham was awake to the situation and the War Department on July 25, 1861, issued orders for accepting one regiment of infantry and five companies of cavalry from Cali-

---

[461] — *Idem*, October 12, 1861.

[462] During the Summer of 1861 the "C. O. C. & P. P. Ex. Co." extended its lines into the Colorado mountains. A daily coach service was maintained to Central City, and a semi-weekly one to the South Park. – *Rocky Mountain News*, June 24, and August 8, 1861.

fornia to protect the overland mail route.[463] With this precaution taken, no Indian difficulties upon the route developed during 1861. There was some little interference, however, from another source. Confederate troops committed depredations upon the Hannibal and St. Joseph railroad, and the service was somewhat interrupted. To prevent this, the Postmaster-general ordered the service from Omaha to Fort Kearny increased to a daily schedule. This provided an alternate route through Iowa over which the mails were transported when the Missouri route proved unsafe. The only inconvenience experienced was a slight delay in transmission.[464]

After the Civil War began, disloyal postmasters and clerks were removed from office, and disloyal contractors were deprived of their contracts.[465] The overland service, however, was but little affected by such actions.

During the summer and autumn of 1861 the service was satisfactorily performed, despite the difficulty occasioned by accumulations of mail at the eastern end.[466] The paper mail was usually carried through in twenty-eight days and the letter mail in twenty.

However, as winter approached, greater difficulties were encountered. The storms of December began to retard and then to interrupt the service. Friends of the Central route were liberal and blamed the unusual weather without condemning the route. They had contended that the route was practicable for year-round travel and refused to believe otherwise. The *Alta*

---

[463] San Francisco *Bulletin*, August 3, 1861; August 13, 1861.
[464] Postmaster-general's *Report*, 1861, p. 561. Also, San Francisco *Bulletin*, August 13, 1861; September 11, 14, 1861.
[465] Postmaster-general's *Report*, 1861, p. 582.
[466] Salt Lake City correspondence of August 27th, in San Francisco *Bulletin*, September 6, 1861.

California, in January, 1862, commented editorially upon the six months of success of the daily mail, saying that though the winter was the most severe in a decade, every trip except one had been made within schedule time.[467]

On the other hand the champions of the southern route were quick to declare the service a failure. A correspondent of the Los Angeles *Star*, writing from Sacramento, California, December 11, 1861, said:

"The Daily Overland Mail is a failure – a gigantic humbug and swindle – and yet the papers up here will not say anything upon the subject. While the Southern route was a complete success, that same miserable sectional jealousy that has brought ruin upon our country, would not let it live, because it happened to pass south of Mason and Dixon's line. . . If the Mail Company cannot perform the service let the steamers bring us our mail."[468]

Later the same Los Angeles paper recommended the route by Mohave and Santa Fé, or at least a diversion south from Salt Lake City via Las Vegas, Nevada, during the winter months.[469] In January a memorial to Congress was prepared embodying this proposal.[470]

But after making allowance for sectional bias, the fact remains that the service was slow and very irregular during the first winter. The *Alta California* admitted in the latter part of January that it had been about a week since the last mail came in from the east.[471] A Washington correspondent writing in February, complains:

---

[467] *Alta California*, January 14, 1862.
[468] Hayes *Collection* (Bancroft Library, University of California) R 47: 410.
[469] Los Angeles *Star*, December 21, 1861.
[470] — *Idem*, January 11, 1862.
[471] *Alta California*, January 27, 1862.

"Letters now arrive only occasionally and newspapers semi-occasionally. A paper comes once a week, thirty-five days old, and is so chafed and dirty as to be illegible. I am aware that there is a good reason and excuse for the present irregularity and bad condition in that the elements seem to have conspired against the company for the past two months, and it is for this reason that the Department does not fine them daily." [472]

However, when it was reported early in February that Congress had stricken out the appropriation for daily overland mail because of inefficiency of service and for economy, the California legislature immediately passed a resolution "that the daily overland mail is of vital importance to the people of the Pacific Coast, . . . that the late interruption, occasioned by floods of unprecedented severity, should not operate to the prejudice of the present route." The legislature also declared "that the daily overland mail company's numerous stations are a necessity to the continuance of the overland telegraph." [473]

During March and April there was little or no improvement. A Saint Louis correspondent writes in March that letters are thirty to forty days on the route, that old papers come soaked and worn, and that "friends of the El Paso route are crowing loudly over the failure of the Central route." He says that people are going back to the ocean, and that unless the speed is increased upon the daily mail route, the past winter's record will kill it.[474]

---

[472] Correspondence of February 13th, in *Alta California* of March 24, 1862.

[473] U. S. Senate. *Miscellaneous Documents*, 37th congress, second session, no. 85, 1, 2.

[474] Saint Louis correspondence of March 3, 1862, in *Alta California* of March 31, 1862. The Washington correspondence of April 30th says that

Between the snow and the mud the stage-coaches had a difficult time. In the mountains the roads drifted full of snow and occasionally teams got off the track and were lost. Sleighs were employed over the heaviest snow stretches. The rains and mud were often as bad on other stretches of the road. Deep, stiff mud in places made the empty coach a full load for the team, and passengers were compelled to walk. Mail bags full of government documents were frequently employed to fill in "chuck-holes" in the worst patches of the road.[475]

There was also considerable difficulty in the spring of 1862 due to the management of the eastern end of the line. The Central Overland California and Pike's Peak Express Company had become financially involved and its case was in the hands of the court. A year before, the company was in financial straits and had borrowed money from Ben Holladay, giving him a mortgage upon the line and its equipment.[476] Holladay continued his advances to the company as its revenue was inadequate to meet necessary outlays. Finally the line was forced to the wall and at public sale Holladay purchased it for $100,000 on March 21, 1862. The company at that time owed him $208,000.[477] Holladay was a vigorous and efficient organizer and set to work with the object of placing the system upon a pay-

---

no one pretends to rely upon the mails. "Letters are from forty to fifty days getting through and newspapers seldom come at all." – *Alta California*, May 27, 1862.

[475] *Alta California*, April 15, 1862.

[476] Bela M. Hughes, in a letter to John Doniphan, under date of May 2, 1892 (found in the library of the State Historical and Natural History Society of Colorado) says that when he was elected president of the company on April 26, 1861, he did not know that it was so heavily involved in debt.

[477] — *Idem*, pp. 2, 3. Hughes continued in control of the line at Holladay's request, for another year, and then became attorney for Holladay.

ing basis. In May he went westward upon his line supervising its conduct, and visiting Denver and other places of importance. Accompanied by Governor Evans of Colorado he visited Central City and the other mining camps in the vicinity of Berthoud Pass.[478]

In April arrangements were made with the Pacific Mail Steamship Company to carry via Panama all mail matter placed on board.[479] It was expected that only the printed matter would be sent by water, but in a short time all matter took the ocean route.[480] This was due in part to Indian depredations[481] that were being encountered in addition to the almost formidable difficulties of snow, rain and mud. The service was interrupted for several weeks but by the middle of June it was resumed, and the postmasters were ordered to forward letters to and from the Pacific Coast by the land route, as had been the rule until the preceding April.[482] It was August however, before all the back mails of March and April which had not been destroyed, were delivered at the places of designation.[483] But the resumption was not complete or thorough going and much mail continued to go by water.[484]

We noted above that the "C. O. C. & P. P. Ex. Co."

---

[478] *Rocky Mountain News*, May 26, 1862.

[479] *Alta California*, April 16, 1862.

[480] — *Idem*, April 19, 1862. Messrs. Forbes and Babcock of San Francisco received the following message from Allan McLane, President of the Pacific Mail Steamship Company, dated New York, April 14, 1862: "On and after the steamer of the 21st of April, take from the Overland Agent for transportation home all mail matter."

[481] These depredations will be discussed in the following chapter.

[482] *Alta California*, July 10, 1862. First regular mail left Saint Louis June 19th.

[483] — *Idem*, August 6, 1862.

[484] The *Alta California* of June 19, 1862, says that the postmaster of San Francisco has decided to send the mail by the ocean because of the severe storms prevailing in the eastern section of the road.

had financed an exploring expedition from Denver to Salt Lake City via Berthoud Pass in the summer of 1861, and that the report was favorable to the route. However, the cost of opening a road and building new stations was so great as to prevent a transfer of the line as had been proposed. In the first session of the Colorado legislature a charter was granted to the "Colorado and Pacific Wagon, Telegraph, and Railroad Company," giving it a rather exclusive monopoly upon the Berthoud route.[485] Later it was charged that this grant was one of the factors which prevented the establishment of the daily mail over this new course.[486] But the people of Colorado kept up the agitation. It was necessary to advertise the route and build a road upon it and then, they were certain, all the emigration would come to or through Colorado. The benefits to be derived were evident. "Open this wagon road and the telegraph and railroad will follow it as sure as the sun rises and sets." [487]

The passage of the Pacific Railroad bill by Congress in July, 1862, gave impetus to the movement. Upon the very day that the news reached Denver a party set out to survey a route over the Rocky Mountains and the *Rocky Mountain News* exclaimed: "Denver will yet be the great half-way station between New York and San Francisco." [488]

---

[485] Colorado Legislature *Session Laws*, Act approved November 6, 1861. The bill had a rather shady history. It was contended that the incorporators had no other object than extortion of money from the express company that had explored and surveyed the route. It was also suggested that this bill figured prominently in the log-rolling or deal which made Colorado City instead of Denver the first capital of Colorado. – *Rocky Mountain News*, October 31, 1861, and subsequent dates.

[486] — *Idem*, July 31, 1862.

[487] — *Idem*, May 27, 1862. See also the issues of April 16, 1862, and April 22, 1862.

[488] — *Idem*, July 1, 1862.

In June, 1862, Governor Evans of Colorado, F. M. Case, W. N. Byers, and others had gone to Berthoud Pass to study its availability as a wagon road and railroad route. The grade was admitted to be very steep but it was thought to be practicable. Governor Evans called a meeting at the Denver City Hall at which the matter was discussed, and a subscription started, to provide for a thorough study of the route. Engineer F. M. Case now made a survey of the proposed line but his report was rather disappointing. He found the grade of Clear Creek too steep to be followed with the maximum grade allowed for the railroad (116 feet to the mile). The altitude of the pass was determined to be 11,495 feet (It is 11,300 feet) and the presence of snow in summer indicated that a tunnel would be necessary.[489] The railroad and overland mail projects via Berthoud Pass were given somewhat of a chill and were postponed.

But during July an important change in the overland mail route was effected. This was the transfer of the line from the North Platte road to the Cherokee Trail.[490] The Indian disturbances during the preceding April and May upon the northern course was the

[489] —*Idem*, July 24, 1862. Report of F. M. Case.

This pioneer dream of a railroad route directly west from Denver is only now being realized. With the completion of the Moffatt Tunnel under the continental divide Denver will for the first time be placed upon a direct trans-continental railroad route. The tunnel is to be over six miles long and will be completed in 1926, or 1927.

[490] The Cherokee Trail probably derived its name from a party of Cherokees headed by Captain Evans of Arkansas, who made their way to California via this route, having begun their journey April 20, 1849. See Grant Foreman's "Early Trails through Oklahoma," in *Chronicles of Oklahoma*, vol. iii, 110. See also, R. P. Bieber in *Mississippi Valley Historical Review*, vol. xii, 363. This party however was not the first to take this route. General Ashley in going to the Green River rendezvous in 1825 took this trail. Stansbury was guided over this trail eastward in 1850 by James Bridger.

THE MILLION DOLLAR MAIL IN OPERATION 231

excuse given the Post Office Department for transferring the line. Twenty days interruption in service was allowed by the Department. The chief reason, perhaps, for changing the route was to shorten it. Such a change had been seriously considered the year before, and would no doubt have been made had not the Berthoud Pass route diverted the company's attention.

This new route followed up the South Platte River to the mouth of the Cache la Poudre and up the valley of this affluent to the famous Virginia Dale. The line now crossed the Black Hills, traversed the Laramie Plains, rounded Elk Mountain, and descended to the North Platte at a point near the mouth of Sage Creek. After crossing the North Platte the road led westward to and through Bridger's Pass, skirted the Red Desert, descended Bitter Creek to the Green and then up Black's Fork to Fort Bridger, where the old line of travel was intersected.[491] This overland stage route approximates the Union Pacific railroad and the Lincoln Highway of today through southern Wyoming. From Laramie westward to Bitter Creek the old stage route lies from ten to twenty miles to the south of its modern counterparts, but from that point on to Fort Bridger the three roads form close parallel lines.

Upon July 21st the daily mail service was inaugurated upon the new line and the road was said to be in excellent condition. A branch line from Latham

---

[491] W. A. Smith went over the route and described it in a letter written from Green River May 28th.—*Rocky Mountain News*, June 27, 1862. This newspaper also gives a description of the route in the issue of July 29, 1862, and adds: "The saving in distance between Julesburg and Salt Lake City is said to be 150 miles; whilst the route is better in many respects, particularly in the supply of wood, water, and grass."

An admirable piece of work upon the identification of this route, along with other western trails, has been done by A. B. Hulbert in his *Crown Collection of American Maps*, Series IV.

(where the main line crossed the Platte to follow the Cache la Poudre) supplied Denver with a tri-weekly service. In August the Colorado Legislature passed a special act granting to Holladay's "Overland Stage Line" [492] the right to build bridges and operate ferries upon the route and to collect tolls for the use of these facilities.[493] Presently a further improvement was effected for the Colorado settlers. On September 3d Ben Holladay wrote to a Denver newspaper:

"Permit me, through your columns, to return my thanks for the liberal charter granted to the Overland Stage Line by the legislature of Colorado, and also for the generous support extended to the line by the citizens. In view of these facts, I have instructed my agents to change the route from its present course, to one bearing via Denver to Laporte, so that hereafter you will have the great through mails passing direct through your city. I am happy to announce that the new route to Salt Lake City realizes the most favorable expectations and is already in such fine running order that I was enabled to make the trip from Salt Lake City to Latham in four days. Ben Holladay. Prop'r Overland Stage Co."[494]

The first through coach from the west reached Denver on September 12th and the Camp Weld Artillery with its Fort Donelson pieces fired a grand salute in honor of the Overland Stage. The daily mail from the east now came along the "cut-off" road which left the Platte in the vicinity of present Fort Morgan and followed an almost direct course to Denver. From this

---

[492] Holladay's line now came to be known as the "Overland Stage Line." In October, 1862, and subsequently the advertisements of the company in the *Rocky Mountain News* were run with this title.

[493] Colorado Legislature, second session. Act approved August 14, 1862.

[494] *Rocky Mountain News*, September 11, 1862.

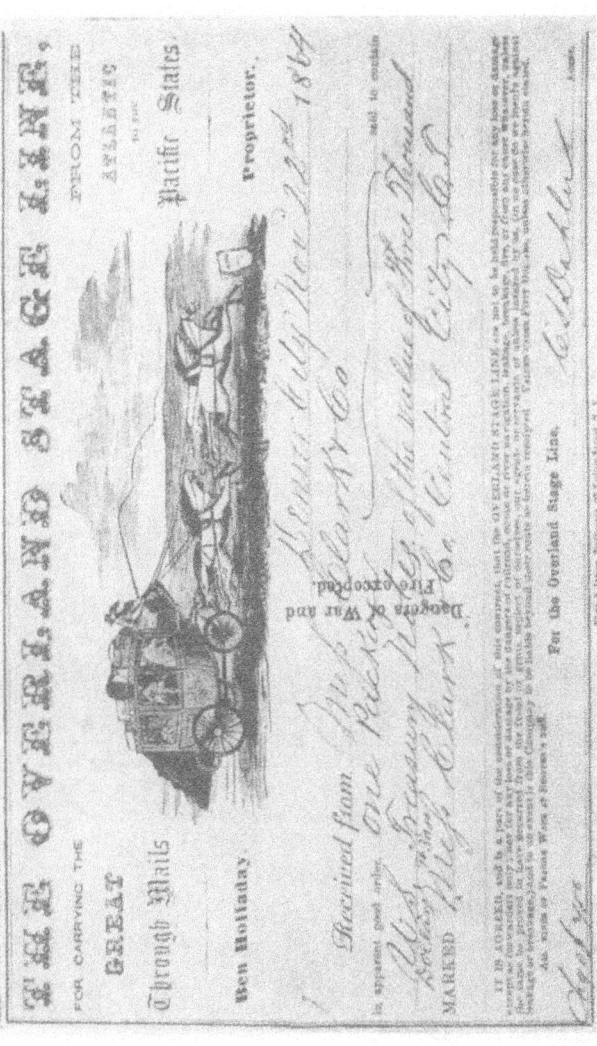

OVERLAND STAGE LINE RECEIPT

point the line ran northward to La Porte, skirting the foothills of the Front Range.[495] The modern highway from Denver to Laramie, Wyoming, follows almost in the very tracks cut by the old overland stage more than sixty years ago.

During 1861 and 1862 the great daily overland mail was the outstanding stage-coach service to the West. There was however, another line, which ran from Kansas City to Santa Fé. This traversed the Santa Fé Trail – the oldest highway into the West. Wagons had been first employed on this trail in 1822 and a monthly mail service was established in 1850. In 1861 the mail was being carried on a weekly schedule, but the remuneration was not large and the facilities rather meagre.[496] W. H. Ryus was a driver on this line. He writes:

"In July, 1861, I was employed by Barnum, Vickery, and Neal to drive over what was known as the Long Route, that is, from Fort Larned to Fort Lyon, two hundred and forty miles, with no station between. We drove one set of mules the whole distance, camped out, and made the journey, in good weather, in four or five days. In winter we generally encountered a great deal of snow, and very cold air on the bleak and wind-swept desert of the Upper Arkansas, but we employees got used to that, only the passengers did any kicking. We had a way of managing them, however, when they got very obstreperous; all we had to do was to yell Indians; and that quieted them quicker than forty-rod whiskey does a man.

"We gathered buffalo-chips to boil our coffee and

---

[495] An interesting description of the route from Denver to Salt Lake City was given in the *Rocky Mountain News* (November 13, 1862) by Edward Bliss, one of the editors, who accompanied B. M. Hughes over the line.

[496] U. S. House. *Executive Documents*, 37th congress, second session, vol. xi, no. 137, 572. The compensation was $54,999 per annum.

cook our buffalo and antelope steak, smoked for a while around the smouldering fire until the animals were through grazing, and then started on our lonely way again. Sometimes the coach would travel for a hundred miles through the buffalo herds, never for a moment getting out of sight of them. Often we saw fifty thousand to a hundred thousand on a single journey out or in. The Indians used to call them their cattle, and claimed to own them. . . The Indians on the plains were not at all hostile in 1861-62; we could drive into their villages." [497]

A branch line was extended to Fort Wise (later Fort Lyon) in February, 1861, and this was continued on up the Arkansas to Canon City, Colorado, in June of the same year.[498] With the mail line established in 1860 from Denver to Colorado City (later Colorado Springs) there was now nearly a through connection between Denver and Santa Fé – a gap of forty miles between Colorado City and Canon City being the only missing link. The old Taos Trail running northward from New Mexico had been used by trappers since the days of the fur trade. With the discovery of gold in the Pike's Peak region many supplies had been brought in from the south to the mining camps and there naturally arose a call for mail facilities between the territories of New Mexico and Colorado. It was a long road that a letter must take in 1860 in going from Denver to Santa Fé for the only mail service was by way of Kansas City.[499] During the spring of 1861 a private pony express was operated weekly between Denver and

---

[497] In Inman, Henry. *The Old Santa Fe Trail*, 154.

[498] U. S. House. *Executive Documents*, 37th congress, second session, vol. xi, no. 137, pp. 572, 579. Additional pay of $5,696 and $5,000 respectively were allowed for these extensions.

[499] *Rocky Mountain News*, January 11, 1860; August 20, 1861.

THE MILLION DOLLAR MAIL IN OPERATION 237

New Mexico, and during part of the year a military express ran from Canon City to Fort Garland in the San Luis valley.[500] For a time in the spring of 1862 the mail contractor from Denver to Colorado City continued the trip to Pueblo and thus connected with the Kansas City and New Mexico mails. But when no through passengers were being carried the contractor was not inclined to continue the journey to Pueblo, since no remuneration was being received for this service.[501] At last, in the autumn of 1862, arrangements were made for a through line from Denver to Santa Fé. It took a rather indirect route, however, going by way of Bent's Fort. The service was in the hands of Cottrell, Vickroy and Company and their first coach arrived in Denver September 28, 1862.[502]

During the latter part of August, Indian troubles occurred in Minnesota, and a general Indian War was anticipated, believed to be stimulated by Secession emissaries.[503] In view of this situation the overland mail was suspended and remained inoperative for three weeks.[504] Upon being resumed the service was considerably improved. During November the overland service to San Francisco anticipated the carriage by water by from three to five days.[505]

In his annual report of December, 1862, the Postmaster-general stated that the service in the past had not been satisfactory, but he expressed the belief that it would be made so. The importance of the line was growing more manifest, as new mines were continually

---
[500] — *Idem*, February 27, 1861; May 11, 1861; August 20, 1861.
[501] — *Idem*, March 22, 25 ,1862.
[502] — *Idem*, October 2, 1862.
[503] *Alta California*, August 29, 1862.
[504] — *Idem*, September 20, 1862.
[505] — *Idem*, November 24, 1862.

being discovered in the region traversed by the route. "As an agency in developing these resources for the government the mail line is indispensable," he contended, "and every needful protection and support should be given to the Company, and some allowance made for failures in the beginning undertaking." [506]

---

[506] Postmaster-general's *Report*, 1862, 126, 127.

Chapter XI

The Indian Peril

"Lo! the poor Indian whose untutored mind
Saw God in the forest, and heard him in the wind."

PARODY:

"Hi! the filthy redskin and his filthier squaw
Who cares for nothing but fill their dirty paws."

The latter quotation appeared in a western newspaper as a parody upon the preceding verse and reflects somewhat the Westerner's attitude toward the Indian during the sixties, as contrasted with that of the Easterner who saw the Indian with more romantic and far-distant eyes. It does not become our duty here to argue the merits of the different points of view.

The Indian wars were the inevitable results of the contact of two different and incompatible civilizations. Both could not exist on the same soil; naturally the stronger would replace the weaker. Occasional conflicts had occurred from the day when the first explorers and trappers penetrated the Indian domain. But so long as the white incursions were temporary and infrequent the Indian's sway was not threatened and the conflict was postponed. However, when the miner, farmer, and stockman took up their permanent homes in the West, a new era dawned.

The "Indian's cattle" were his food and shelter and as he saw the buffalo slaughtered, he read his fate in the whitened bones on the prairie. The long gray line of white-man's wagons seemed an endless chain, carrying an innumerable host toward the land of the setting sun. In those white-topped caravans were inexhaustible supplies of food, varieties unlimited, that appealed to the Indian's newly developed tastes. Why should he permit them all to pass him by, and with their rumbling to frighten away his game? And now the slowly-moving ox-train was supplanted by the flying stage-coach. Would there ever be an end? Should he not stop the stream before it overwhelmed him? His primitive mind was grasping the situation and a decision was forthcoming.

Overland staging had met some Indian difficulties previously, but not until the sixties did these become chronic. The isolated depredations of the fifties were but preliminaries to the general uprisings of the middle sixties. During 1861 no Indian difficulties of consequence occurred, but in the following year depredations were committed which gave a foreboding of greater conflicts to come.

In March, 1862, it was reported that General Halleck had been ordered to send troops to protect the overland mail route, and in early April, that General Craig was to have charge of these troops.[507] However, some of the Indians bestirred themselves before the troops arrived. By April 4th sixty head of stock were reported stolen from the region immediately east of Fort Bridger.[508] The marauders burned the stations between Fort Bridger and the North Platte, destroyed mail and coaches, drove off the stock and killed several men. At other points on the route mails accumulated; while at some places mail bags were cut open, their

---

[507] *Rocky Mountain News*, March 28, 1862; April 4, 1862.
[508] *Alta California*, April 4, 1862. These were stolen from the stations at Split Rock, Dry Sandy, Rocky Ridge, and Red Butte.

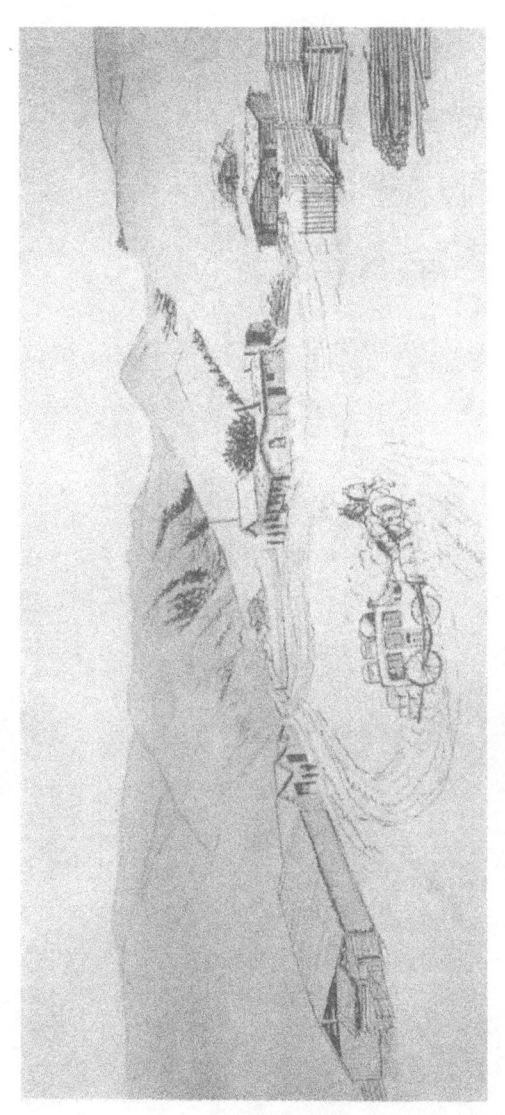
BRIDGER PASS STATION, ON THE OVERLAND STAGE ROUTE
From an original drawing

contents rifled and "the stations [were] knee-deep with loose and opened letters." [509]

One of the most prominent encounters occurred on the Sweetwater in Wyoming. The mail party, consisting of nine men and two coaches, left Atchison April 2, 1862. On the 17th they were attacked by the Indians. Mr. T. S. Boardman, one of the party, writes of the engagement:

"We drove to the top of a slight elevation to the left of the road; the other coach was driven up along side, distant about ten feet; mules badly frightened; one of them was shot through the mouth, and the bullets whistling rapidly among them, it was thought best to let them go. They were accordingly cut loose and were soon drove up a canon to the southwest of the road, by some ten or twelve Indians. Everything that could afford protection, mail sacks, blankets, buffalo robes, etc., were thrown out of the coaches and from the front boots, and were placed upon the north and south sides between the coaches, against the wheels and along the east side of us, behind which we barricaded ourselves. James Brown who was standing by the hind wheel of one of the coaches, then received a shot in the left side of the face. . . Lem Flowers (Division Agent) was then struck in the hip. . . Phil Rogers received two arrows in the right shoulder. . . James Anderson was shot through the left leg, and William Reed through the small of the back. . .

"The bullets pattered like hail upon the sacks that protected us. We returned the fire with the rifle and our revolvers whenever we got sight of any of the foe, reserving most of our revolver shots for their charges.

---

[509] G. W. Pence in the *Silver Age* (Carson City, Nevada), June 19, appearing in the *Alta California*, June 23, 1862.

They charged upon us twice, but the volleys that we poured upon them repelled them. About four o'clock P.M. they withdrew in parties of two and threes . . . We soon determined to get away if we could, with the wounded to the next station."

They uncoupled one of the coaches, spread some blankets on the running gears and attempted to draw the wounded to safety upon this improvised ambulance. However, this process was slow and hard and was soon given up. Instead, the wounded were helped along by a man on each side.

"After a fatiguing walk of eight miles we reached the station of Three Crossings. Here we found the station keeper, wife and three children, and the men employed by the Company, who informed us that Indians – probably the same band – had stolen all the mules and eight head of cattle the night before." Here the station house and stable were made into a fort. Some of the cattle returned, and on the 21st these were yoked to a wagon and the party moved westward, reaching Fort Bridger on the 2nd of May, where the wounded were properly cared for in the hospital.[510]

News of these disturbances were soon telegraphed east and west and preparations made to punish the Indians and protect the mail route. The Colorado troops, who would have been the logical ones to handle this situation, were busily engaged with General Sibley's Confederate army in northern New Mexico. Their service in that field was important and decisive. General Sibley was defeated and turned back from further invasion.[511] Brigham Young telegraphed to the Utah

---
[510] *Alta California*, May 26, 1862.
[511] Whitford, W. C. *Colorado Volunteers in the Civil War.*

Delegate at Washington that "The militia of Utah are ready and able as they ever have been to take care of all the Indians, and are able and willing to protect the mail if called upon to do so."[512] April 24th, Lieutenant-general Wells of the N. L. Militia of Utah ordered Colonel R. T. Burton and a detachment to accompany and guard the eastbound stage. April 28th, President Lincoln called upon ex-Governor Young to raise a company of one hundred men for ninety days' service in the vicinity of Independence Rock.[513] The company was immediately raised and with equipment and supplies departed on May 1st for the region of the hostilities. When the troops arrived the Indians had disappeared, and after thirty days of service this company was mustered out.[514]

On May 15th Brigadier-general Craig proclaimed martial law upon the plains for the better protection of the mail and the commerce of the prairies.[515] By this date also, eighty cavalry from the east had passed Fort Laramie on their way westward, and another company had arrived at Fort Kearny.[516] Early in April the 3d Regiment of California volunteers under Colonel Connor were put under orders to prepare to march to Utah about May 10th. They were to garrison the forts and protect the Overland Mail route.[517] However, Colonel Connor did not take up his line of march until July, and it was not until August 6, 1862,[518] that he assumed command of the Military District of Utah, estab-

---

[512] Quoted in Tullidge, *History of Salt Lake City*, 252.
[513] — *Idem*, 254.
[514] — *Idem*, 259.
[515] *Rocky Mountain News*, May 28, 1862.
[516] *Alta California*, May 16, 1862.
[517] — *Idem*, April 6, 1862.
[518] Tullidge, *History of Salt Lake City*, 274.

lishing himself at Camp Douglas on the outskirts of Salt Lake City.

In the summer of 1862 settlers in Colorado were disturbed over the possibility of Indian difficulties and began to call for the return of their troops from New Mexico for the defense of their own homes.[519] Some plundering had been done on the South Platte north of Denver and Governor Evans, Indian Agent Vaile, and some troops under Colonel Leavenworth repaired to the scene. The Indians were induced to leave immediately for their hunting grounds on the Republican River.[520] In July reports again indicated difficulties in that direction but troops sent for relief found small cause for complaint,[521] and in the fall of this year the Colorado settlers felt secure from Indian attack.[522]

The Indian troubles in Minnesota during the summer of 1862 were very serious, but they did not reach so far south as the overland mail line.

In 1862 troops were stationed on the South Pass route of the overland mail line and Fort Laramie was the principal military stronghold. With the change to the Bridger Pass route in July, Fort Laramie was left to the north of the mail line and it became necessary to establish another fort to guard the coaches. A good site was selected at the north base of Elk Mountain where the Cherokee Trail rounded the Medicine Bow Range. The fort established here in the fall of 1862 was named in honor of General Halleck. Troops were stationed also at other points along the route, while at

---

[519] *Rocky Mountain News*, June 30, 1862.

[520] — *Idem*, June 24, 1862.

[521] It appeared that the settlers wanted to be rid of the Indians whose horses were eating up the grass on the bottoms. — *Rocky Mountain News*, July 11, 1862.

[522] — *Idem*, September 25, October 30, 1862.

Salt Lake City Colonel Connor was in control with a regiment of California volunteers.

The telegraph line still ran via the South Pass route; hence the troops had two lines of communication to keep open. On this northern route an attack was made upon Pacific Springs Telegraph Station November 24th and one man was killed. Telegrams were sent east and west for troops, but the Indians already had disappeared and driven the stock before them.[523]

In January, 1863, Colonel Connor with about three hundred men fought the Battle of Bear River in southern Idaho. He severely defeated an equal number of Bannocks and Shoshones, completely breaking their power in that region. The War Department commended the volunteers for their gallant service and their Colonel was commissioned a Brigadier-general.[524] News of this engagement was received with joy by settlers in the West. When, during the following month, news was received of Indian depredations in northwestern Colorado a Denver newspaper asked: "Would it not be better to employ a few more men like Colonel Connor, and wipe the treacherous vagabonds from the face of the earth? . . . It requires no prophet to foresee that our increasing perplexities with the different Indian tribes will eventually lead to their extermination." [525] But agencies for peaceable solution of the problems were at work, and early in 1863 Indian deputations were taken to visit the national capital. Representatives of the Arapahoes, Apaches and Cheyennes left Fort Lyon on the Arkansas River in February.[526] During the same month seven Ute chiefs

---
[523] — *Idem*, December 11, 1862. Quoting *Deseret News* of Nov. 26th.
[524] Whitney, O. F. *Popular History of Utah*, 190.
[525] *Rocky Mountain News*, February 26, 1863.
[526] — *Idem*, February 26, 1863.

were housed at Camp Weld near Denver, preparatory to making their eastward journey. The *Rocky Mountain News* says of them in its issue of February 14th: "Those Ute chiefs are stopping in a Sibley tent near the Sutler's store in Camp Weld. A guard of three with drawn swords are daily guarding the tent. They have a few Navajo scalps which are as thick as a buffalo hide. These are intended for a present to Father Abraham when they call upon him in the White House." On the 22d these Utes departed for Washington accompanied by Colonel Head and escorted by companies D and H of the Colorado regiment.

During the same spring, troubles arose on the line west of Salt Lake City. In March, 1863, Eight Mile Station, in western Utah, was attacked and the station keepers were killed.[527] When the eastbound coach arrived the Indians were waiting for it. Not until the coach was within twenty-five yards of the house did the driver, Hank Harper, recognize their hostile intentions. He quickly plied his whip, turned the horses from the road and tried to make a detour around the station, but it was too late to save himself. He was caught by a bullet from the assailants and dropped into the front boot. The passenger beside the driver was hit and also fell into the boot. Then Judge G. N. Mott, newly-elected Delegate to Congress from Nevada, crawled out of the coach, got the lines, and drove successfully to Deep Creek.[528] Though the driver had been killed, the mail was not interrupted. On May 19th the Indians again attacked the coach in the same

---

[527] — *Idem*, April 9, 1863. Also, Egan, W. M., ed. *Pioneering the West*, 200, 260.

[528] Howard R. Egan, who was at Deep Creek at the time, writes: "They got the dead driver out and laid him beside the door where he was when we got back. The other man, when they saw that he was still alive, they car-

vicinity and the driver, W. R. Simpson, was killed. Major Egan, who sat beside the driver took the lines and continued the drive. Soldiers were accompanying this stage, but as the Indians were hid in the rocks the soldiers' return fire was ineffective.[529] The coach approaching Salt Lake City from the west was attacked June 10th. The driver and an employee were killed and scalped, and the mail was cut to pieces.[530] On July 8, 1863, the Indians executed a surprise attack upon Canyon station near Deep Creek in Western Utah. Five men were killed and the station was burned.[531]

In the mid-summer of 1863 the Utes caused some

---

ried into the house. This man lived and when well enough to travel went east to his home and friends although he had lost about a tablespoonful of his brains. . ." Next morning Egan and others went to Eight Mile Station to see what had been done. He thus describes the work of the savages: "The Cook was lying just outside of the space between the rooms, stripped, scalped, and cut all over his body. They had even cut his tongue out before, or after, death, I don't know which, but I think it was before, because they had dobbed his face with blood and then covered that over with flour to make him a white man again. We had some trouble in finding Mr. Wood, who was the Overland Mail hay-stacker, in haying time, and hustler the rest of the year — a good steady young man. After about one hour hunting around, we found him. He laid about seventy-five yards north of the house and about thirty yards west of the road in the rabbit brush. They had taken off every stitch of clothing and left him as naked as he was when born. They had not cut and slashed his body as they had the other man's, probably because they had killed him before they got him." – Egan, *op. cit.*, 261.

[529] San Francisco *Bulletin*, May 22, 1863. Egan, *op. cit.*, 200. Denver *Commonwealth*, June 18, 1863.

[530] San Francisco *Bulletin*, June 11, 1863.

[531] W. M. Egan, then a boy of twelve years, was with his older brothers freighting grain for the stage teams and passed Canyon Station the day before the attack. Howard R. Egan describes the assault on Canyon Station thus: "The Indians waited till the men had been called to breakfast in the dug-out, and were all down in the hole without their guns, all except the hostler, William Riley, who was currying a horse just outside the north door of the stable at the time of the first alarm, and he was shot through the ankle and the bone broken short off. He started down the canyon on the run, but did not get far before he was caught and killed.

"The men at breakfast were mostly all killed as they came out of the dug-out to reach their arms that were stacked in the south end of the barn. Not

little excitement in the vicinity of Fort Halleck. When news of the disturbances reached Denver an Indian expedition was immediately planned. Sixty wagons were loaded with sixty days' rations and six companies of the First Colorado Cavalry under Major Wynkoop, prepared for the movement. They were to go via Camp Collins to Fort Halleck.[532] It appears that Utes came to the fort about the first of July begging provisions. They then commenced running off the stock belonging to the Overland Stage Company and were followed once or twice without success. Then seventy troops were sent after them and after riding thirty miles they came upon the Indians hidden behind breastworks on a wooded hill. A rather sharp engagement followed and the Indians were finally dispersed. One soldier was killed and four were wounded, while the Indian loss was estimated at from twenty to sixty.[533] With the arrival of the Colorado troops and of others from the East the Utes disappeared and no further trouble was had with them.

In July, 1863, Governor Doty of Utah and General Connor made a peace treaty with the Indians at Fort Bridger. Goods were distributed to the tribes and they agreed not to molest the overland travel.[534] The troops along the line however, were undoubtedly a more effective guarantee of peace than the treaty signed at the

---

one of them ever reached his gun. One man, though wounded, tried to escape by running down the canyon as Riley did. He got further away, but was caught and killed, and, as he was some bald on the top of his head, and a good growth of whiskers on his chin, they scalped that and left him where he fell. . . They took the clothes off of every man and left them just where they fell all this had been done without a shot being fired by the whitemen. A most complete surprise and massacre."-Egan, *op. cit.*, 263-264.

[532] Denver *Commonwealth*, July 2, 1863.
[533] —*Idem*, July 16, 1863.
[534] *Alta California*, August 14, 1863; October 6, 1863.

fort.[535] Peace reigned along the mail line in the fall of 1863, but when suggestions came that some of the troops be removed to other fields, this editorial appeared in the Denver *Commonwealth* of September 17, 1863:

"There are at present in this district, the First Colorado Cavalry and eight companies of the Eleventh Ohio, and the country they occupy and protect is more than 500 miles square. There is the telegraph line from Julesburg via Fort Laramie to Bridger – on this the Eleventh Ohio are stationed. There is the Overland Stage route from this place via Fort Halleck to Bridger. A battalion of the First Colorado but recently returned from a 700 mile tramp after a band of Utes that had been committing numberless depredations on this route in the vicinity of Fort Halleck. . .

"In the South there is the Arkansas route to New Mexico to guard from 125 miles east of Fort Lyon to beyond the Raton Mountains. Recently, three trains arrived at Fort Lyon, having been completely stripped of their lading by an encampment of 2,000 to 3,000 Kiowas and Comanches on the road between Lyon and Larned. The trainmasters aver that the Indians had white men, women, and children captives. Major Anthony with 125 men has gone down on the road to protect the immense amount of stuff going over it to New Mexico.

"Besides these routes of travel and trade, on which Indians are eternally depredating, there are four regular posts to be garrisoned – Lyon, Garland, Halleck,

---

[535] A description of the distribution of the troops under General Connor is given in a letter from Salt Lake City, printed in the San Francisco *Bulletin*, November 30, 1863. The distribution of the troops about Fort Halleck is given in the Denver *Commonwealth*, August 20, 1863.

and Laramie, the control of the disloyal element in our midst, and occasional irregular services, such as protection of emigrants to the northwestern mines. So far we have been enabled to get along without serious outbreaks of any kind, but the presence of No. 1 troops is all that has restrained the Indians from open hostility. . .

"Colorado from her geographical position, from her tried loyalty, and on account of her valuable resources should receive ample protection. We are utterly opposed to stripping this country of troops. An ounce of prevention is worth a pound of cure."

During 1862 and 1863 the plains Indians had acquired many firearms and horses and, to observant men, it was evident that a general uprising was being planned. Governor Evans of Colorado repeatedly communicated to the authorities at Washington evidence in substantiation of this fact.[536] He was kept informed as to developments by Elbridge Gerry,[537] a trader with an Indian wife, who resided north of Denver on the South Platte River. In early September, 1863, Governor Evans made an effort to meet the plains Indians at the head of the Republican River and make a treaty of peace. He sent Gerry to gather the Sioux, Arapahoes, and Cheyennes at the appointed place while he, accompanied by a company of the first Colorado Cavalry, brought out provisions for the feast. But the Governor's emissary found the Indians insolent or indifferent, and neither persuasion nor bribery could induce them to come to the proposed council. They

---

[536] Smiley, J. C. *Semi-Centennial History of the State of Colorado*, vol. i, 413. Also Governor Evans's correspondence published in the *Rocky Mountain News*, August 25, 1864.

[537] Gerry was a grandson of Elbridge Gerry who signed the Declaration of Independence. He was an educated man.

asked Gerry what was wanted of them, and when he replied that the Governor desired them to settle down on their reservation and live as white men, they replied: "Well, you can just go back to the Governor and tell him we are not reduced quite that low yet."[538] The attempted conference was a complete failure. Governor Evans had hopes for better success with the Utes and left in October with Mr. Nicolay, Lincoln's private secretary, for Conejos on the upper Rio Grande to treat with the Utes and Comanches.[539] This treaty at Conejos was more successful and the Indians agreed to accept a reservation in the Gunnison River country. The influence of Ouray, chief of the Utes, was a vital factor in keeping peace between his tribe and the whites. His visit to Washington in the spring previous had impressed him with the unlimited military power of the whites and he continued to advocate peace. Ouray was a great Indian chief and friend of the white men and his service is fittingly commemorated by the placing of his picture in the dome of the Colorado capitol.

But among the plains Indians there was no Ouray to counsel discretion. In April, May, and July respectively, General Mitchell, Commander of the Nebraska District, held three councils with the Sioux on the Platte River but each ended in failure.[540]

In the spring of 1864 detachments of the First Colorado Cavalry came into collision with some of the plains Indians. Late in April one hundred of these troops had a sharp engagement with mounted Chey-

---

[538] "Interview with Ex-Governor Evans" in 1884. (Bancroft MS.), p. 11. See also Denver *Commonwealth*, August 27, September 24, 1863.

[539] Denver *Commonwealth*, October 1, 1863.

[540] Ware, E. F. *The Indian War of 1864*, 146, 198, 219, *et seq*.

ennes not far from Fort Larned and about the same time a smaller body of soldiers encountered other Cheyennes who were said to be running off stock from Fremont's Orchard on the South Platte. Other troops were now sent from Denver against the South Platte marauders, and, at Cedar Canon on an affluent of the South Platte, these Indians were routed and one hundred horses recovered.[541] As a part of Colorado's Volunteers were in the east doing duty in the Missouri campaign, Governor Evans now appealed to the Department of Kansas and to New Mexico for additional troops. He was informed that there were none to spare and so set about to organize a state militia. In early June, horses were stampeded from freighters on the "cut-off" road east of Denver and on the 11th a savage assault was made on a ranch thirty miles southeast of Denver. Mr. Hungate, his wife, and two children were murdered and scalped. Their mutilated bodies were brought into Denver and placed on exhibition.[542] Feeling naturally ran high and rumors spread fast that all the settlements were to be attacked.[543] Denver was almost in panic and the "people were gathering guns and fixing for a defense and gathering women into the second story of Kountze's bank to keep them from being massacred."[544] The governor ordered all business houses closed at 6:30 p.m. and all able-bodied citizens to meet for drill at seven o'clock.[545]

On July 17th some Indian raids were made on the

---

[541] Smiley, J. C. *History of Colorado*, vol. i, 414. *Rocky Mountain News*, May 4, 1864. G. B. Grinnell in his *Fighting Cheyennes*, pp. 134-138, gives the Indian side of the story.
[542] Denver *Commonwealth*, June 15, 1864.
[543] Howbert, I. *Memories of a Lifetime in the Pike's Peak Region*, 100.
[544] Evans's *Interview, op. cit.*, 18.
[545] Governor Evans's order in *Commonwealth*, June 22, 1864.

stage route along the South Platte. From Junction (now Fort Morgan, Colorado) came the report that two emigrants were killed at Bijou Ranch, eighty-five miles from Denver, and seventeen horses run off. The same band of Indians continued down the road and ran off the stage company's stock at Junction, and sixty horses from Murray's, the first station below Junction. "The soldiers from Living Springs left the Junction this morning at two o'clock and overtook them about twenty-five miles southeast of here on Beaver Creek. Only five Indians were with the stock. These five were killed and nearly all the stock recovered. None of the soldiers were harmed. All the stage stock was recovered." Another raid was made near Valley Station. "The women and children are all leaving for Denver. Dead cattle, full of arrows, are lying in all directions. A general Indian war is anticipated." "Valley Station, July 18, 2½ p.m. The stage has just come down and the passengers say that they found two men killed and scalped on the road at Beaver Creek, about a mile above the station."[546]

General Mitchell, stopped all the immigrant and freight teams in the vicinity of Julesburg upon hearing of the Indian depredations above, in order that the trains might come through in sufficient force to protect themselves.[547]

On the same day that the South Platte raids occurred (July 17th), a skirmish was had at Fort Larned on the Arkansas route. The day following, the Indians attacked a train at Walnut Creek, fifteen miles below

---

[546] *Rocky Mountain News*, July 18, 1864. The issue of July 23d gives more details regarding these raids and summarizes the results. Five men were killed, and 130 horses stolen, of which all but 53 were recovered.
[547] — *Idem*, July 22, 1864.

Larned, and killed ten men. They also scalped a man and a boy without killing them, these having escaped with life by feigning death.[548]

The most widespread outbreak of the summer occurred in August. On the 8th, an attack was made upon some trains at Plum Creek, thirty-five miles east of Fort Kearny. Fourteen men were reported killed and some women and children taken prisoners. Three trains were robbed and burned.[549] Three men were killed near Gilman's Ranch, and nine miles below Cottonwood another was shot on the following day. On the 10th the valley of the Little Blue was raided, trains were captured, and Mrs. Eubanks, her two children and Miss Roper carried away by the marauders.[550] The westbound coach arrived at Fort Kearny on the 10th and the passengers reported "not a living soul on the road within fifty miles of Kearny, and not a hoof of stock to be found."[551] The same day it was reported from Omaha that the coach had passed several burned trains and eleven dead bodies; that six whites were killed at Thirty-two Mile Creek the night before; and that the stock had been stolen from Cottonwood, ninety miles west of Kearny.[552]

Governor Evans of Colorado now made a special effort to raise a militia force. He issued a proclamation: "Patriotic citizens of Colorado: — I again appeal to you to organize for defense of your homes and families against the merciless savages. . . Any man who kills a hostile Indian is a patriot; but there are Indians who are friendly and to kill one of these will

---
[548] — *Idem*, August 1, 1864.
[549] — *Idem*, August 9, 1864.
[550] Grinnell, *op. cit.*, 148.
[551] *Rocky Mountain News*, August 10, 1864.
[552] — *Idem*, August 11, 1864.

THE INDIAN PERIL

involve us in greater difficulty. It is important therefore to fight only the hostile, and no one has been or will be restrained from this."[553] The *Rocky Mountain News* added: "A few months of active extermination against the red devils will bring quiet and nothing else will."[554]

Governor Evans had sent messengers to the Indian tribes thought to be friendly, directing them to rendezvous at Fort Lyon, Fort Larned, Fort Laramie, or Camp Collins, where subsistence and protection would be provided. The effort met with little or no response, and the Governor now "authorized all citizens of Colorado, either individually or in such parties as they may organize, to go in pursuit of all hostile Indians. . . and hold to their own private use and benefit, all property of said hostile Indians that they may capture."[555] Appeal was made to the War Department and the Governor was authorized to raise a regiment of "one hundred day men" to fight the Indians.[556]

The overland mail was of course interrupted by this general outbreak.[557] On the 15th it was reported from Fort Kearny that there was no immediate prospect of the mails being resumed between that point and the Missouri River as the country was deserted to within forty miles of Atchison. General Curtis however, was gathering and sending up the Platte all the troops he could get and was determined that the route should be protected.

---
[553] — *Idem*, August 10, 1864.
[554] — *Idem*, August 10, 1864.
[555] — *Idem*, August 11, 1864.
[556] — *Idem*, August 13, 1864.
[557] — *Idem*, August 24, 1864. "The last eastern mail arrived ten days ago. No more need be expected for some time to come."

On the Arkansas River between Bent's Fort and Boone's, a stage station was attacked on the 16th and the stock killed. The next day three men were killed and one woman was captured, fourteen miles below Boone's.[558] A general attack upon the frontier settlements of Colorado was planned by the Indians to take place about August 22d. Friendly Indians told Elbridge Gerry of this, and he immediately rode sixty miles to Denver to tell the Governor. Messengers were sent to the settlements and defensive preparations made. The Indians finding that their secret had leaked out, refrained from the contemplated attack.[559]

One mail was brought through from the east, arriving at Denver August 25th. It brought news of excitement and Indian depredations in Nebraska and Kansas equal to those in Colorado.[560] During these troubles the mail stage running between Denver and Santa Fé was escorted by troops whenever it made its infrequent trips.[561] Hope of early resumption of mail service across the plains was given a blow when the postmaster at Denver on September 2d received orders from Washington to forward all mail for the east to San Francisco to be sent by water. The postmaster protested that there was not sufficient cause for interruption of the service, and the Denver newspaper criticized Holladay, saying that he had refused to restock the line until the mail contract was awarded to him.[562]

West of Denver the mail service continued in operation. About seventy-five passengers and a large amount

---

[558] — *Idem*, August 24, 1864.
[559] — *Idem*, August 26, 1864. Evans's MS., *op. cit.*, 16; Howbert, *op. cit.*, 110.
[560] — *Idem*, August 25, 1864.
[561] — *Idem*, August 31, 1864.
[562] — *Idem*, September 3, 1864.

of mail accumulated at Latham, on the South Platte. Mr. Root, who was the mail agent at that station at the time, says that one hundred and nine sacks of mail, weighing in all about two or three tons, accumulated at his station. When rumor came of an intended attack these sacks were piled up to the ceiling about the room to constitute breastworks for defense.[563] A great amount of mail accumulated at Atchison for a time, but was finally returned to New York and sent to California by the ocean route. Upon reaching San Francisco the mail intended for Salt Lake City, Denver and other intermediate points, was forwarded eastward upon the stage, and after a delay of several weeks and a transportation of several thousand additional miles, finally arrived at its destination.[564]

Some minor contacts between Indians and troops along the mail route occurred in early September, but nothing of consequence took place. On September 19th a mail coach left Denver for the East via the Arkansas route, and four days later one departed over the Platte road.[565] The first mail from the East arrived in Denver on the 29th, and during October regular mail service was again resumed.

On August 29, 1864, a letter had been written by "Black Kettle and other Chiefs," making a peace overture.[566] Major Wynkoop went from Fort Lyon to the Cheyenne village on the Smoky Hill and recovered four white prisoners. He then brought the chiefs to

---

[563] Root and Connelley, *Overland Stage to California*, 333. Mr. Root is living today in Topeka, Kansas. He is 89 years old.

[564] One of the largest consignments of this back mail arrived at San Francisco the first of October. It consisted of 70,000 letters and 180 sacks of newspapers.—*Alta California*, October 3, 1864.

[565] *Rocky Mountain News*, September 19, 24, 1864.

[566] Grinnell, *op. cit.*, 152.

Denver where they had a talk with Evans, Chivington, and others late in September; but little was accomplished. Winter was coming on and many of the Indians were now ready for peace and rations; but General Curtis telegraphed that no peace was to be made without his authority. Most of the military officers were for chastising the Indians severely before peace was made. Plans in this direction culminated in the attack at Sand Creek on November 29, 1864, which has been called either a "Battle" or a "massacre" according to the point of view of the writer.[567] The number of Indians killed on this occasion has been variously estimated at from one hundred to six hundred.

The fugitives from the Sand Creek encounter sent messengers to the Sioux and Arapahoes inviting them to join in a return attack. These other tribes joined the Cheyennes and early in January, 1865, they set out toward Julesburg. About one thousand warriors were in the party that made this attack on January 7th. They attempted to lead the soldiers from Fort Rankin (later Fort Sedgwick, about a mile west of Julesburg) into the sand hills to surround them, and did succeed in killing fourteen of the troops. The Indians now swooped down upon the mail and supply station of Julesburg. Just before the Indians charged in from the hills the westbound coach arrived at the station and the passengers alighted to get breakfast. Upon seeing the Indians swarming into the valley the whites rushed to

---

[567] A lengthy report upon this affair is the "Report of the Joint Special Committee appointed under the joint resolution of March 3, 1865." The accounts by Grinnell and by Howbert are instructive and give the story from opposite points of view. News of the fight reached Denver December 7th and caused great rejoicing. On the 22d the soldiers arrived and paraded before their admiring fellow citizens.—*Rocky Mountain News*, December 7, 8, 22, 1864.

THE INDIAN PERIL 263

Fort Rankin and safety. The Indians now plundered the coach and the supply stores at Julesburg, the squaws bringing in extra ponies to carry away the sacks of flour, sugar, and shelled corn. The paymaster who had come in on the morning coach abandoned his box of greenbacks in his flight to the fort. The Indians knocked open the box but were disappointed to find that it contained nothing but bundles of "green paper." Some of these they hacked into pieces and threw into the air.

Two discharged soldiers traveling eastward in a one-horse wagon were attacked and killed. "They had some scalps and Indian relics from Sand Creek, about which they had talked a great deal on the road."[568] When the Indians opened their valises they found the scalps of Little Wolf and White Leaf, two Cheyennes who were killed at Sand Creek. "Little Wolf's scalp was recognized at once by a peculiar little shell which he had always worn, still attached to the hair. White Leaf's scalp was known by the light color of the hair. The white men had many other trophies from Sand Creek, which they were taking home to the States, and when the Indians saw all these things they were so angry that they cut the bodies of the dead to pieces."[569]

After plundering most of the day the Indians moved off to camp on the headwaters of the Republican.[570] News of this attack caused great excitement in Denver,

---

[568] *Rocky Mountain News*, January 16, 1865.

[569] Grinnell, *op. cit.*, 184. Grinnell adds that Touching Cloud, who was living in 1909, was of this Indian party. Grinnell gives the soldier party killed as numbering nine. Surgeon Hamilton, who attended the wounded in these raids says there were two soldiers returning with Indian trophies.– *Rocky Mountain News*, January 16, 1865.

[570] Grinnell, *op. cit.*, 179. *Rocky Mountain News*, January 7, 9, 1865. The telegraph operator telegraphed from Julesburg on the 10th that the bodies of 13 soldiers and 5 citizens were brought in, and that 55 Indians were killed.

and Acting Governor Elbert telegraphed to Governor Evans who was in Washington: "The Indians are again murdering travelers and burning trains on the plains. Get authority to raise a regiment of cavalry for one year's service. We must have five thousand troops to clean out these savages or the people of this territory will be compelled to leave it. Everything is already at starvation prices. The General Government must help us or give up the Territory to the Indians."[571]

Passengers who started east from Denver were compelled to return, since the coaches were not being run past Julesburg. But on January 14th a large train of 105 wagons and 300 men left Denver for the East. It was protected by a military escort with cannon.[572] It carried a large mail and got through in safety. The day following its departure the American Ranch was attacked and burned by Indians and seven bodies were found in the ruins. Wisconsin Ranch and Godfrey's Ranch were also attacked but no one was killed. Acting Governor Elbert now called for six companies of volunteer militia to open the road to Julesburg.[573] Supplies were scarce in Colorado, flour going to $27 per hundred and bacon and sugar to fifty cents per pound.[574]

On January 28th the Indians again made a concerted attack upon the South Platte and completely wrecked seventy-five miles of the road, burning stations and ranches, capturing wagon trains and destroying the telegraph line. At Valley Station over five hundred head of cattle were driven off, and one hundred tons

---

[571] *Rocky Mountain News*, January 9, 1865.
[572] — *Idem*, January 14, 1865; January 19, 1865, they reached Valley Station in safety.
[573] — *Idem*, January 17, 1865.
[574] — *Idem*, January 19, 1865.

of hay burned. The Indians crossed the river on the ice and remained encamped on the north side for six days while their warriors raided the South Platte valley. At two points only, Fort Rankin and Valley, were troops stationed at the time of these raids, and these forces were not strong enough to check the Indians.[575] Two large wagon trains of supplies were captured west of Julesburg and the Indians revelled in quantities of flour, sugar, rice, coffee, shoes and clothing. On February 2d a large band of Indians again plundered Julesburg and then set fire to the buildings.[576] The Indians now turned northward, crossing the North Platte and moving toward the Powder River country. On the 6th Colonel W. O. Collins of the Eleventh Ohio Volunteer Cavalry fought a battle with them at Mud Springs, and again on the North Platte two days later. His force, however, was not sufficiently large to accomplish anything decisive. The Indians now moved off northward to the Powder River where they encamped to enjoy their spoils.[577]

Ben Holladay had urgently appealed to the Government at Washington in January for additional protection for his overland stages, saying that if Julesburg were sacked the Overland Mail would necessarily be suspended until spring.[578] In February a similar plea came from Utah. It was suggested that military posts be established every hundred miles east of Denver of such strength as would defy attack. Emigrants and

---
[575] Grinnell, *op. cit.*, 183. *Rocky Mountain News*, January 28, 1865. *Alta California*, January 30, 1865.
[576] *Alta California*, February 7, and March 21, 1865. Birge in his *The Awakening of the Desert*, 126, says that the loss in the attack was $115,000. Barnes, in his *From the Atlantic to the Pacific, Overland*, 25, says that 6000 bushels of corn were destroyed at Julesburg.
[577] *Rocky Mountain News*, February 21, 1865. Grinnell, *op. cit.*, 185-194.
[578] Washington correspondent in the *Alta California*, January 28, 1865.

mails could then be escorted from post to post in times of difficulty and each post would also serve as a nucleus for settlers. "This periodical stopping up of the road is getting to be a decided nuisance and promises to become intolerable, falling with especial weight upon the citizens of the Territory." [579]

On February 3d a large accumulated mail of eighty-six sacks weighing about six tons was forwarded eastward from Denver. This was carried in five coaches, escorted by forty soldiers. Passengers on the coaches, and east-bound travelers with twenty additional teams accompanied the mail. [580]

On February 6th Colonel Moonlight who had replaced Colonel Chivington in command of the District of Colorado, announced that martial law would be proclaimed in Colorado on the 8th, and business houses be closed until 360 men were furnished to protect the road to Julesburg. [581] These men were duly raised and placed upon the line. Captain Murphy with one hundred men began on the 10th to repair the telegraph line west of Julesburg. They "traveled fifty miles, and put up eight miles of poles and twelve miles of wire in fifty hours." [582] The first message over the wire from Omaha brought good news. Major-general Dodge was in command of the Kansas and Nebraska Department. He had telegraphed the officials of the mail line to resume service at once and promised that ample protection would thereafter be afforded to mail, freight and emigrant travel to the West. Two thousand troops were being forwarded to escort travel along the

---
[579] Found in the *Alta California*, February 17, 1865.
[580] *Rocky Mountain News*, February 3, 1865.
[581] Martial law was suspended in Denver February 20, 1865.
[582] *Rocky Mountain News*, February 13, 1865. Ware, *op. cit.*, 532.

Platte.[583] About the middle of February mail coaches began to be dispatched from Saint Joseph westward,[584] and by March 8th the regular daily schedule was resumed.[585]

With the termination of the Civil War more troops were available for service on the Plains. A Saint Louis letter of June 22, 1865, remarks:

"The Government authorities are forwarding numerous regiments of cavalry to the Plains. Not less than ten regiments mostly of Sheridan's old Cavalry command have left here for Fort Leavenworth, and others are going. Two thousand are now enroute from Cincinnati. We shall soon have more troops on the Plains than ever before. General Pope has informed parties from Denver that he meant to use every man in his command if necessary to keep open the overland route to California. General Dodge, who is in immediate command of the department of Kansas and Colorado, has given the same assurance." [586]

Among the troops who came to the plains were some former Confederate soldiers who had enlisted for service against the Indians. These were called "Galvanized Yankees." [587] With the presence of regular soldiers on the line and the disappearance of many of the Indians the five companies of Colorado militia who had

---
[583] *Rocky Mountain News*, February 13, 1865.

[584] The diary of mail agent, Frank Root, from February 16th to 25th appears in the *Rocky Mountain News* of March 1, 1865.

[585] — *Idem*, March 8, 1865. *Alta California*, March 18, 1865.

[586] *Alta California*, July 23, 1865. Mr. Barnes, who was a passenger on the stage to Salt Lake City from the east in June, 1865, says that from about 150 miles out from Fort Kearny a government escort of two to four horsemen accompanied each stage night and day. – Barnes, D. *From the Atlantic to the Pacific Overland*, 25.

[587] *Rocky Mountain News*, June 26, 1865. Mr. Bowles who arrived in Denver on this date, told of passing one regiment of these soldiers.

been stationed on the road from Denver to Julesburg were brought back to Denver and discharged at the end of April.[588]

Throughout the summer of 1865 Indian troubles were slight and infrequent except upon the Cherokee Trail.[589] On Sage Creek, near Bridger's Pass, two emigrants were killed on June 2d and the country was raided for fifty miles along the mail line. On the 8th a station near Fort Halleck was attacked and five of the seven men stationed there were killed. Horses were driven off and the station was burned.[590] During the month of June the mail company lost 87 head of stock between Cherokee and Sulphur Spring Station, west of Fort Halleck.[591] Mail service was now reduced to a tri-weekly in this region, and between Fort Halleck and Sulphur Spring the soldiers furnished the transportation.[592] Mail accumulated at Fort Halleck and a number of large government wagons were employed to transport it under escort to Green River.[593] At this time there occurred the Platte Bridge Fight and other difficulties on the North Platte west of Fort Laramie,

---

[588] — *Idem*, April 28, 1865. The issue of April 12th describes these militia companies and gives their location.

[589] An attack upon Gilman's station was reported in the *Rocky Mountain News* of May 13, 1865, and a little difficulty on the Little Blue in the issue of May 24, 1865.

[590] — *Idem*, June 8, 12, 1865.

[591] While Bob Spotswood was division superintendent and located at Virginia Dale an Indian attack became imminent. The Indians were becoming familiar with firearms. "Their knowledge of a cannon was limited, but their respect for it enormous." Spotswood and his men got the rear wheels and axle of a wagon, fastened two joints of stove pipe in position so that the whole resembled a cannon. When the doors of the shed were swung open and this "artillery" was pushed into position and loading begun, the Indians beat a hasty retreat. – Sanford, A. B. *Story of Bob Spotswood's Life* (MS. in library of State Historical and Natural History Society of Colorado).

[592] *Rocky Mountain News*, June 26, 1865.

[593] Root and Connelley, *op. cit.*, 311.

but these only indirectly affected the mail line on the Cherokee Trail.[594] On July 29th Valley Station was attacked and two men were killed.[595] In August there was a recurrence of trouble in the neighborhood of Fort Halleck and Fort Collins. In the attacks of August 4th on the section between Big Laramie and Rock Creek, twelve whites were killed and two captured. The Hospital Steward at Fort Halleck, E. N. Lewis, told how one of the captured men was scalped and tied to a wheel of a wagon; that bacon was then piled around him and he was burned in its flame.[596] On September 1st one man was killed and cattle and horses were stolen from the Big Thompson, between Fort Collins and Denver.[597] As winter approached, the difficulties subsided, and a peace treaty was signed by General Sanborn with a large number of Indian chiefs on the Arkansas.[598]

Hereafter Indian disturbances played a smaller part in the story of the overland mail. Although there were some rather widespread Indian troubles in 1867 (to be discussed in the last chapter) the Indian peril for the through overland mail had largely passed with the summer of 1865.

---

[594] An account of the Indian troubles on the Platte in 1864-5 is given in Hebard, G. R., and E. A. Brininstool. *The Bozeman Trail*, 119-153.
[595] *Rocky Mountain News*, July 31, 1865.
[596] — *Idem*, August 10, 16, 1865.
[597] — *Idem*, September 1, 1865.
[598] — *Idem*, September 11, 16, 1865.

Chapter XII

The Mail in the Middle Sixties[599]

Despite the isolated Indian depredations during 1863 the overland mail service throughout the year was carried on in a satisfactory manner. The Postmaster-general reported in December: "The service on this route has been performed during the past year with commendable regularity and efficiency, and no accident, Indian hostility, or other casualty has occurred to prevent or retard the safe and prompt transmission of mails and passengers, the trips being, with rare exceptions, accomplished within the schedule time." [600]

Notwithstanding the splendid preparations for the winter service,[601] the coming of the deep snow and its accompanying difficulties, made humanly impossible the maintenance of regular and efficient service. In January, 1864, a resolution of inquiry relative to the failures of the overland mail during the preceding two

---
[599] This chapter covers approximately the same period as does the previous one, but it was thought best to follow the Indian problem through without interpolations of unrelated data.

[600] Postmaster-general's *Report*, 1863, 12.

It was in 1863 that the postage rate on letters was first made uniform throughout the United States. The act of March 3, 1863 fixed the rate at three cents per half ounce on all domestic letters. Just previous to this time letters to the Pacific Coast were paying a postage rate of ten cents. The postage rates to the Pacific Coast during the period here considered were as follows: before 1851, forty cents per half ounce letter; 1851-5, six cents; 1855-1863, ten cents; 1863-1883, three cents.

[601] A letter from Ruby Valley, Nevada, under date of October 18, 1863, says that the Overland Mail Company has on the route between that point and Salt Lake City 30,000 bushels of grain for use during the succeeding winter and spring. Good stock and good men are also provided. In the *Alta California*, Oct. 26, 1863.

months was introduced in the United States Senate. There was considerable delinquency, but appearances were kept up by getting through in fairly regular time, packages destined for the newspapers. Subscribers, seeing that the newspapers were getting overland packages, could not definitely determine whether it was failure of the mail service or negligence of their friends in the East, that was accountable for the non-receipt of letters.[602]

The mail failures were not due entirely to the stage service. The following dispatch was received at San Francisco, February 2, 1864: "New York, January 30th. Mails have accumulated by stoppage of Hannibal and St. Joseph Railway from snow. We forward by last and next steamer about sixteen days' mail."[603] Criticism of the mail service was not limited to the overland route. The New York *Tribune* complains that "the mails are in a horrible condition all over the country," and says that the Postmaster-general is blamed unjustly or at least excessively; and explains that the inefficiency is due to the overcrowding of the railroads.[604]

San Francisco newspapers, eager friends of the overland mail service, were quick to place the blame for failures upon the East. The *Bulletin* remarks: "When the Eastern roads are open again the Western will hurry mails to their destination." The same journal continues:

"An overland daily mail has always been a favorite of the California public. That when it fails during a

---

[602] The San Francisco *Bulletin* of January 18, 1864, describes the situation thus.

[603] — *Idem*, February 2, 1864.

[604] — *Idem*, February 1, 1864.

THE MAIL IN THE MIDDLE SIXTIES 275

month or two of the winter to serve us as handsomely as it always does in summer, it does so from no fault of those who undertake to maintain it, is a gratifying consideration. . . . It would be a misfortune indeed if, for any cause save and except the completion of long sections of railway between the Missouri and the Pacific we should be deprived of this method of getting to and from the Atlantic States in person or by correspondence." [605]

When the cold and snow abated somewhat, the spring high water continued the work of retardation, and it was not until in June that the service became regular and good time was again made.[606]

The contract under which the daily overland mail was established and was being conducted was to expire June 30, 1864. In the October previous the Postmaster-general had advertised for bids for the performance of the service.[607] John A. Heistand, of Pennsylvania,

[605] — *Idem*, February 2, 1864.
[606] — *Idem*, June 16, 1864.
[607] U. S. House. *Executive Documents*, 38th congress, second session, no. 24, pp. 10, 11. See Postmaster-general's *Report*, 1863, 10. The stations on the route as advertised follow:

"ROUTE NUMBER 14258. From Atchison, by Lancaster, Kinnekuk, Kickapoo, Long Chain, Seneca, Laramie Creek, Guittard's, Oketo Otoe, Pawnee, (Nebraska Territory) Grayson's, Big Sandy, Thompsons, Kiowa, Little Blue, Liberty Farm, Lone Tree, Thirty-two-mile Creek, Summit, Hook's, Fort Kearny, Platte Station, Craig, Plum Creek, Willow Island, Midway, Gilman's, Cottonwood Springs, Cold Springs, Fremont Springs, Elk Horn, Alkali Lake, Sand Hill, Diamond Springs, South Platte, Julesburg, (Colorado Territory) Antelope, Spring Hill, Dennison's, Valley Station, Kelly's, Beaver Creek, Bijou, Fremont's Orchard, Eagle's Nest, Latham, Cache La Poudre, Sherwoods, Laporte, Bouer, Cherokee, (Idaho Territory), Virginia Dale, Willow Springs, Big Laramie, Little Laramie, Cooper Creek, Rock Creek, Medicine Bow, Fort Halleck, Elk Mountain, Pass Creek, North Platte, Sage Creek, Pine Grove, Bridger's Pass, Sulphur Springs, Waskie, Duck Lake, Dug Springs, Laclede, Big Pond, Black Buttes, Rock Point, Salt Wells, Rock Springs, Green River, Lone Tree, (Utah Territory), South Bend, Church Buttes, Millerville, Fort Bridger, Muddy, Quaking Asp Springs, Bear River,

was the lowest bidder, at $750,000 per year.[608] His bid was subsequently withdrawn and contracts were finally made with Ben Holladay for the service from the Missouri River to Salt Lake City at $365,000; and with William B. Dinsmore, president of the Overland Mail Company, for the service from Salt Lake City to Folsom City, California, for $385,000 per year. The contracts were to run from October 1, 1864, to September 30, 1868. The trips were to be made in sixteen days eight months in the year, and in twenty days the remaining four months. They were to carry through letter mail, mail matter prepaid at letter rates, and all local and way mails.[609] Arrangements were made to have the paper and document mail for the Pacific Coast carried by sea at $160,000 per annum.[610] This made a total of

Needle Rock, Echo Canyon, Hanging Rock, Weaver, Daniel's, Kimball's, and Mountain Dale to Salt Lake City, 1220 miles, and back daily.

"UTAH TERRITORY. 14620. From Salt Lake City, by Travellers' Rest, Rock Wells, Joe Dug Out, Fort Crittenden, No Name, Rush Valley, Point Lookout, Simpson's Springs, River Bed, Dug Way, Black Rock, Fast Springs, Boyd's Willow Springs, Canyon Station, Deep Creek, Prairie Gate, Antelope Springs, Spring Valley, Shell Creek, Gold Canon Butte, Mountain Springs, Ruby Valley, (Nevada Territory) Jacob's Wells, Diamond Springs, Sulphur Springs, Robert's Creek, Camp Station, Dry Creek, Cape Horn, Simpson's Park, Reese River, Mount Airy, Castle Book, Edwards's Creek, Cold Springs, Middle Gate, Fair View, Mountain Well, Still Water, Old River, Bisby's, Nevada, and Desert Wells, to Virginia City, 558 miles, and back, daily. Nevada Territory. From Virginia City, by Carson, Genoa, Fridays, Yanks, Strawberry, Webster Moss, Sportsman Hall, and Placerville to Folsom City, 140 miles."

[608] U. S. House. *Executive Documents*, 38th congress, second session, no. 24, 15. The *Rocky Mountain News*, in hearing of the contract award, comments as follows in its issue of June 30, 1864: "The probability is that Mr. Heistand was playing stool pigeon for Mr. Holladay. If so, he ought to be histed. At any rate the great western autocrat [Holladay] has unquestionably become the assignee of Mr. Heistand's contract. For four years more Colorado, Utah, and Nevada belong to Ben Holladay for a footstool and may the Lord have mercy upon them."

[609] Postmaster-general's *Report*, 1864, 782.

[610] — *Idem*, 783. This was done in conformity with act of March 25, 1864.

THE MAIL IN THE MIDDLE SIXTIES 277

$910,000 per year for the transportation of the entire mail, as compared with $1,000,000 under the contract of 1861. Also, it should be noted that this sum was paid in the depreciated greenbacks that were worth but about half their face value in gold. The reduced price would not have been possible had it not been for the increase in the passenger and express traffic upon the line. It was averred by some that the contractors could afford to run the coaches for the passenger and express traffic alone. Extra coaches were frequently required to carry the passengers, and the coaches generally ran full.[611]

Much of the travel on the eastern end of the line was to Denver, Colorado. On the western end there was considerable travel and express transportation between California and the region of Virginia City, Nevada. The Comstock mines were flourishing and business was brisk. In the early summer of 1864 three separate companies were operating daily stages from California to the Nevada Mines.[612] The Pioneer Stage Company carried the daily overland mail as far as Virginia City. The route taken was by way of Placerville, Strawberry Valley, Genoa and Carson City. This line was exceptionally well equipped and did a flourishing business. The California Stage Company was the principal competitor. Its stages ran from Sacramento to Virginia City via the Henness Pass route. "The Pacific Stage and Express Company" operated a line of six-horse Concord coaches over the same route; but by July 22, 1864, their advertisement drops from the papers and

---
[611] *Alta California*, July 25, 1864.
[612] See advertisements in San Francisco *Bulletin*, June 21, 1864, to July 15, 1864.

the California Stage Company announces a new arrangement with six-horse coaches.[613]

During 1863, 1864, and 1865 mail coaches were running on a weekly schedule from Kansas City to Santa Fé. The course ran along the Arkansas to Bent's Fort and then turned southwestward along the mountain division of the old Santa Fé Trail, crossing the Raton Pass and going by Fort Union. The line was not very well equipped and it took about a month to make the round trip.[614] In November, 1863, Mr. Morehead rode the stage to Santa Fé. He writes: "They then had a change of animals at Fort Larned and Fort Lyon. Conductors, drivers, and passengers camped out every night and did their own cooking. At Larned we encountered a heavy snow storm and had to abandon our coach and take a light canvas-covered wagon. We were nine days going 240 miles, the distance between Fort Larned and Fort Lyon. Then again we encountered deep snow in crossing the Raton Mountains, between Bent's old fort and Fort Union, and thence to Santa Fé." [615]

The contract under which the daily mail had been carried from Sacramento, California, to Portland, Oregon, expired September 15, 1864. This service had been performed since January 1, 1861, by the California Stage Company for $90,000 per year.[616] The compensation was insufficient and the company operated the line at a loss. When bids were again called for the only bidder was the California Stage Company

---

[613] San Francisco *Bulletin*, July 22, 1864. The California Stage Company was a large concern, operating stages to all parts of Oregon and Nevada territories. A. G. Richardson was superintendent in 1864.

[614] Inman, Henry. *The Old Santa Fe Trail*, 158.

[615] Connelley, W. E. *Doniphan's Expedition*, 620.

[616] U. S. House. *Executive Documents*, 37th congress, second session, no. 137, 546. (Serial 1139.)

THE MAIL IN THE MIDDLE SIXTIES 279

at $250,000 per year. This figure was deemed extravagant by the Postmaster-general and he contracted for service to June 30, 1865, only.[617] When the next bids were opened the same company was again the only bidder, this time at a figure of $300,000. The Postmaster-general declined to accept the bid and made a contract with other parties at $225,000 per year.[618]

In 1864 the Overland Mail Company was running the mail from San Francisco southward to Los Angeles. The service was complained of. One passenger writes: "Their stages are old, rickety, mud wagons, . . . If the Stage Company, for $25 through fare, and enormous way fare (at which prices they run full) in addition to the $44,000 paid them by the Government for carrying the mail, cannot give better coaches and teams they had better sell out." [619]

Discoveries of gold in Montana and Idaho caused the usual stampedes into those sections and the demand for postal service consequently arose. Private expresses as usual preceded the regular United States mail to the mining camps. In July, 1863, a weekly pony express was established from Fort Bridger to Bannock City (Montana), and letters were carried through in seven days for fifty cents each.[620] Oliver and Company's Express carried mail and passengers from Salt Lake City to the Montana mines in the spring of 1864.[621] The Post Office Department contracted for a tri-weekly mail service over this route to begin July 1, 1864. Ben Holladay received this contract, and although there

---
[617] Postmaster-general's *Report*, 1864, 783. Also, *Alta California*, September 26, 1865.
[618] Postmaster-general's *Report*, 1865, 3.
[619] Letter from Los Angeles in San Francisco *Bulletin*, March 2, 1864.
[620] Denver *Commonwealth*, July 2, 1863.
[621] — *Idem*, June 22, 1864.

was some delay in getting the coaches to the line on account of the flood in the South Platte,[622] the regular service was in operation by August. Holladay now cut the stage fare from Salt Lake City to Virginia City, Montana, down to $25 in greenbacks to run Oliver and Company off the line.[623]

Mining developments in western Idaho made necessary, means of communication to that region, and Holladay received a contract in 1864 for a tri-weekly mail service from Salt Lake City northwestward to Boise and Walla Walla.[624] From Salt Lake City this line and the one to Virginia City ran over the same route northward eighty-three miles to Bear River Junction, passing through Ogden and Brigham City. Here the route forked, the Montana road going northward via Fort Hall, while the Idaho-Oregon route turned northwestward via Malad and Boise. In the fall of 1866 General Rusling traveled over this latter route. He described the country from the Junction to Boise as wild and sterile. "There were no settlements anywhere except the isolated stage stations, and but little travel beyond the tri-weekly stages."[625] The stage was ferried across the Snake River on a rude boat and the coach continued over the famous Oregon Trail to the Columbia. In 1867 the mail service on this line was increased to a daily schedule.[626]

The Indian depredations of 1864 and 1865 induced

---

[622] The flood in Cherry Creek and the South Platte did considerable damage in Denver. The *Rocky Mountain News* establishment and the city hall were washed away and the city records were never recovered. Several lives were lost. This is known in Denver history as the "Big Flood."

[623] *Rocky Mountain News*, August 29, 1864.

[624] —*Idem*, July 15, 1864. Root and Connelley, *op. cit.*, 485.

[625] Rusling, J. F. *Across America*, 214.

[626] Postmaster-general's *Report*, 1867, 6.

THE MAIL IN THE MIDDLE SIXTIES 281

the Utahans to take steps to establish a line of commerce to the head of navigation on the Colorado River, and thence by water to the Pacific Coast. In his message of January, 1865, Brigham Young expressed the hope that this line of communication would be found practicable, and said that steps had already been taken to build a warehouse at the head of navigation on the Colorado River.[627] Nothing however, came of the project as the river was not well fitted for steam navigation.

We have mentioned in a previous chapter the work of the contractors on the overland mail line in exploring a route from Denver westward to Salt Lake City in 1861, and how the Cherokee Trail instead of the Berthoud Pass route was taken in 1862. When the Central Overland California and Pike's Peak Express Company was dissolved, W. H. Russell, its former president, came to Colorado and engaged in a project for building a toll road over the continental divide west of Denver. In the fall of 1862 the "Clear Creek and Hot Sulphur Springs Wagon Road Company" was organized and work commenced.[628] The work was suspended in December and resumed the following spring, but the money subscribed was exhausted before the road reached the summit of the divide. The project now slumbered for two years and then was revived by Bela M. Hughes, agent of Ben Holladay. The right to build a road from Denver to Middle Park by way of Boulder Creek was granted Holladay and his associates

---

[627] *Alta California*, February 3, 1865. In the summer of 1922 the writer interviewed a Utah pioneer, Joseph Burgess, now residing at Saint George, Utah, who as a boy accompanied the expedition down the Virgin River to the Colorado to establish a settlement.

[628] *Rocky Mountain News*, October 30, 1862; November 6, 1862. A new pass was discovered near the head of Clear Creek and named "Vasquez Pass" in honor of Louis Vasquez, an old trapper.

by the Colorado Legislature, and in April 1865, Hughes came west to select a route. His expedition set out from Salt Lake City, June 3d, to work out a practicable roadway eastward.[629] He was accompanied by Colonel Johns of the California Volunteers with 150 men and 22 wagons. The route followed was that explored by the Berthoud-Bridger expedition of 1861. Nearly four months were consumed in selecting the course and making it passable for wagons. They reached Denver September 28th, and the *Rocky Mountain News* of that day, in welcoming them said:

"They have done a great work for our Territory and the nation. For the nation, in opening up an infinitely more feasible route, and saving nearly 200 miles of travel to Salt Lake City, avoiding the desert Bitter Creek country, and leading travel through green pastures and beside cool waters; for Colorado, in opening a route which will bring through the very heart of our richest mining country all the immense travel which now goes by the Cheyenne and South Passes, thereby avoiding us entirely."

On October 4th Hughes wrote: "I have adopted the Berthoud Pass and will complete the road over it in May and the whole road by June next. All reports about our abandoning the road and its not being eligible, are utterly false."[630] Despite these good intentions the road was not finished or used as anticipated.

In 1864 D. A. Butterfield (not to be confused with John Butterfield of the Overland Mail Company) began a freight and forwarding business that presently developed into an organization competing with Holladay's overland mail line. He announced the inaugur-

---
[629] — *Idem*, June 15, 1865.
[630] — *Idem*, October 26, 1865.

ation of his forwarding business in July, together with a statement by A. Byram of the famous freighting firm, that ample transportation would be provided.[631] In December his "fast freight line" was established and in the following spring "Butterfield's Overland Despatch" was organized into a joint stock company, backed by New York capital.[632] On the 9th of May, 1865, the city council of Leavenworth voted $4,000 to Butterfield's Overland Despatch to aid it in opening a line of communication on the Smoky Hill route.[633] The company made preparations for opening such a line of travel during the summer. A thirty-wagon train set out from Fort Riley, Kansas, on July 4th, to select the road and establish stations. A military escort of 250 men under Major Pritchard accompanied the party.[634] This train was presently followed by coaches for passenger and express traffic.

The first coach on the new route arrived at Denver September 23, 1865, and received a hearty welcome.

[631] — *Idem*, July 18, 1864.

[632] — *Idem*, December 10, 1864; April 6, 1865.

[633] — *Idem*, May 22, 1865. This was not Leavenworth's first attempt to divert the plains travel through this city. Some of the Pike's Peakers had followed the Smoky Hill route in 1858 and 1859, but scarcity of water on the western end gave the route a bad name. In the spring of 1860 Leavenworth employed the pioneer gold prospector, W. Green Russell, to seek out a good route westward. Russell and party of thirty-five left Leavenworth April 2d and arrived at Denver May 4th. A favorable report on the road was made but still travelers preferred the Platte route. – *Rocky Mountain News*, May 9, 1860; May 30, 1860.

[634] Major Eaton, who was employed by the company to lead its expedition, tells how he would throw up a mound, drive stakes and place the number of the station on them, and lay claim to the land for his company. – *Rocky Mountain News*, August 1, 1865. The expedition reached Denver August 7th, and the men were high in their praise of the new route. Eaton reported water at frequent intervals, no alkali, and good grass most of the way. He said the route was one hundred per cent better than the Platte route. – *Idem*, August 8, 1865. See also the issue of September 6, 1865, for favorable report by Lieutenant Fitch.

A procession of carriages and horsemen and the First Colorado band greeted the new arrival. A banner was carried with this inscription: " 'Westward the course of Empire takes its way.' The energy of our old townsman Col. D. A. Butterfield proves him the Hercules of Express men. Welcome Dave and your Express."

The company set about building stations and procuring coaches. It was announced that during the following year they would extend their route from Pond Creek via Fort Lyon and the McFerren trail to Santa Fé and from Denver westward to Salt Lake City via Berthoud Pass.[635] These projects never materialized. The company's short line from Denver to the mining camp of Central City seems to have become the most regular and profitable part of its enterprise.

On October 2, 1865, one of their coaches was attacked by Indians, and was plundered and burned after the passengers had escaped.[636] In November one of the stations (Blufton) was burned and two men killed. The coach at Smoky Hill Station was also attacked, but the Indians were repulsed.[637] Troops were now provided for the route and in December a tri-weekly service was announced,[638] but it appears that such a schedule was never maintained. The line did, however, become a competitor of Holladay's line. A Saint Louis correspondent wrote in November: "The route from Denver to Atchison is now a race course. . . The time is frequently inside of five days, whereas six days was once thought good time.[639] One trip was made on the Holladay line in three days, eleven hours, and fifteen

---

[635] — *Idem*, September 28, 1865.
[636] — *Idem*, October 16, 1865.
[637] — *Idem*, December 1, 4, 1865.
[638] — *Idem*, December 19, 1865.
[639] *Alta California*, December 17, 1865.

minutes.⁶⁴⁰ The Holladay company now reduced the fare from Denver to Central City from $6 to $1 in order to force out the new intruder, but the new line continued to operate throughout the winter between these points. Across the plains, however, its service became very irregular and was for a time suspended. In January the company was reorganized in conformity with a charter from the Colorado legislature.⁶⁴¹ In February it was announced that difficulties had been overcome and that the line was being re-opened. Hardly had the coaches been put in motion again before the service was suspended and the line disposed of.⁶⁴² The Overland Despatch Company had no mail contract, received insufficient military protection, and had a powerful competitor. The Holladay company was too strong for the new enterprise and finally defeated it. Butterfield's Overland Despatch had received the encouragement or support of the big express companies of the East, but these did not come to the rescue at the critical juncture. An account of the situation and of Holladay's procedure is given by Mr. Root:

"The express companies doing business in the West and California had for years been pressing Holladay for through rates and a pro rata on express business; but he would not listen to them, and held them at bay on the east at the Missouri River, and on the west at Salt Lake City, Wells, Fargo and Company having

---

⁶⁴⁰ *Rocky Mountain News*, November 3, 1865. *Alta California*, December 13, 1865. The Saint Louis correspondent attributed this speed to the presence of the rival line on the Smoky Hill route.

⁶⁴¹ *Rocky Mountain News*, January 19, 1866.

⁶⁴² The advertisement of the company was resumed in the *Rocky Mountain News* of February 7, 1865, under "The Overland Despatch Company," with Butterfield's name omitted. On March 14th the advertisement disappears from this newspaper.

gained control of the old Overland Mail Company from Salt Lake to Sacramento. The express managers found they could make terms with the Butterfield Overland Despatch from the Missouri River to Denver, this would leave only the gap of six hundred miles from Denver to Salt Lake City. They had threatened to fill in this gap by stocking a line themselves. As late as February, 1866, they had entered into no binding arrangements with the B. O. D. Company, but Holladay was afraid they would, and, this accomplished, they might carry out their threat to stock the line from Denver to Salt Lake and accomplish their purpose of a through line in opposition to the overland line of Holladay's.

"Mr. Holladay quietly formed his plans; he instructed David Street, his general agent in the West, to send a competent practical stage man and a clerk over the line of the B.O.D. Co. as passengers" and make a careful examination of the property. This was done, and Mr. Street with the data left for New York. "The next day after his arrival in New York, Mr. Holladay received from the three great express companies – the American, United States, and Wells, Fargo & Co. – an identical note (or round robin it might be termed), demanding a through rate and some division of territory or business, accompanied by the threat that, in case of a failure to comply, they would stock the gap in their lines, viz., between Denver and Salt Lake City." Holladay sent for the president of the Park Bank (who was president of the B. O. D. Co.), to dine with him. He was able to make satisfactory arrangements with him for the purchase of the line, since he had so much data upon it. After making the arrangements he "turned to his secretary and said: 'Answer those express companies and tell them to stock and be d—'"[643]

It was in March, 1866, that Holladay purchased the Butterfield Overland Despatch. The service was suspended for a time,[644] but about the first of May it was revived and in August was made the regular route for the California mail.[645]

During the year 1865 the service on that portion of the overland mail line west of Salt Lake City was performed with reasonable regularity, but upon the section east of that city it was rather irregular. At times the service was very good; but Indian disturbances, high water, or bad roads, contributed to produce a slow and irregular service much of the time.[646]

However, there were some special trips that were made with remarkable dispatch. In October, 1865, Louis McLane, Superintendent of Wells, Fargo and Company's Express, rode from San Francisco to Salt Lake City in three days, seventeen hours, and twenty minutes. "The Pioneer stages brought him from Shingle Springs to Virginia City in thirteen hours, and forty-five minutes; and the Overland stages from Virginia City to Salt Lake City in sixty-four hours and thirty minutes."[647]

Hon. Schuyler Colfax and party also made commendable time on their overland journey in the summer of 1865. From Atchison to Denver (653 miles) was

---
[643] Root and Connelley, *op. cit.*, 404.

[644] St. Louis letter of March 20th in *Alta California*, April 17, 1866. Also St. Louis letter of March 19th in *Alta California*, April 28, 1866.

[645] Root and Connelley, *op. cit.*, 55. Denver letter of May 27th in *Alta California*, June 28, 1866.

[646] Postmaster-general's *Report*, 1865. 3.

[647] Salt Lake City letter of October 8th, in *Alta California*, October 10, 1865.

made in four and one-half days. "From Salt Lake City to Virginia City, Nevada, 575 miles, the ride was made in seventy-two hours, on which a drive of eight miles was covered in thirty-two minutes. A stretch of seventy-two miles – into Placerville – was made in seven hours including stops." [648]

The winter of 1865-6 was said to be the most severe since that of 1861, but the mail was carried with fair speed and regularity. A letter from Ruby Valley, Nevada, under date of December 29th says that the snow was fifteen inches deep on the level, and from three to fifteen feet where the road crosses the summits.

"Notwithstanding these difficulties the Overland Mail Company's stages arrive and depart with their usual regularity, making the trip from Salt Lake City to Virginia in 120 hours; distance six hundred miles. This Company never was in finer condition for winter service, having an abundance of grain for their horses, as well as hay; plenty of provisions for their men, and sleighs and light coaches distributed so well along the route that it is impossible for snow or anything else almost to stop them. Unfortunately the Company east of Salt Lake City have lost the continuity, but this is nothing very new for them." [649]

The record of December was hardly kept up in January and February, and complaints again arose over the slowing up of the mail. But with the coming of spring, conditions again improved.

MAIL SERVICE IN THE CONFEDERATE STATES

A law passed by Congress February 28, 1861, authorized the Postmaster-general to discontinue the pos-

---
[648] Root and Connelley, *op. cit.*, 54.
[649] Found in the *Alta California*, January 8, 1866.

THE MAIL IN THE MIDDLE SIXTIES 289

tal service on routes where in his opinion it could not be safely continued, or the postal revenues collected. July 12, 1861, Postmaster-general Blair reported to Congress the "Discontinuance of the mail service in all the so-called seceded States with the exception of that on the route in the western counties of Virginia where the inhabitants remained loyal to the Union." [650] For a time, correspondence was carried by express companies, but this privilege was of short duration.[651] Postmaster-general Blair issued an order August 26, 1861, directing the officers and agents of the Post Office Department to put an end to all written intercourse with the seceded states.[652]

We have noted in the foregoing chapters how persistently Southern statesmen in Congress fought against the increase in postal expenditure. Senators Toombs of Georgia, Yulee of Florida, Hunter of Virginia, and others were strongly against using the Post Office Department as a pioneering, military, or expansionist agency, and were for making the Department self-supporting, as it had been in its earlier years. There had been a constant fight during the preceding decade over this principle. Accordingly, when the constitution of the Confederate States was drafted they planned to settle that question once and for all. To the simple provision of the United States Constitution that Congress shall have power "to establish post offices and post roads," they added this proviso: "but the expenses of the Post Office Department after the first day of March

---

[650] U. S. House. *Executive Documents*, 37th congress, second session, no. 55, vol. v. (Serial no. 1131.) Mr. Blair to Speaker of the House of Representatives, February 17, 1862.

[651] San Francisco *Bulletin*, July 8, 1861.

[652] Moore, F., editor. *Rebellion Record*, vol. iii, 29.

in the year of our Lord 1863, shall be paid out of its own revenue." [653]

John H. Reagan of Texas was made Postmaster-general in President Jefferson Davis's Cabinet.[654] President Davis reported to the Confederate Congress April 29, 1861, that "the Postmaster-general had already succeeded in organizing his department to such an extent as to be in readiness to assume the direction of our [their] postal affairs."[655] Reagan addressed to the different postmasters the following order on May 20, 1861:

"You are hereby instructed, as the postal service of the Government of the United States within the Confederate States will be suspended after the first of June next, to retain in your possession subject to the further orders of this department, for the benefit of the Confederate States, all mail bags, locks and keys, etc., . . . and all property belonging to or connected with the postal service, and to return forthwith full inventory of the same. You will also report to the Chief of the finance bureau of this department your journal and ledger account, etc. . . . exhibiting the final balance in your possession."[656]

Great difficulties were encountered in the conduct of the mail service in the Confederacy. President Davis explained in his message of November 18, 1861:[657]

"The absorption of the ordinary means of transportation for the movements of troops and military supplies; the insufficiency of the rolling stock of railroads for the accumulation of business resulting both from military

---

[653] *Constitution of the Confederate States of America.*
[654] Moore's *Rebellion Record*, vol. ii, 354.
[655] Richardson, J. D. *Messages and Papers of the Confederacy*, vol. i, 79.
[656] Moore, F., editor. *Rebellion Record*, vol. i, 325.
[657] Richardson, J. D. *Messages and Papers of the Confederacy*, vol. i, 138.

operations and the obstruction of water communication by the presence of the enemy's fleet; the failure, and even refusal, of contractors to comply with the terms of their agreements; the difficulties inherent in inaugurating so vast and complicated a system as that which requires postal facilities for every town and village in a territory so extended as ours, have all combined to impede the best-directed efforts of the Postmaster-general whose zeal, industry and ability have been taxed to the utmost extent."

But despite difficulties the officials were able to report a gradual improvement towards a self-supporting department.[658] President Davis was able to say in his message to Congress, December 7, 1863:

"The Postmaster-general reports the receipts of that Department for the fiscal year ending June last to have been $3,337,853.01 and the expenditures for the same period, $2,662,804.77. The statement thus exhibits an excess of receipts amounting to $675,058.34 instead of a deficiency of more than $1,000,000 as was the case in the preceding fiscal year. It is gratifying to perceive that the Department has thus been made self-sustaining in accordance with sound principle, and with the express requirement of the Constitution." [659]

The question of evasion of military service through acquiring mail contracts attracted some attention in 1863 and 1864. On October 1, 1862, the Confederate Congress repealed the act of April 21, 1862, which had exempted mail contractors from military service.[660] But because of the depreciation in the Confederate currency

---
[658] — *Idem*, vol. i, 192. President Davis's Message of February 25, 1862; vol. i, 237, message of August 18, 1862; vol. i, 296, message of January 12, 1863.

[659] — *Idem*, i, 379.

[660] *War of the Rebellion, Official Record*, series iv, vol. iii, 122.

the Post Office Department encountered such difficulty in obtaining contractors that the Postmaster-general and President Davis recommended exempting contractors again. This was accomplished by the law of April 14, 1863, and again the army men objected. General Lee in a letter of September 10, 1864, complained to the Secretary of War of the evasion of military duty by persons procuring mail contracts at nominal sums.[661]

The postal service of the South collapsed with the Confederacy early in 1865, and the United States Post Office Department began again to extend its lines into the southern states.

---

[661] The case of one Leftwich of Richmond was cited. He obtained a contract for an unimportant line in Alabama. He resided in Virginia and employed someone else to perform the service. The Postmaster-general says it was costing him at the rate of $6,000 per year to have the service performed. Three contracts were made for the compensation of one mill, one cent, and ten cents respectively. – *War of the Rebellion, Official Record*, series iv, vol. iii, 657, and iii, 72.

Chapter XIII

In the Days of the Stage-coach

In the middle sixties the overland mail reached its greatest proportions and achieved its greatest success. It is perhaps fitting, therefore, that we should pause here in our chronological story, to say something of the presiding genius of the overland mail during these palmy days, and to describe the overland mail as an institution.

Ben Holladay was born in Kentucky in 1824, and in the thirties and forties resided in western Missouri. Upon the outbreak of the Mexican War he obtained contracts for supplying the troops that were to travel to Santa Fé. His promptness made him a favorite contractor and he was able to make unusual profits. At the close of the war he bought a large amount of government war material – oxen, wagons, etc. – at a low figure, and the following year took a train to Salt Lake City with $70,000 worth of goods. He was on good terms with the Mormons and disposed of his merchandise at a favorable margin. In 1850 he drove a herd of cattle to California, fattened them near Sacramento, and sold them to the Panama Steamship Company at a profitable figure.[662]

Holladay was very well acquainted with the West before he went into the staging business. He had advanced money to Russell, Majors, and Waddell and

---

[662] Letter of John Doniphan, attorney for Holladay, written in the Saint Joseph *Catholic Tribune* of June 22, 1895. Quoted in Root and Connelley, *op. cit.*, 448-450.

had come into possession of their stage property in 1862. He bid successfully for the service to Salt Lake City in 1864, and from this point he ran lines into Idaho and Montana.[663] He operated stage lines to the mining regions about Denver also. The Western Stage Company's line from Omaha to Fort Kearny was purchased by Holladay,[664] and in 1866 he bought the Butterfield Overland Despatch operating along the Smoky Hill route to Denver. In all he controlled nearly five thousand miles of stage lines.[665] Bela M. Hughes, long Holladay's attorney, said of him: "He had the friendship and support of President Lincoln and Postmaster-general Blair, and backed by ample means, with rare courage resolved to make the line a success, and he did so."[666]

Ben Holladay made money fast and spent it lavishly. After he had accumulated a snug fortune he went to New York to live, where he built a magnificent residence a few miles out on the Hudson. Subsequently he built an elegant mansion at Washington and resided there during the sessions of Congress. While holding so many important government contracts it was to his interest to be at hand when matters vitally affecting his business interests were under consideration in Congress. During this same period he also owned and operated steamship lines to Oregon, Panama, Japan and China.[667]

J. F. Rusling, who crossed the continent in the stagecoach in 1866, thus describes the proprietor of the line:

---

[663] Rusling, J. F. *Across America*, 206, 40.
[664] Root and Connelley, *The Overland Stage to California*, 206.
[665] — *Idem*, 486.
[666] Hughes Manuscript (in library of State Historical and Natural History Society of Colorado), p. 5. (Written May 2, 1892.)
[667] — *Idem*, 444. See also advertisements of these lines in San Francisco newspapers of 1863 and 1864.

BEN HOLLADAY
President of the Overland Stage Line

"He was a man apparently of about forty-five, tall and thin, of large grasp and quick perceptions, of indifferent health but indomitable will, fiery and irascable when crossed and a Westerner all through. Apparently he carried his vast business very jauntily, without much thought or care, but he crossed the continent twice each year, from end to end of his stage routes, and saw for himself how matters were getting on." [668]

Henry Villard described him as "a genuine specimen of the successful Western pioneer of former days, illiterate, coarse, pretentious, boastful, false, and cunning." [669] Mark Twain tells a story with reference to Holladay. A youth who had crossed to California in the overland stage was subsequently traveling in the Holy Land with an elderly pilgrim who thus tried to impress upon the young man the greatness of Moses, the guide, soldier, poet, lawgiver of ancient Israel:

"Jack, from this spot where we stand, to Egypt, stretches a fearful desert three hundred miles in extent — and across that desert that wonderful man brought the children of Israel! — guiding them with unfailing sagacity for forty years over the sandy desolation and among the obstructing rocks and hills, and landed them at last, safe and sound, within sight of this very spot; . . . It was a wonderful, wonderful thing to do, Jack! Think of it!

"Forty years? Only three hundred miles? Hump! Ben Holladay would have fetched them through in thirty-six hours" [670]

Under Holladay's supervision the overland mail line was very thoroughly organized and efficiently con-

---

[668] Rusling, *op. cit.*, 208.
[669] Quoted in Paxson, *The Last American Frontier*, 186.
[670] Mark Twain, *Roughing It*, 42. (1913 edition.)

ducted. Over the entire system there was a general superintendent of the lines, a Washington agent, an attorney and a paymaster.[671] The main line was divided into three grand divisions – Atchison to Denver, Denver to Salt Lake City, and Salt Lake City to Placerville. Over each of these a division superintendent was placed. He had charge of three minor divisions, somewhat over six hundred miles of the route. This position was one of considerable importance, and an "experienced, level-headed driver" was usually selected to fill the post.

The division agent, "boss" of about two hundred miles of the route, had charge of all company property within his territory. He hired and dismissed the drivers, stock tenders, blacksmith, harness-maker, etc.; distributed the supplies along the line; and supervised, generally, the running of the stages and the conduct and care of the stations.[672] Mark Twain says of him:

"It was not absolutely necessary that the division agent should be a gentleman, and occasionally he wasn't. But he was always a general in administrative ability, and a bull-dog in courage and determination, otherwise the chieftainship over the lawless underlings of the Overland service would never in any instance have been to him anything but an equivalent for a month of insolence and distress and a bullet and a coffin at the end of it."[673]

Next in rank and importance to the division agent was the conductor or messenger. His beat also was about two hundred miles. He sat with the driver, and when necessary rode the entire distance without other

[671] Rusling, *op. cit.*, 207.
[672] Root and Connelley, *op. cit.*, 76.
[673] Mark Twain, *Roughing It*, 38.

rest than that which he could get while perched upon the coach. He had entire charge of the mail and express matter until he delivered them to the next conductor and received his receipt for them. He was usually a man of intelligence, decision, and considerable executive ability.

Of all the employees the driver was the most interesting character of the stage-coach days. Mr. Frank Root, a conductor on the stage-coach in the sixties, writes of this class:

"With few exceptions, the drivers were warm-hearted, kind, and obliging. Many of them capable of filling other and more important positions. The most of them were sober, especially while on duty, but nearly all were fond of an occasional 'eyeopener' . . .

"Quite a number of the boys were experienced in their business, having driven in a dozen or more different states and territories. Several were holding the reins of four- and six-horse stage teams in the West long before a railroad had reached the 'Father of Waters.' Now and then there was one to be found whose locks and beard were silvered from having sat on the box and weathered the wintry blasts of a third of a century or more, driving on various lines between the Alleghanies and the Rockies. . .

"Nearly every driver I knew seemed more or less fascinated with his chosen occupation, sitting on a stage box, and when once in the business it appeared as if they never could retire from it. There apparently was some sort of a charm about stage-driving that they never could resist. Old drivers frequently told me that." [674]

---
[674] Root and Connelley, *op. cit.*, 267-271.

Mr. Rusling says of the drivers:

"We talked a good deal, or essayed to, with the drivers but . . . they were a taciturn species. Off the box they were loquacious enough, but when mounted with four or six in hand, they either thought it unprofessional to talk, or else were absorbed too much in their business. . . They each had their fifty or sixty miles, up one day and back the next, and to the people along the route were important personages. . . They were fond of tobacco and whiskey and rolled out ponderous oaths, when things did not go to suit them. . .

"As bearers of the United States mail they felt themselves kings of the road and were seldom loth to show it. 'Clar the road! Git out of the way thar with your bull teams!' was a frequent salutation." [675]

Mark Twain's remarkable picture of the stage driver and his position, contains truth as well as humor:

"The driver tossed his gathered reins out on the ground, gaped and stretched complacently, drew off his heavy buckskin gloves with great deliberation and insufferable dignity — taking not the slightest notice of a dozen solicitous inquiries after his health, and humbly facetious and flattering accostings, and obsequious tenders of service, from five or six hairy and half-civilized station-keepers and hostlers who were nimbly unhitching our steeds and bringing the fresh team out of the stables — for, in the eyes of the stage-driver of that day, station-keepers and hostlers were a sort of good enough low creatures, useful in their place, and helping to make up a world but not the kind of beings which a person of distinction could afford to concern himself

---

[675] Rusling, *op. cit.*, 42.

with; while, on the contrary in the eyes of the station-keeper and the hostler, the stage-driver was a hero – a great and shining dignitary, the world's favorite son, the envy of the people, the observed of the nations. When they spoke to him they received his insolent silence meekly, and as being the natural and proper conduct of so great a man; when he opened his lips they all hung on his words with admiration (he never honored a particular individual with a remark, but addressed it with a broad generality to the horses, the stables, the surrounding country *and* the human underlings); when he discharged a facetious insulting personality at a hostler, that hostler was happy for the day; when he uttered his one jest – old as the hills, coarse, profane, witless, and inflicted on the same audience, in the same language, every time his coach drove up there – the varlets roared, and slapped their thighs, and swore it was the best thing they'd ever heard in all their lives. And how they would fly around when he wanted a basin of water, a gourd of the same, or a light for his pipe! – but they would instantly insult a passenger if he so far forgot himself as to crave a favor at their hands. They could do that sort of insolence as well as the driver they copied it from – for, let it be borne in mind, the Overland driver had but little less contempt for his passengers than he had for his hostlers.

"The hostlers and station-keepers treated the really powerful conductor of the coach merely with the best of what was their idea of civility, but the *driver* was the only being they bowed down to and worshipped. How admirably they would gaze up at him in his high seat as he gloved himself with lingering deliberation, while some happy hostler held the bunch of reins aloft, and waited patiently for him to take it. And how they would bombard him with glorifying ejaculations as he cracked his long whip and went careering away." [676]

Nearly every driver fairly worshipped his whip, and considered it worth almost its weight in gold. He hated to lend it even to his most intimate friend or to a companion driver. Some had the stocks ornamented with silver ferrules. Some drivers were so expert in handling their whips that they could sit in their seats and pick a fly off a lead horse with the lash, while going at a lively trot.[677]

The stock tenders and other underlings at the stations were usually low, rough characters – the dregs of society, many of whom were fugitives from justice.

The stations came to be established at intervals of from ten to fifteen miles. Every fifty miles or so were "home stations," where the driver's route ended, and where passengers could obtain meals. Those intervening were called "swing stations" and consisted of a stable, granary, and a room for one or two stock tenders. The "home stations" were more commodious, consisting of sleeping rooms, dining room, telegraph office, barn, etc. At the headquarters of each division were coach and repair shops, blacksmith and harness shops, etc. A horse-shoer and harness-repairer with separate team and outfit, traveled from station to station plying his trade. At Atchison, Denver, Salt Lake City, and other important points, shops on a large scale were established, where the general repairing was done with material from the manufactory at Concord.[678]

The stations along the Platte were usually one- to

---

[676] Mark Twain, *op. cit.*, 21-22.
[677] Root and Connelley, *op. cit.*, 271.
[678] —*Idem*, 487.

three-room structures built of hewn logs, with sod roofs and dirt floors. Adobe or stone were employed in some of the buildings farther west. Mark Twain found the stations rather uninviting:

"The station buildings were long, low huts, made of sundried, mud-colored bricks, laid up without mortar. The roofs which had no slant to them worth speaking of, were thatched and sodded or covered with a thick layer of earth, and from this sprung a pretty rank growth of weeds and grass. It was the first time we had ever seen a man's front yard on top of his house. The buildings consisted of barns, stable-room for twelve or fifteen horses, and a hut for an eating-room for passengers. This latter had bunks in it for the station-keeper and a hostler or two. You could rest your elbow on its eves, and you had to bend in order to get in at the door. In place of a window there was a square hole about large enough for a man to crawl through, but this had no glass in it. There was no flooring, but the ground was packed hard. There was no stove but the fireplace served all needful purposes. There were no shelves, no cupboards, no closets. In a corner stood an open sack of flour, and nestling against its base were a couple of black and venerable tin coffee pots, a tin teapot, a little bag of salt, and a side of bacon. . . The table was a greasy board on stilts, and the tablecloth and napkins had not come – and they were not looking for them, either." [679]

Ranches developed at some of the stations and much of the hay used along the route was grown by the ranchers. Often the grain had to be transported long distances, and a train of wagons was kept busy on each

---

[679] Mark Twain, *op. cit.*, 23, 24.

division hauling and distributing provisions, forage, and other necessary supplies.[680]

Mr. Root says that from forty to eighty tons of hay were consumed annually at each station, and that it cost from fifteen to forty dollars per ton. The cost of grain he estimated at over one-half million dollars per year, since there was a freight expense of about ten cents per pound in supplying distant stations.[681]

The Concord coach was an institution in the development of the West. This famous vehicle was manufactured by the Abbott-Downing Company of Concord, New Hampshire, a firm founded in 1813, which during the fifties and sixties, supplied coaches for all the important stage lines of the West. The coach usually employed on the "Overland" had provision for nine inside passengers, three to a seat, and one or more on the outside. The front seat faced backward, and the middle seat was often a removable stool-like arrangement with little or no support for the back. The rear seat was the most desirable.

The body of the coach was built of stout white oak, braced with iron bands. It was suspended upon two leather thoroughbraces extending lengthwise of the coach and attached at each end to a standard protruding up from the axle. These thoroughbraces were made of straps of leather placed on top of each other to a thickness of about three inches. This leather swing was used in the absence of steel springs to absorb the jars, and it permitted the coach to rock slightly forward and back. Behind the body was the triangular "boot"

---

[680] Root and Connelley, *op. cit.*, 487, say that the general manager of the line chartered, in the later sixties, seven Missouri River steamboats in one day at Saint Louis to load with corn for the "Overland."

[681] — *Idem*, 74.

THE CONCORD STAGE-COACH
The type of stage-coach used in pioneer days to transport mail

for mail, express, or baggage, and at the front, under the driver's seat was another leather compartment for the carriage of similar articles.

Mr. Rusling writes: "The Concord coaches quite surpassed our expectations, both as to comfort and speed. They were intended for nine inside – three seats full – and as many more outside as could be induced to get on." [682] Mark Twain writes of the one in which he rode: "Our coach was a great swinging and swaying stage of the most sumptuous description – an imposing cradle on wheels." [683]

Some of the coaches were built with an extra seat a little above and in the rear of the driver, and another seat facing backward, at the extreme rear of the upper deck. On such a coach, from fifteen to seventeen passengers were taken occasionally.[684]

The Monday coach out from Atchison was called the messenger coach, no mail arriving from the east on Monday. This coach was filled with express packages and carried a strong iron box containing the treasure and most valuable articles. On the regular coaches the safe was carried in the front boot, under the driver's box.

The mail was usually carried in the front and rear boots, but was strapped on top and piled inside when the occasion required. It was charged that at times mail was carried under the coach between the axles and the body, and that mail was thus ruined when streams were forded.

Over the mountainous stretches the regular Concord coach was exchanged for a "mountain mud-wagon,"

---

[682] Rusling, *op. cit.*, 41.
[683] Mark Twain, *op. cit.*, 7.
[684] Root and Connelley, *op. cit.*, 49.

which with its low canvas top was less likely to capsize in crossing the mountain regions.[685] There were on the main line about one hundred coaches, most of which were in constant use. During the middle sixties these cost, when delivered, about one thousand dollars apiece.[686]

The coach was drawn by four or six horses, depending upon the nature of the road and the distance between stations.[687] Holladay was himself a great lover and judge of stock, and it was his aim to have the line equipped with the best stage horses available. The wheelers working on the mountain lines were enormous fellows, and where possible the six horses were of the same shade, and tapered in size from the wheelers to the leaders. Spirited horses were selected for the runs out of stations where they were much observed.[688] Mr. Root, mail messenger, writes:

"Most of the teams were well matched, although among a few there was a decided contrast. Some of them, perfect in build, were the most lovely white, while others, just as nicely matched, were of a jet black. Then there were some nicely matched, beautiful bays — both of dark and light shade; there were also some equally fine teams of chestnut color; a number of handsome roans; the most lovely dapple-grays; occasionally a team of buckskins; and some splendidly matched sorrels and iron-grays."[689]

Mr. Rusling was happily surprised with the stage teams:

---

[685] Rusling, *op. cit.*, 143.
[686] Root and Connelley, *op. cit.*, 76.
[687] Birge, J. C. *The Awakening of the Desert*, 415, 416.
[688] — *Idem*, 410.
[689] Root and Connelley, *op. cit.*, 494.

"The animals . . . were our standing wonder; no broken-down nags like our typical stage-horses east; but, as a rule, they were fat and fiery. . . Wirey, gamey, as if feeling their oats thoroughly, they often went off from the stations at a full gallop; at the end of a mile or so would settle down to a square steady trot." [690]

Horses were used almost exclusively on the overland stage, but sometimes mule-teams were used to pull across sandy stretches.

No part of the line was more splendidly equipped or efficiently conducted than that between Placerville and Virginia City, Nevada. The "Pioneer Stage Company" was the sub-contractor on this part of the route. During the "palmy days" of the Comstock Lode there was much travel over this road and the competition that developed resulted in improved service. Bancroft, the Pacific Coast historian, writes of this line:

"A sprinkled road over which dashed six fine sleek horses, before an elegant Concord coach, the lines in the hands of an expert driver, whose light hat, linen duster, and lemon-colored gloves betokened a good salary and an exacting company, and who timed his grooms and his passengers by a heavy gold chronometer watch, held carelessly, if not conspicuously, on the tips of his fingers – these were some of its conspicuous features." [691]

On the main lines there were approximately twenty-five hundred horses and mules, most of which were in regular use. From eight to twelve were kept at each station. During the Civil War, while the Government was buying cavalry horses, these animals were valued

---
[690] Rusling, *op. cit.*, 41.
[691] Bancroft, H. H. *History of Nevada, Colorado, and Wyoming*, 230.

at near half a million dollars. The harness was of the very best Concord make, and cost during this period about one hundred fifty dollars for a complete set of four.[692]

There was considerable passenger travel on the overland mail stages in the sixties. The fares from Atchison in the early part of 1863 were: to Denver $75; to Salt Lake City $150; to Placerville, $225.[693] As the greenbacks depreciated, fares were increased. In 1865 the fare from the east end was $175 to Denver, and $350 to Salt Lake City. By 1866 the fare (in currency) from Fort Kearny to Denver was $150; to Salt Lake City, $300; to Nevada, $450; and to California, $500.[694] During the years immediately following, the fares were reduced about to the original level.[695] The advance in the fare was more nominal than real, and made little difference in the amount of the passenger traffic. The passenger fare included the transportation of twenty-five pounds of baggage, but the cost of meals was extra.[696] These varied from time to time and from place to place, and ranged from fifty cents to two dollars.[697]

---

[692] Root and Connelley, *op. cit.*, 74.

[693] —*Idem*, 64.

[694] Rusling, *op. cit.*, 41. The *Alta California* of April 27, 1866, says, "The fare to Salt Lake City from Placerville is $125 in coin, and from Salt Lake City to Virginia City, Montana, $175 in currency."

[695] The *Territorial Enterprise* of Nevada says, under date of May 24, 1868: "The rates of passage on the Overland stages have been reduced 25 per cent. The following are the present rates, in currency: To Omaha, $225; to St. Helena, Montana, $240; to Salt Lake City, $120. This is better than no reduction at all, but the present figures do not strike us as being low enough to strike anybody dumb."—*Alta California*, May 26, 1868.

[696] Barnes, *From the Atlantic to the Pacific, Overland*, 21. Baggage to Salt Lake City (over 25 pounds) was $1.50 per pound.

[697] Rusling, *op. cit.*, 42, says: "Halts were made twice a day for meals, forty minutes each. . . Our meals were fair for the region; generally

Almost every coach carried passengers and at times passage was booked days in advance and extras were sometimes run. It was often charged that the company neglected the mail transportation to carry passengers.[698]

One can hardly imagine worse punishment than riding day and night continuously for twenty days in a crowded coach. One passenger draws this pen picture:

"A through ticket and fifteen inches of seat, with a fat man on one side, a poor widow on the other, a baby on your lap, a bandbox over your head, and three or four more persons immediately in front, leaning against your knee, makes the picture, as well as your sleeping place for the trip."[699]

Another traveler tells how certain passengers put hay on the flat top of the coach, put their blankets over, strapped themselves on by ropes tied to the railings, and got good sleep while the passengers inside, packed like sardines, got none.[700]

There were all kinds of passengers, but they were usually more exclusive than those on the cars of today. Occasionally private parties of two, four, or six, would charter a coach and lay in a supply of "good things" that could not be procured on the route. They usually had air pillows which were inflated to provide a soft place for the head.[701]

Mr. Root says that the mail pouches, carried west-

---

coffee, beef-steak or bacon, potatoes, and saleratus biscuit hot; but the prices — one dollar and one dollar and a half per meal — seemed extortionate."

[698] Barnes, *op. cit.*, 35. Barnes wrote from Denver, June, 1865: "I have seen the stages pass through here loaded with passengers and not carry a pound of mail, while perhaps two weeks' mail, or more, lay heaped in the office."

[699] — *Idem*, 8.

[700] Rusling, *op. cit.*, 44.

[701] Root and Connelley, *op. cit.*, 66.

ward daily, usually ran as follows: to San Francisco, two; to Sacramento, one to two; to Virginia City and Carson City, Nevada, one each; to Salt Lake City, one to two; and to Denver, two. In addition there was a one way-pouch which was opened at the few post offices along the route.[702]

---

[702] — *Idem*, 52.

Chapter XIV

Final Years and Passing of the Overland Stage

From its inception the stage-coach service to the Pacific Coast had been looked upon as but a temporary expedient. The fond hope had ever been for the railroad and its band of steel to unite the East and West. By the year 1866 the trans-continental railroad was making headway, and for the stage-coach, the beginning of the end had come.

The earliest of the Pacific railways had been chartered in 1862, but not until the land grants and bond subsidies were increased in 1864 did active organization begin.[703] By the summer of 1866 railroad building had progressed sufficiently to make itself felt somewhat in overland communication. On August 15th, the eastern terminus of the overland mail line was changed by the Postmaster-general from Atchison to Manhattan, Kansas, the railroad having reached that point.[704] By this change a gain of 168 miles was effected in the stage service. The mail was now carried to Denver via the Smoky Hill route, the one used by the Butterfield Despatch Company, which Holladay had bought out in the March previous. As the railroad advanced westward along this route the stage terminus accordingly receded.

In the meantime the railroad from Omaha was built

---

[703] Paxson, F. L. *The Last American Frontier*, 325.

[704] Postmaster-general's *Report*, 1866, 4. Saint Louis letter of August 17th, in the *Alta California* of September 15, 1866.

westward to Fort Kearny,[705] and so, when the gap between the railroads east of Omaha was practically filled, the Postmaster-general ordered, on November 13th, a daily coach service from Fort Kearny to Denver also.[706] This gave two daily lines to Denver, from which point a single daily line continued westward.

During 1866 there were Indian disturbances on the Powder River road leading into Montana,[707] and on December 21st, Captain Fetterman and his command of seventy-eight men were killed near Fort Philip Kearny.[708] But on the Overland Route the Indians were, in general, peaceful. A Saint Louis correspondent explains the frequency of Indian War rumors thus:

"There are so many parties in and out of business on the Plains who desire an Indian War as a means of speculation, that they are ever busy circulating stories to the effect that the warriors of such and such a tribe have put on their war paint, and declared hostility to death against the whites." [709]

George E. Cook, treasurer of the Overland Company, wrote August 25th:

"Testimony of General Sherman that the Indians were not only quiet but well disposed and friendly and the fact that our mail coaches are daily passing from the Missouri River to Salt Lake, without the first cause of molestation, since last year, certainly offers strong evidence of their peaceable disposition." [710]

---

[705] *Alta California*, September 4, 1866.

[706] Postmaster-general's *Report*, 4. In November, 1866, there was a gap of thirty-five miles from Woodbine, Iowa, to Council Bluffs. This was bridged by a stage line. All mail for the far West from the Northern section was now sent via Chicago and Omaha. – *Alta California*, November 23, 1866.

[707] *Alta California*, August 31st; September 6th, 1866.

[708] Paxson, *op. cit.*, 274.

[709] *Alta California*, October 11, 1866.

[710] — *Idem*, October 10, 1866.

FINAL YEARS OF THE OVERLAND STAGE

In the latter part of 1866 Holladay disposed of his entire overland mail holdings; and a consolidation of the "Holladay Overland Mail and Express Company," the "Overland Mail Company," the "Pioneer Stage Company," and "Wells, Fargo and Company," was effected under the name of "Wells Fargo and Company." [711]

Wells Fargo and Company had been founded in 1852 by Henry Wells, William G. Fargo, John Livingston, D. N. Barney, and others to conduct an express and banking business, and had had a rapid growth.[712] This consolidation gave them practically exclusive control of all express and stage routes between the Missouri River and the Pacific Coast, with numerous branch lines in Nevada, Montana, Idaho and Colorado.[713] They were now capitalized at $10,000,000 and Louis McLane was elected president.[714]

---

[711] — *Idem*, November 4, 1866. Root and Connelley, *The Overland Stage to California*, 56, 489. The "Overland Mail Co." was the remnant of the John Butterfield Company which had established and operated the first great overland mail line, running from St. Louis to San Francisco via El Paso, Texas. This company had been moved to the central route in 1861 and conducted the part of the route west of Salt Lake City. The Pioneer Stage Company was founded by Louis McLane and operated between Shingle Springs, California, and Virginia City, Nevada, and did a big business during the sixties.

[712] Stimson, A. L. *History of the Express Companies*, 180. *Pamphlets of California Commerce*, vol. iii, no. 16: "Catalogue, Historical exhibit, etc., at the World's Columbian Exposition," Chicago, 1893. Henry Wells began his career as an expressman at Albany, New York. In 1845 Wells and Company was organized, and conducted an express business west from Buffalo. In 1850 they combined with Livingston and Fargo and Butterfield; and with Mason and Company to form the American Express Company, of which Mr. Wells was elected president.

William G. Fargo was born in Pompey, New York, in 1818. He made his start as an employee of the Auburn and Syracuse Railroad. He was a partner in Wells and Company in 1845, and secretary of the American Express Company in 1850, and helped form Wells, Fargo and Company in 1852.

[713] Root and Connelley, *op. cit.*, 56.

[714] *Alta California*, November 4, 1866. *Pamphlets of California Commerce*, vol. iii, no. 16.

The Indian depredations early in 1867 were virtually a continuation of the Sioux difficulties in the Powder River country, of the December previous. The mail from Fort Laramie to Fort Philip Kearny (237 miles northward) was attacked January 11, 1867, and the wagons and mules were lost.[715] A few months later, Chief Red Cloud attacked a wood train near Fort Philip Kearny but was repulsed by Major Powell and his men who formed a barricade with the iron, bullet-proof bodies of their army wagons.[716]

Depredations continued during the spring and summer. The Indians attacked a party of stagemen in Bridger's Pass June 4th, killed two men, and drove off the stock for forty-five miles east from Sulphur Springs.[717] Two days later, Bridger's Pass Station was burned and Plum Creek Station, one hundred fifty miles east of Julesburg, was attacked and the operator killed and scalped. A dispatch said, "Central City has raised $5,000 to be paid for Indian scalps at the rate of $25 a scalp, with ears attached." [718]

The Overland route was seriously obstructed from the western terminus of the Union Pacific railroad to the Green River.[719] Papers were submitted by the contractor to the Post Office Department showing that "from April 1, to August 15, 1867, the Indians robbed him of 350 head of stage stock; burned twelve of his stations, with large amounts of grain and hay; destroyed three coaches and express wagons, severely wounded several of his passengers; and killed outright thirteen of his most reliable employees." [720]

---

[715] *Alta California*, January 13, 1867.
[716] Paxson, *op. cit.*, 283.
[717] *Alta California*, June 6, 1867.
[718] — *Idem*, June 10, 1867.
[719] — *Idem*, June 9, 1867.
[720] Postmaster-general's *Report*, 1867, 5.

The mail lines were supported by the military but notwithstanding this, the Denver postmaster reported that no mail reached his office from February 23 to March 2 and that there were eighteen failures during the month of March. From June 8th to September 1st regular trips were made on alternate days, the reduction in the service being caused by the loss of stock.[721]

There was much controversy at this time in regard to relations with the Indians. In general the West wanted a stern policy of punishment or of extermination. The East, moved by philanthropic motives, considered the white man the aggressor and hence stood for peaceful measures. Some wanted the management of Indian affairs transferred to the war department, while others thought civilians would be more successful in dealing with wild tribes. Indian agents blamed the military for the sad state of affairs, and the army men reversed the charge.

At the bottom of the difficulty, however, were the inevitable consequences of the westward migration of the whites. The Indians were being compressed, their reserves curtailed, their best hunting grounds depleted. At the time when their natural food was disappearing they had come to learn of the white man's diet and of the ease with which it could be procured by thievery. No moral teachings restrained them. What other recourse was there than pillage, or war for their hunting grounds? So the wars had continued with intervals of peace. The Indians early learned to fight in the summer and proffer peace in the fall in order to get annuities and rations for the winter.

The army had now been given a chance to settle the Indian question but the war had dragged on "with no

---
[721] — *Idem*, 5.

definite results, save to rouse the passions of the West, the revenge of the Indians, and the philanthropy of the East."[722] Now the Government determined upon another course and a peace commission was formed by the Act of July 20, 1867. It was to collect and deal with the hostile tribes, to secure the safety of the overland routes, and arrange permanent homes for the tribes off the main lines of travel.

The Peace Commission sat for fifteen months and made some important treaties with the Indians, securing their relinquishment of lands along the overland routes. The white claim to the Powder River valley was surrendered and a great northern reserve created in the Black Hills of southern Dakota.[723] In the meantime the Union Pacific railroad had been pushed westward with vigor, reaching Cheyenne by the end of 1867.[724] The country of the most hostile Indians was now crossed by the railroad, and the overland stage during the remainder of its existence was comparatively free from Indian disturbances. The mail to Santa Fé was more fortunate than the "Overland" during 1867, but it also was besieged by the Indians during the greater part of the summer. Several stations were robbed of their stock and the mail was necessarily delayed.[725]

The Postmaster-general reported in December, 1867, that the complaints in reference to the overland mail service during the spring and summer of that year had been more numerous and pressing than at any other time since the route was established. It was charged

---

[722] Paxson, *op. cit.*, 288.
[723] — *Idem*, 302.
[724] — *Idem*, 332.
[725] Postmaster-general's *Report*, 1867, 5.

FINAL YEARS OF THE OVERLAND STAGE 323

that the Indian disturbances had not been sufficient to justify the great irregularity and the interruptions that had prevailed; but the Postmaster-general was convinced from the reports of General Sherman and others, that the failures had been unavoidable under the circumstances.[726]

By the close of the year 1867 the two railroads had replaced a major part of the coach service east of Denver. The Union Pacific had reached Cheyenne, Wyoming; and the Union Pacific, Eastern Division, (Kansas Pacific) had reached Hays City, 571 miles west of Saint Louis. On the Pacific side, the Central Pacific Company had reached Cisco, 94 miles distant from Sacramento.[727]

During these years when the first trans-continental railroad was being pushed across the continent, and the mail service by stage-coach was being replaced, branch and parallel lines of coaches were opening new paths and marking the routes for new railroads. In 1867 a mail line was established along the old Butterfield or Southern Route from Western Texas to California (approximately the route of the Southern Pacific Railroad). Service was already being performed from Mesilla on the Rio Grande, a little north of El Paso, to Tucson, Arizona; but the Postmaster-general now extended it to Los Angeles, and made it tri-weekly.[728] This extension was very beneficial to persons living along the line, since previously it had been necessary to send letters for California eastward to Saint Joseph,

---

[726] — *Idem*, 4.

[727] Paxson, *op. cit.*, 332.

[728] Postmaster-general's *Report*, 1867, 6. A semi-weekly mail already existed from Los Angeles via San Bernardino and La Paz to Prescott, Arizona. Los Angeles *Republican*, February 8, 1868. *Alta California*, February 22, 1865.

and then back over the overland route via Salt Lake City to the Pacific Coast.

With a view to affording more direct mail communication between Chicago, Saint Paul, and other important points, and the territories of Montana, Idaho, and Washington, a route from Fort Abercrombie to Helena was advertised for the spring lettings of 1867, and duly awarded to contract for a three-times-a-week service. By this route about six hundred miles in distance would be saved between Chicago and Helena, as compared with the more indirect one via Salt Lake City. Unfortunately, however, Indian hostilities were prevalent; and the little mail matter entrusted to this line was conveyed on ponies, traveling over some portions of the route only at night.[729] The Postmaster-general considered the service as performed to be of no value to the Department and discontinued it March 30, 1868.

The mail line from Salt Lake City through Idaho to The Dalles, Washington Territory, was improved in 1867 from a tri-weekly to a daily service.[730]

The winter storms of 1867-8 caused delay in the mail service as usual. Across the Sierras, both the Donner

---

[729] Postmaster-general's *Report*, 1867, 6. Congress intervened, however, and authorized a post-coach service over the route. An advertisement was issued inviting proposals for a tri-weekly service in four-horse coaches. A contract was accordingly entered into with Leech, Piper, and Montgomery, of Pennsylvania, at $194,000 per annum, the service to commence January 1, 1869, and continue to June 30, 1872. (Postmaster-general's *Report*, 1868, 8.) However, no service was performed and the contract was annulled. (U. S. House. *Executive Documents*, 41st congress, second session, no. 314.)

[730] Postmaster-general's *Report*, 1867, 6. When it was re-let in October, 1868, the same service was secured for $149,000 per year, a reduction of $164,000 from the amount of the previous contract.—Postmaster-general's *Report*, 1868, 8. After the first trans-continental railroad was completed in 1869, this route was changed so as to begin at Indian Creek on the Central Pacific railroad, instead of at Salt Lake City. This made a saving of 110 miles, reducing the distance to 765 miles.—U. S. House. *Executive Documents*, 41st congress, second session, no. 314, p. 420.

FINAL YEARS OF THE OVERLAND STAGE 325

Lake and the Placerville-Lake Tahoe routes were employed. Sleighs were used for the transportation over the higher altitudes, seventy-five miles of good sleighing being reported during the early part of January.[731]

During the year 1868 the trans-continental railroad building proceeded more rapidly than ever before. The Central Pacific was now over its hardest grades and in the late summer was able to make rapid progress across Nevada. The railroad followed the Humboldt River and hence was a hundred miles or more north of the overland stage route, which ran via Austin, Nevada. West of Cheyenne the Union Pacific pushed forward, unchecked by the continental divide. Four hundred twenty-five miles were added to its track during the year.[732] But by the end of the year there still remained about four hundred miles of stage service between the railroads.

In November, 1868, the terminus of the Union Pacific was at Bryan, Wyoming. From this point the old stage route was followed to Salt Lake City, via Fort Bridger, Bear River City, and Echo Canyon. West of the Mormon metropolis the stages proceeded south of the Great Salt Lake via Rush Valley, Simpson Spring, Deep Creek, Ruby Valley, and Diamond Mountain to Austin. From here a newly opened route was followed directly northward to Argenta on the Central Pacific.[733] Passengers and most of the mail took this route from Austin, but some of the heavy matter continued to be sent westward to Wadsworth by freight teams.[734]

---

[731] Nevada *Territorial Enterprise*, January 11th, in the *Alta California* of January 15, 1868.

[732] Paxson, *op. cit.*, 334.

[733] A series of articles "Across the Continent," signed "Gould," in the *Alta California*, November 14, 17, 19, 20, 22, 1868.

[734] *Alta California*, December 5, 1868. It was reported that "eight bull-

The original Holladay contract of 1864, now in the hands of Wells, Fargo and Company, expired October 1, 1868. A new contract was let to Carlton Spaids of Chicago for the service, but he failed to fulfill it, and after considerable delay and difficulties, arrangements were finally made with Wells, Fargo and Company to continue the service. They were to receive $1,750,000 per year, subject to deduction as the railroad progressed.[735] The railroad was completed sooner than anticipated, and the total amount paid them for the service from October 1, 1868, to May 10, 1869, was $455,804.64.[736] In fact, almost everyone was surprised at the rapid progress made in the building of the first trans-continental railroad. When Wells, Fargo and Company bought out Holladay in 1866 they expected a half dozen years of staging before the railroad would be completed. In this, of course, they were disappointed, and it is said they lost heavily in consequence."[737]

---

team loads of overland mail matter have been despatched from Austin for Wadsworth, as freighting teams in sufficient numbers to carry the enormous mass of back mails are not running between Argenta and Austin at present."

[735] Postmaster-general's *Report*, 1868, 6, 7. Brigham Young had offered to carry 1500 pounds of mail daily both ways between the termini of the railroad for $559,375, and ten cents per pound per hundred miles for all additional mails. The Union Pacific Railroad Company offered to contract for one year for $1,500,000 without reduction of pay as the railroad advanced.

[736] Postmaster-general's *Report*, 1869, 5.

[737] Root and Connelley, *op. cit.*, 489, say that Wells, Fargo and Company "had on hand when the two roads united, between $50,000 and $75,000 worth of surplus stagecoaches, and these they closed out to Gilmer and Salisbury for less than one-third the original cost." They still continued to operate quite a number of branch lines in various parts of the West. From the record of government mail contracts of 1869 (U. S. House. *Executive Documents*, 41st congress, second session, no. 314), we find the following among those operated by Wells, Fargo and Company: From Bear River Junction to Virginia City, Montana, 302 miles, three times per week each way for $47,500. (Page 264 in above document.) From Austin to Argenta, Nevada, 100 miles and back daily, for $4950, (p. 253); from Helena, Montana, to

FINAL YEARS OF THE OVERLAND STAGE 327

The overland mail service during the winter of 1868-9 was very unsatisfactory. Evidence before the Committee on Public Expenditures showed that thousands of pounds of mail matter had been destroyed or left uncared for week after week, along the line.[738] The first mail from the east in three weeks came into Salt Lake City March 8th in five coaches.[739]

The old stage road, to the south of the Great Salt Lake and more than a hundred miles south of the Central Pacific railroad in Nevada, was held to as long as possible, for along it the contractors already had their stations.[740] It was not until April 10th, when the approaching railroads were but one hundred ten miles apart, that the stages began running directly between the termini.[741] There was little to encourage a stage company to its best efforts. The stage service was now but a temporary expedient, and an impatient public endured it complainingly.

Writing of the overland stage service in 1868 and 1869 is like relating the story of a defeat or chronicling the incidents of decline. Our interests naturally incline to the rising thing, the improved facility, and we *endure* or despise that which is no longer the best. In the fifties and early sixties the six-horse coach was the pride of the West, now it was spoken of with contempt. The "magnificent Concord coach" had become the "terrible rattling stage." And when the golden spike was driven at Promontory Point on May 10, 1869, the fare-

---

Fort Benton, 141 miles, tri-weekly, for $17,850 (p. 400); from Phil Sheridan to Denver, 201 miles, daily, for $79,000 per year (p. 418).

[738] Washington correspondence, January 31, 1869, in *Alta California*, March 6, 1869.

[739] *Alta California*, March 17, 1869.

[740] —*Idem*, April 3, 1869.

[741] —*Idem*, April 10, 1869.

well note was struck. The continent was spanned with steel and the Overland stage-coach was replaced forever.

Though its going is not regretted, as a memory it persists. A quarter century after the coach had gone, the following appeared in the Atchison *Champion*:

"There are few if any of the things of the fading past to which in our reminiscent moods, we revert more fondly than the old stage-coach. That vehicle of travel so popular with the generations who have fallen asleep. . .

"The old stage-coach! How well we remember it, and how vividly we recall its appearance, conjuring up out of the depths of memory all the experiences associated with the journeys we took in it. It seemed to us then the very incarnation of cosiness and comfort, the embodiment of all that was best in the line of transportation. It was so far superior to the old springless lumber wagon and the ox cart that we deemed it a rare luxury to have both the occasion and the means to ride in it. . . But the old stage-coach has ended its career – made its last trip. Here and there what remains of it stands beneath the rickety shed of a wayside inn, a relic of bygone days – weather-worn, storm-broken, its doors gone, its sides and back smashed in, its boot the poor, forlorn remnant of its former proud and glorious self. Ghosts of a buried past now hide in it. Shades of the occupants it carried once have enwrapped it. Spectral forms of the road-agents who once surrounded it to rifle the contents of its boot now troop around it when nightly shadows enfold it. . .

"The imperious and impressively confident driver – Bill, Hank, Joe, Dave, is gone. From his nerveless hands the lines have fallen, and the shrill notes of his horn have died away on the air of the vanished years. Poor thing! There it stands, under the old tavern shed, wretched, dismantled, forlorn. No one hails its coming with eager, beating heart; no one weeps as it rumbles away with its precious freight of affection and friendship. Decay and rust settled down upon it years ago and pre-empted it, and a strange mustiness now dominates it. The blasts of winter have frayed its trappings; the winds of autumn have shredded its curtains. Its chains, once so bright, are tarnished with the rust of decades, but their links bind us to a well-remembered past. Its gloss which shone in the suns that set in that far yesterday, is blurred and faded out." [742]

The overland stage was shortlived, its days being numbered before it began. It was the last link between the old and the new, in overland transportation. Along with the buffalo and the roving Indian it lived its day and passed. But its services are not to be despised or minimized. For twenty years its record is interwoven with that of the development of the Trans-mississippi West.

The stage-coach followed the pioneer trails; and the mail service, meagre and infrequent as it was at first, was nevertheless a connecting link with the old home. The arrival of the mail was ever an occasion of importance to the remote settlements of the West. And the people's representatives at the National Capital were generally attentive to Western requests. Often it was debated in Congress whether the Post Office Department should be strictly a business establishment, providing postal service only where the lines would be self-supporting, or whether its mission was also to act as an agency of civilization and of national expansion,

---

[742] Quoted by Root and Connelley, *op. cit.*, 598, 599.

looking for returns not only in immediate postal receipts but in the development of the Commonwealth. Generally the latter view prevailed at Washington, and a paternal interest in the West, and a willingness to invest for the future, characterized most of the legislation relating to the Trans-mississippi region. Mail lines were run not only to the sparsely settled regions where postal receipts were small, but through regions uninhabited, where it was hoped that with this encouragement, settlements would spring up.

The guarding of the mail lines and the protection of emigrant travel went hand in hand. Regular mail service was a sign of security and a preliminary to increased migration.

Scarcely a railroad line was projected which did not follow a post route; and over most of these roads, stage-coach wheels cut deep the track before rails of steel were laid.

More recently has come the motor car, and the old trails are re-born. With more fidelity than the railroads, have the automobiles followed the stage-coach routes of other days. The air-mail pilot of today follows a more direct course than did his grandfather who cracked his whip over a Concord coach and six, but from his position among the clouds he may see below, gas-propelled specks coursing along turnpike roads or paved highways, chasing the phantoms of the stage-coach which rattled and jolted over the identical trail but sixty years ago.

The fortified mail station with its stock tenders, extra teams, and stores of supplies is gone, and in its place stands a freshly-painted, grass plotted modern station, where the present carriers pause to replenish supplies.

But the facility of *modern* conveyance does not blind

us to the service of the *old*, of the days when the West was new. The Overland stage-coach is now a symbol of a past era, but in its day it ranked high in service to its generation; and we today may cherish it as a promoter of settlement and a precursor of railroads into the West.

Bibliography

Bibliography of references cited

ALBRIGHT, George Leslie. Official explorations for Pacific railroads (Berkeley, California, 1921).
ALTER, J. Cecil. James Bridger (Salt Lake City, 1925).
BANCROFT, H. H. History of Arizona and New Mexico, 1530-1888 (San Francisco, 1889).
——— History of California (San Francisco, 1886-90), 7 vols.
——— Chronicles of builders of commonwealth (San Francisco, 1891-2), 7 vols.
——— History of Nevada, Colorado, and Wyoming, 1540-1888 (San Francisco, 1890).
——— History of Utah (San Francisco, 1889).
——— Early records of Utah, July 1847 to December 1851 (Ms. Bancroft library, University of California).
——— Incidents in Utah history, 1852-1854 (Ms. Bancroft library).
——— Utah biographical sketches (Ms. Bancroft library).
——— Utah jottings (Ms. Bancroft Library).
——— Interview with Governor Evans of Colorado (Ms. Bancroft library).
BARNES, Demas. From Atlantic to Pacific overland (New York, 1866).
BAYLES, W. Harrison. Postal service in thirteen colonies: in *Journal of American History*, vol. v, 429-458.
BIEBER, R. P. The Southwestern trails to California in 1849: *Mississippi Valley Historical Review*, vol. xii, 342-376.
BIRGE, J. C. Awakening of desert (Boston, 1912).
BONSAL, Stephen. Edward Fitzgerald Beale: pioneer in path of empire, 1822-1903 (New York, 1912).
BOWEN, Eli. United States post office guide (New York, 1851).
BOWLES, Samuel. Across the continent (Springfield, Mass., 1865).
BRADLEY, Glenn D. Story of pony express (Chicago, 1913).
BRETZ, J. P. Some aspects of postal extension into West: in Amer. Hist. Assn. *report*, 1909, 143 ff.

BRISBIN, J. S., editor. Belden, the White Chief (Cincinnati, 1870).
CARVALHO, S. N. Incidents of travel and adventure in Far West (New York, 1857).
CHANNING, Edward. History of United States (New York, 1907-1921), 5 vols.
CHITTENDEN, H. M. History of American Fur Trade of Far West (New York, 1902), 3 vols.
CHORPENNING, George. Statement and appendix of claim of George Chorpenning against United States, 1889. (pamphlet).
CLELAND, R. G. History of California: the American period (New York, 1922).
CLEMENS, Samuel Langhorne (Mark Twain). Roughing It (Chicago, 1872).
CODY, William F. Autobiography of Buffalo Bill (New York, 1920).
COMAN, K. Economic beginnings of the far west (New York, 1912), 2 vols.
COOKE, P. St. Geo. Conquest of New Mexico and California (New York, 1878).
COY, Owen C. Pony Express antedated: in *Grizzly Bear*, February, 1917.
CUSHING, Marshall Henry. Story of our post office (Boston, 1893).
DALE, H. C. The Ashley-Smith Explorations (Cleveland, 1918).
DAVIS, J. P. Union Pacific Railway; a study in railway politics, history ,and economics (Chicago, 1894).
DAVIS, W. W. H. El Gringo; or New Mexico and her people (New York, 1857).
DAWSON, T. F. Scrap-books. (Newspaper and Magazine clippings, Library of State Historical and Natural History Society of Colorado).
DELLENBAUGH, F. S. Fremont and '49 (New York, 1914).
[DENVER] Commonwealth, 1863 to 1864.
DESERET News [Salt Lake City, Utah], 1851 to 1855.
DUNBAR, Seymour. History of Travel in America (Indianapolis, 1915), 4 vols.
GOODWIN, Cardinal. Trans-mississippi West, 1803-1853 (New York, 1922).
GREELEY, Horace. Overland Journey (New York, 1860).
GREGG, Josiah. Commerce of Prairies: or journal of a Santa Fe

trader (New York, 1844), 2 vols. (reprinted, and edited by R. G. Thwaites, in Early Western Travels series, vols. 19 and 20).

GRINNELL, G. B. Fighting Cheyennes (New York, 1915).

GWIN, W. H. Memoirs on History of United States, Mexico, and California (Dictated for Bancroft Library, 1878. Ms.).

HALL, Frank. History of State of Colorado (Chicago, 1889-95), 4 vols.

HAYES Collection (Newspaper clippings, Bancroft Library, University of California).

HEAP, Gwinn H. Central Route to Pacific from the valley of Mississippi to California (Philadelphia, 1854).

HARRISON, Benjamin. This Country of Ours (New York, 1897).

HEBARD, Grace R. and Brininstool. The Bozeman Trail (Cleveland, 1922), 2 vols.

HODDER, F. H. Railroad background of the Kansas-Nebraska act: in *Mississippi Valley Historical Review*, vol. xii, 3-22.

HOUGH, Emerson. Passing of Frontier (New Haven, 1921).

HOWBERT, Irving. Memories of a lifetime in Pike's Peak region (New York, 1925).

HUGHES, Bela M. Letter to John Doniphan (Denver, Colorado, May 2, 1892. In library of State Historical and Natural History Society of Colorado).

HULBERT, A. B. Crown Collection of American Maps, Series IV, vols. 1 and 2. (Colorado Springs, Colorado, 1925).

INMAN, Henry. Great Salt Lake Trail (New York, 1898).

——— Old Santa Fe Trail (New York, 1899).

KIMBALL, Everett. National Government of United States (New York, 1920).

KUYKENDALL, R. S. History of Early California Journalism (Berkeley, California, 1918. Ms.).

LARIMER, W. H. H. Reminiscences of General William Larimer and of his son William H. H. Larimer, two of founders of Denver City (Lancaster, Pa., 1918).

LITTLE, Feramorz. Mail Service across plains (Salt Lake City, 1884. Ms.).

[LITTLE Rock, Arkansas] Gazette, 1849.

[Los Angeles, California] Southern Vineyard, 1854 to 1856.

MCDONALD, William. Select Documents illustrative of history of United States, 1776-1861 (New York, 1898).

McMaster, J. B. History of people of United States from revolution to Civil War (New York, 1898-1913), 8 vols.

Majors, Alexander. Seventy Years on frontier (Chicago, 1893).

Moore, Frank, editor. Rebellion Record (New York, 1864-71), 12 vols.

Parrish, Randall. Great Plains, romance of western American exploration, warfare and settlement, 1527-1870 (Chicago, 1907).

Paxson, F. L. History of American Frontier, 1763-1893 (Boston, 1924).

——— Last American Frontier (New York, 1910).

Rees, James. Footprints of a letter carrier (Philadelphia, 1866).

Rhodes, J. F. History of United States since compromise of 1850 (New York, 1893-1904), 7 vols.

Richardson, A. D. Beyond the Mississippi (Hartford, Conn., 1867).

Richardson, J. D. Compilation of messages and papers of Confederacy (Nashville, 1905), 2 vols.

——— Compilation of messages and papers of Presidents, 1789-1897 (Government Printing Office, 1899), 10 vols.

Root, F. A. and Connelley. Overland Stage to California (Topeka, 1901).

Roper, D. C. United States Post Office (New York, 1917).

Rusling, J. F. Acrosss America, or great west and pacific coast (New York, 1875).

Sacramento Union, 1851-1859.

[St. Joseph, Mo.] Daily News. History of Buchanan Co. and St. Joseph, 1898.

Sanford, A. B. Story of Bob Spotswood's Life (Library of State Historical and Natural History Society of Colorado. Ms.)

[San Francisco] Alta California, 1849-1869.

San Francisco Bulletin, 1855 to 1869.

[San Francisco] California Star, 1847, 1848.

San Francisco Herald, 1850 to 1856.

Shinn, C. H. Story of the Mine (New York, 1896).

Simpson, J. H. Report of explorations across great basin of territory of Utah (Washington, 1876).

Smiley, J. C. History of Colorado (Chicago, 1913), 2 vols.

Smith, William. Colonial Post Office: in *American Historical Review*, vol. xxi, 258-275.

SOPRIS, S. T. First Stage Coach (Ms. in library of State Historical and Natural History Society of Colorado).
STIMSON, A. L. History of Express Companies (New York, 1858).
TEXAS Almanac for years 1859, 1860, 1861, 1867, 1868, 1869 (Galveston, Texas, 1859-69).
THWAITES, R. G. Early Western Travels series (Cleveland, 1904-1907), 32 vols.
TULLIDGE, E. W. History of Salt Lake City (Salt Lake City, 1886).
TWITCHELL, R. E. Leading Facts of New Mexican History (Cedar Rapids, Iowa, 1912), 2 vols.
U. S. CONGRESSIONAL Globe, 32d congress, first sessions, 2 vols.
────── 32d congress, second session, 2 vols.
────── 33d congress, first session, 2 vols. in 3 parts.
────── 33d congress, second session, 2 vols.
────── 34th congress, first session, 3 vols. and appendix.
────── 34th congress, third session, 2 vols. and appendix.
────── 35th congress, first session, 2 vols. and appendix.
────── 35th congress, second session, 2 parts.
────── 36th congress, first session, 4 parts.
────── 36th congress, second session, 2 parts and appendix.
U .S. HOUSE. Executive Documents, 32d congress, first session, no. 56. Serial no. 643. (Mail contracts).
────── 33d congress, second session, no. 86. (Mail contracts).
────── 34th congress, first session, no. 122. (Mail contracts).
────── 35th congress, first session, no. 96. (Abstract of offers for carrying the mails).
────── 35th congress, second session, no. 109. (Mail contracts).
────── 35th congress, second session, no. 108. (Pacific Wagon Roads).
────── 35th congress, second session, no. 28. (Veto message of President Buchanan).
────── 35th congress, second session, no. 30. (Serial no. 1004). (Case of Carmick and Ramsey).
────── 36th congress, first session, no. 86. (Serial no. 1057). (Offers and contracts for carrying the mails).
────── 36th congress, second session, no. 73. (Serial no. 1101). (Abstract of offers for carrying the mails).
────── 37th congress, second session, no. 137. (Serial no. 1139). (Offers for carrying the mails).

——— 37th congress, second session, no. 55. (Serial no. 1131). (Relative to discontinuance of mail service in seceded states).

——— 38th congress, second session, no. 24. (Serial no. 1223). (Advertisements, bids, and correspondence relative to Overland California mail contract of 1864).

——— 40th congress, second session, no. 201. (Serial no. 1341). (Contracts with Benjamin Holladay, 1864).

——— 40th congress, third session, no. 14. (Serial no. 1372). (Letter of Postmaster-general relative to contracts for overland mail, 1868).

——— 41st congress, second session, no. 314. (Serial no. 1427). (Mail contracts).

U. S. HOUSE. Reports, 36th congress, first session, no. 268.

U. S. SENATE. Executive Documents, 32d congress, first session, no. 50. (Reports relative to the contracts for ocean mail to California).

——— 32d congress, first session, no. 1, part ii. (Serial no. 612).

——— 41st congress, third session, no. 44. (Serial no. 1440).

U. S. SENATE. Miscellaneous Documents, 32d congress, first session, no. 63.

U. S. SENATE. Reports, 36th congress, first session, no. 259. (Serial no. 1068). (Report on bill for relief of Hockaday and Liggett).

U. S. LAWS from 1789 to 1815, 5 vols. (Published by John Bioren and W. John Duane, 1815).

U. S. STATUTES at Large. (Boston, 1845-1868), 15 vols.

U. S. POSTMASTER-GENERAL's Annual Report of:

1847, H. Ex. Docs. 30th cong., 1st sess., no. 1, vol. i (Ser. 503).
1848, H. Ex. Docs. 30th cong., 2nd sess., no. 1, vol. i. (Ser. 537).
1849, H. Ex. Docs. 31st cong., 1st sess., no. 5, vol. iii. (Ser. 569).
1850, H. Ex. Docs. 31st cong., 2nd sess., no. 1, vol. i. (Ser. 595).
1851, H. Ex. Docs. 32nd cong., 1st sess., no. 2, vol. ii. (Ser. 635).
1852, H. Ex. Docs. 32nd cong., 2nd sess., no. 1, vol. i. (Ser. 674).
1853, H. Ex. Docs. 33d cong., 1st sess., no. 1, vol. i. (Ser. 712).
1854, S. Ex. Docs. 33d cong., 2nd sess., no. 1, vol. ii. (Ser. 747).
1855, S. Ex. Docs. 34th cong., 1st sess., no. 1, vol. iii. (Ser. 812).
1856, S. Ex. Docs. 34th cong., 3d sess., no. 5, vol. iii. (Ser. 876).
1857, S. Ex. Docs. 35th cong., 1st sess., no. 11, vol. iii. (Ser. 921).
1858, S. Ex. Docs. 35th cong., 2nd sess., no. 1, vol. iv. (Ser. 977).
1859, S. Ex. Docs. 36th cong., 1st sess., no. 2, vol. iii. (Ser. 1025).

Index

BIBLIOGRAPHY

1860, S. Ex. Docs. 36th cong., 2nd sess., no. 1, vol. iii (Ser. 1080).
1861, S. Ex. Docs. 37th cong., 1st sess., no. 1, vol. iii. (Ser. 1119).
1862, H. Ex. Docs. 37th cong., 3d sess., no. 1, vol. iv. (Ser. 1159).
1863, H. Ex. Docs. 38th cong., 1st sess., no. 1, vol. v. (Ser. 1184).
1864, H. Ex. Docs. 38th cong., 2nd sess., no. 1, vol. v. (Ser. 1220).
1865, H. Ex. Docs. 39th cong., 1st sess., no. 1, vol. vi. (Ser. 1254).
1866, H. Ex. Docs. 39th cong., 2nd sess., no. 1, vol. iv. (Ser. 1286).
1867, H. Ex. Docs. 40th cong., 1st sess., no. 1, vol. iv. (Ser. 1327).
1868, H. Ex. Docs. 40th cong., 3d sess., no. 1, vol. iv. (Ser. 1369).
1869, H. Ex. Docs. 41st cong., 2d sess., no. 1, vol. i. (Ser. 1411).

[VIRGINIA CITY, Nevada] Territorial Enterprise.

VISSCHER, W. L. Thrilling and truthful history of Pony Express (Chicago, 1908).

WAR of the Rebellion: Compilation of official records of Union and Confederate Armies. (Washington, 1880-1901), 70 vols. in 130.

WARE, E. F. Indian War of 1864 (Topeka, 1911).

WHITFORD, W. C. Colorado Volunteers in Civil War (Denver, 1906).

WHITNEY, O. F. History of Utah (Salt Lake City, 1892), 4 vols.
—— Popular History of Utah (Salt Lake City, 1916).

WILLIAMS, N. B. American Post Office in U. S. Senate. Executive Documents, 61st congress, second session, no. 542.

WILSON, J. G. and J. Fiske. Appletons' Cyclopaedia of American Biography (New York, 1887-9), 6 vols.

YOUNG, L. E. Founding of Utah (New York, 1924).

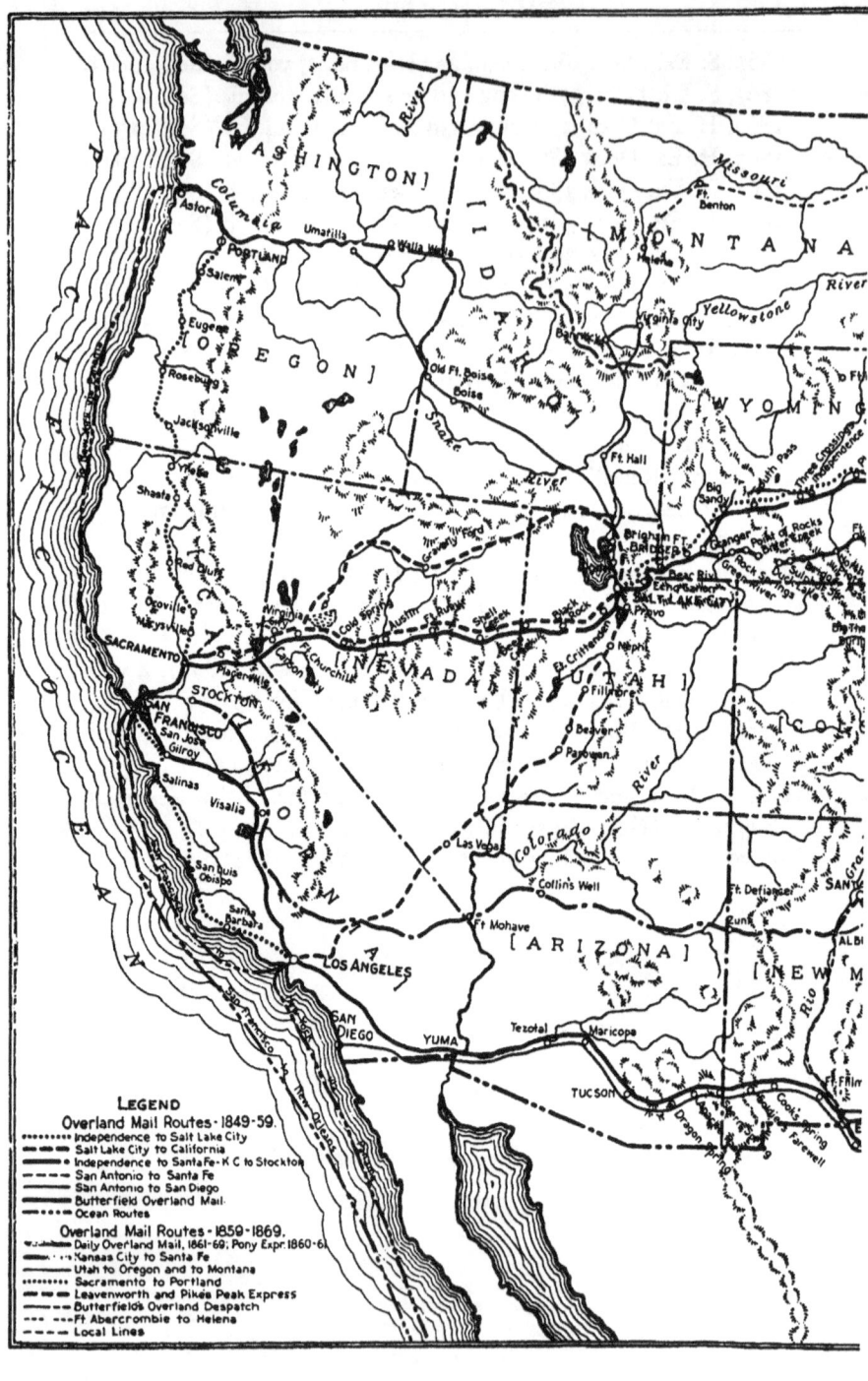

Index

ABBOTT-DOWNING Company: builder of Concord coaches, 306
Adams and Company: 68
Albright, G. L: *Official Explorations for Pacific Railroads*, 80 *footnote*, 335
Albuquerque: 88, 90, 115, 116, 117, 118, 141
Albuquerque mail route: 90 see *Neosho to Albuquerque route*
Alta California: cited in *footnotes* on following pages: 47, 93, 186, 187, 224, 225, 226, 227, 228, 237, 242, 245, 246, 247, 252, 261, 265, 266, 267, 273, 277, 281, 285, 287, 288, 312, 317, 318, 319, 320, 323, 325, 327, 338.
Alter, J. C: *James Bridger*, 221 *footnote*, 335
Alvord, E. S: 160
American Desert: 149
American Express Company: 286, 319 *footnote*
American Historical Review: 19 *footnote*, 20 *footnote*, 338
Anderson, James: 245
Anthony, Major: 253
Apaches: 98, 249
Arapahoes: 249, 254, 262
Arizona: 97, 323
Arkansas: 196
Arkansas River: Indian depredations along, 260
Arrowhead Trail: route of, 69
Articles of Confederation: provision regarding postal service and rates, 24
Ashley, General: 230 *footnote*

Aspinwall, W. H: 40
Atchison: coaches leave, 245, 259, 261, 284, 287, 300, 304, 317
Atchison Champion: 328

BABBITT, ALMOND W: 56
Bailey, G: 92, 95, 96
Baker, James: 221 *footnote*
Bancroft, H. H: *Chronicles of Builders of Commonwealth*, 45 *footnote*, 46 *footnote*, 54 *footnote*, 55 *footnote*, 335
Bancroft, H. H: *Early Records of Utah*, 335
Bancroft, H. H: *History of Arizona and New Mexico*, 335
Bancroft, H. H: *History of California*, 40 *footnote*, 41 *footnote*, 43 *footnote*, 45 *footnote*, 54 *footnote*, 335
Bancroft, H. H: *History of Nevada, Colorado and Wyoming*, 65 *footnote*, 166 *footnote*, 311 *footnote*, 335
Bancroft, H. H: *History of Utah*, 335
Bancroft, H. H: *Incidents of Utah History*, 335
Bancroft, H. H: *Utah Biographical Sketches*, 335
Bancroft, H. H: *Utah Jottings*, 335
Barnes, D: *From Atlantic to Pacific, Overland*, cited in *footnotes* on 265, 267, 312, 313, 335
Barney, D. N: 319
Barnum, Vickery, and Neal: contractors on mail to Santa Fe, 235
Barry, W. T: Postmaster-general, 26
Bayard, William: 55
Bayles, W: "Postal Service in Thir-

teen Colonies," 20 *footnote*, 24 *footnote*, 335
Beale, E. F: 74, 83, 116, 118
Benjamin, Senator: 199
Benson, Ezra: 56
Benton, Senator: 82, 83
Bent's Fort: 70, 237, 278
Berthoud, E. L: 220, 221, 222, 282
Berthoud Pass: discovery of, 221; 222, 223, 228, 229, 230, 231, 282, 284
Bieber, R. P: 231 *footnote*, 335
Birch, James E: 105
Birge, J. C: *Awakening of Desert*, 265 *footnote*, 310 *footnote*, 335
Bishop, Fred: 65
Black Hills: 59, 231; of Dakota, 322
Black Kettle: Indian chief, 261
Blair, Postmaster-general: 289, 296
Blanchard, W. L: 65
Bliss, Edward: 235
Boardman, T. S: 245
Boise (Idaho) : mail to, 280
Bolton, H. E: 16, 26
Bonsal, Stephen: *Edward Fitzgerald Beale*, 335
Bowen, Eli: *United States Post Office Guide*, 335
Bowler, T. F: 75 *footnote*, 117
Bowles, Samuel: *Across the Continent*, 335
Bradley, G: *Story of Pony Express*, cited 170 *footnote*, 178 *footnote*, 179 *footnote*, 190 *footnote*, 335
Bretz, J. P: "Some Aspects of Postal Extension into West," 27 *footnote*, 28 *footnote*, 335
Bridge, Thomas: 159
Bridger, James: 220, 221, 222, 230 *footnote*
Bridger's Pass: trail through, 219, 231, 248, 268, 274 *footnote*; Indian depredations at, 320
Brisbin, J. S: *Belden, White Chief*, 336
Britton, John: 117
Broderick, Senator: 123, 196 *footnote*
Brown, James: 245

Brown, Postmaster-general: 89; selection of southern route for overland mail, 90; liberal to West, 103; biographical sketch of, 103 *footnote*; 104, 108, 113, 115, 119, 121, 122; death of, 134
Brown, Senator: 133
Bruce, E. F: 159, 160
Buchanan, President: 123 *footnote*; message by overland mail, 124, 125, 126; relations of Gwin to, 205; 339
Buffalo Bill's Life Story: 176 *footnote*, 178 *footnote*, 179 *footnote*
Buffaloes: slaughtered, 241
Burgess, Joseph: 281 *footnote*
Burton, R. T: 247
Butterfield, D. A: 282, 284
Butterfield, John: and other contractors, 90; letter to President Buchanan, 95; 125
Butterfield's Overland Despatch: organized, 283; service of, 284, 285, 286; bought by Holladay, 296, 317
Butterfield Overland Mail Route: bids, 88; contract for service on, 90; defense of, 91; criticism of, 92; length and character, 92, 93; first coaches upon, 94; arrival at San Francisco, 95; distances upon, 96; service upon, 96; gains in favor, 98; schedule maintained upon, 99; 121, 122, 124, 125, 126, 132, 135, 161, 166, 186, 189, 195, 199, 200, 207, 208 *footnote*, 209, 210, 212, 213, 214, 217; reëstablished, 323
Byers, W. N: 153, 230
Byram, A: 283

CALIFORNIA: mail service under Mexican rule, 54; first overland mail from, 54; post offices established in, 55, 106; favors mail service, 113; praise Postmaster-general Brown, 121, 130, 173; bid for support of,

INDEX 349

199, 204; troops from, 223; legislature favors overland mail, 226, 261, 274, 277; volunteers of, 282, 285, 287, 295; stage fare to, 312, 323
California Stage Company: 208, 277, 278
California Star: 53, 186 *footnote*, 338
California to Salt Lake City Mail: first established, 63; Humboldt River route, 64, 66; Mormon trail route, 64, 66, 69; method of carriage, 67, 68; extra mail, 67, 109. See *Central mail route*
California Volunteers: 247, 249
Camel expedition: 116
Campbell, A. H: 91
Campbell, Postmaster-general: 44, 103 *footnote*
Cantinas (letter bags): 180
Card, B. C: 157
Carmick and Ramsey: 44, 339
Carson, Kit: 54
Carson valley (Nevada): mail to, 64, 65
Carvalho, S. N: *Incidents of Travel*: 68 *footnote*, 336
Case, F. M: 230
Cass, Senator: 79
Central mail route, via Salt Lake City: mail contracts on, 109, 110; route, 111; new route west of Salt Lake City, 112; service on, commended, 113; winter conditions on, 114; 121, 122, 123, 125, 126, 132, 135, 151, 156, 166, 169, 185, 189, 196, 197, 199, 204, 205, 207, 208 *footnote*, 209, 210, 211; law for daily mail on, 212; winter service on, 226
Central Overland California and Pike's Peak Express Company: chartered by Kansas, 156; operates through to California, 157, 159, 160, 188, 211, 218, 219, 223 *footnote*; in hands of receiver, 227, 228, 281

Central Pacific railroad: 323, 325
Channing, E: *History of United States*, 20 *footnote*, 336
Cheap postage: in England, 29; agitation for in United States, 30; act of 1851, 31
Cherokee Trail: 219, 221, 223, 230; mail upon, 231, 248, 268, 269, 281
Cheyenne: railroad reaches, 322, 323, 325
Cheyenne Indians: 249, 254, 255, 256, 261, 262, 263
Chittenden, H. M: *History of American Fur Trade of Far West*, 71 *footnote*, 336
Chivington, Colonel: 262, 266
Chorpenning, George: 63, 64, 65, 66; act for relief of, 67; 110, 111, 112, 113, 114, 156, 197
Chorpenning, George: *Statement of Claim of*, cited in *footnotes* on 63, 64, 65, 66, 67, 69, 110, 114, 157, 336
Chronicles of Oklahoma: 230 *footnote*
Civil War: not responsible for establishment of overland mail, 213; 217, 224, 246, 247, 267
Clear Creek and Hot Sulphur Springs Wagon Road Company: 281
Cleland, R. G: *History of California, American Period*, 336
Clemens, S. L: see *Mark Twain*
Cody, W. F: *Autobiography of Buffalo Bill*, 336
Colfax, Congressman: 139, 155, 158, 198, 203, 287
Collamer, Senator: 129
Collins, W. O: 265
Colonial postal service: by trading vessels, 19; beginnings of, 19; expense and revenue of, 20; taken over by British Government, 21; produces surplus, 21
Colorado: pioneer newspaper of, 146; influence of mail company in, 151; slow in getting U. S. mail, 155; pioneers of, want daily mail, 218, 229; legislature charters Holla-

day's stage line, 232, 236; troops of, 246; Indian troubles in, 248, 249, 254, 255, 258, 260, 266, 267; legislature grants charter to Holladay, 282; 285, 319
Colorado and Pacific Wagon, Telegraph and Railroad Company: 229
Colorado River: goods shipped on, 106, 117, 281
Colorado *Session Laws*: 229, 232 *footnote*
Colorado State Historical and Natural History Society: 154 *footnote*, 155 *footnote*, 227 *footnote*, 268 *footnote*, 336, 337
Colorado troops: 246, 252, 253, 254, 255, 256, 259
Coman, K: *Economic Beginnings of Far West*, 336
Comanche Indians: 98, 253, 255
Compton, Allen: 57
Conductor (or messenger): 300, 301
Conestoga wagons: 22, 53
Confederate States: mail service in, 288, 289, 290, 291, 292; self-supporting, 291
Connelley's *Doniphan Expedition*: 165 *footnote*, 278 *footnote*
Connor, Colonel: 247, 249, 252, 253 *footnote*
Constitution of Confederate States of America: 290
Cook, George E: 318
Cooke, P. St. George: *Conquest of New Mexico and California*, 336
Corbin, A. R: 125, 126
Cottrell, Vickroy and Company: 237
Coy, O. C: "Pony Express antedated," 336
Craig, General: 242, 247
Crittenden, Senator: 85
Crowninshield, Walter: 166 *footnote*
Curtis, General: 259, 262
Cushing, M. H: *Story of our Post Office*, 336

DAILY OVERLAND MAIL: 185; resolution for, 197; Greeley for, 197; bill for, 198; Hale Bill, 200, 203; Holt against, 208, 209; law providing for, 211; terms, 212; route not designated, 217; route considered, 219, 221; first coach of, 223; Confederate interference, 224; winter service, 225; new route, 231; interrupted by Indian outbreak, 259, 264; service in 1863, 273; list of stations on, 275 *footnote*; contract of 1864, 276; service in 1865, 287, 288; two lines to Denver, 318; in 1867, 322, 324; in 1868, 327
Dale, H. C: *Ashley-Smith Explorations*, cited, 69 *footnote*, 336
Davis, Jefferson: 290, 291, 292
Davis, J. P: *Union Pacific Railway*, 79 *footnote*, 336
Davis, W. W. H: 71, 72, 74 *footnote*
Davis, W. W. H: *El Gringo*, 336
Dawson, T. F: *Scrap-books*, 336
Dellenbaugh, F. S: *Fremont and '49*, 336
Democratic Party: 139, 199
Denver: gold discovered at site of, 145, 146; express agent at, 147; mail at, 148; express road to, 149; many passengers to, 152; town company of, 152; first U. S. mail to, 155, 156; mail lines radiating from, 158, 159; 160, 197, 207, 212, 217, 218, 219, 222, 229, 232, 236, 237, 252; troops from, to fight Indians, 256, 257, 260, 261, 263, 264, 265, 266, 267, 269, 277, 281; reception of Overland Despatch, 284; 285, 286, 287, 296, 300, 304, 312, 314, 317, 318, 321
Denver Commonwealth: 251 *footnote*, 252 *footnote*, 253 *footnote*, 255 *footnote*, 256 *footnote*, 279 *footnote*, 336
Denver to Santa Fe Mail: 237, 253, 260

INDEX 351

Deseret News: 60, 61 *footnote*, 249 *footnote*, 336
Dinsmore, William B: 276
Division agent: 300
Division superintendent of Overland mail line: 300
Dodge, General: 266, 267
Doniphan, John: 277 *footnote*
Doty, Governor: 252
Douglas, Senator: 80, 103 *footnote*, 211
Drumm, Stella M: 81 *footnote*
Dunbar, S: *History of Travel in America*, 22 *footnote*, 23 *footnote*, 97 *footnote*, 105 *footnote*, 108 *footnote*, 336

EATON, Major: 283 *footnote*
Eagan, Howard: 66 *footnote*, 112, 196 *footnote*, 251
Eagan, Howard R: 177 *footnote*, 196 *footnote*, 250 *footnote*, 251 *footnote*
Eagan Trail: Salt Lake to Sacramento, 112
Eagan, W. M: *Pioneering the West*, 112 *footnote*, 177 *footnote*, 178 *footnote*, 197 *footnote*, 250 *footnote*, 251 *footnote*, 252 *footnote*
Elbert, Acting Governor of Colorado: 264
Eleventh Ohio: guard mail line, 253
El Paso: mail from, 74; 81, 89, 90, 93, 105, 111, 113, 122, 195, 199, 200, 207
Emory, Captain: 221
Eubanks, Mrs: captured by Indians, 258
Evans, Captain: 230 *footnote*
Evans, Governor: 228, 230, 248, 254, 255, 256, 258, 259, 260, 262, 264
Evans, Governor: *Interview* with, 255 *footnote*, 256 *footnote*, 260 *footnote*
Express service: authorized by Congress, 27; private, 28, 29, 53, 54, 55 *footnote*, 56, 61, 68; private rates, 146, 155, 156; 158, 159, 160; rates, 160; military, 237; in Confederate States, 289

FAIRBANKS'S Tavern: 19
Fargo, William G: 319
Fetterman, Captain: killed by Indians, 318
Ficklin, B. F: 157, 165 *footnote*, 170
Finlay, Hugh: 23
Finney, W. W: 170, 182
Fitch, Lieutenant: 283 *footnote*
Flowers, Lem: 245
Force, Peter: *American Archives*, 24 *footnote*
Foreman, Grant: 70 *footnote*, 230 *footnote*
Fort Abercrombie: post route from, 324
Fort Abercrombie to Helena Mail: 324
Fort Belknap: 93
Fort Bridger: 58, 175, 219, 231, 242, 246; peace treaty at, 252; pony express from, 279; 325
Fort Chadbourne: 93
Fort Churchill: 171, 175, 182, 185, 186 *footnote*
Fort Collins: 269
Fort Garland: military express to, 237, 253
Fort Hall: 280
Fort Halleck: 248, 252, 253, 268, 269
Fort Kearny: 160, 175, 182, 185, 186 *footnote*, 207, 224, 247, 258, 259, 274 *footnote*, 296, 312, 318
Fort Laramie: 58, 60, post office at, 145; 175, 247, 248, 253, 259, 268, 320
Fort Larned: 235, 253, 256, 257, 259, 278
Fort Lyon (Fort Wise): 235, 236, 253, 259, 278, 284
Fort Miller: 116
Fort Mohave: 116
Fort Morgan (Colorado): 232, 257
Fort Philip Kearny: 318, 320
Fort Riley: 148, 283

Fort Sedgwick (Fort Rankin): 262, 263, 265
Fort Smith (Arkansas): 93, 200
Fort Tejon: 116
Fort Union: 72, 278
Fort Yuma: 81, 89, 105, 108, 111, 207
Fox, J. M: 148
Franking privilege: 132, 133, 202
Franklin, B: deputy Postmaster-general, 21; *Autobiography*, 22 footnote, 23 footnote, 24
Freighting: 54, 68, 147; interrupted by Indian difficulties, 257; 326
Fremont, J. C: 66 footnote, 82, 83

GADSDEN Treaty: mail transportation rights under, 44
Galvanized Yankees: 267
Gerry, Elbridge: 254, 255, 260
Giddings, George H: 74, 108 footnote
Gila River: 93, 106
Gilpin, William: 82, 220
Goodell, Tim: 221
Goodwin, Cardinal: *The Trans-mississippi West*, 336
Goose Creek Mountains: mail difficulties in, 64, 66
Grant, J. M: 54
Grant, W. S: 157
Greeley, Horace: 47, 147, 149, 150, 197
Greeley, Horace: *An Overland Journey* cited, 147 footnote, 149 footnote, 150 footnote, 336
Green River: proposal to bridge, 219, 220, 222, 231, 268, 320
Green, R. F: 117
Green, Senator: 203
Gregg, Josiah: *Commerce of Prairies*, 336
Gregory, John H: 158 footnote
Grinnell, G. B: *Fighting Cheyennes*, 256 footnote, 258 footnote, 261 footnote, 262 footnote, 263 footnote, 265 footnote, 336
Grow, Congressman: 133

Gunnison, Captain: 83
Gwin, Senator: 79, 86, 110 footnote, 122, 123, 131, 140, 165 footnote, 166 footnote, 169, 188, 199, 202, 203, 204, 205, 209, 210, 211, 213 footnote
Gwin, W. H: *Memoirs*, 337

HALE BILL: proposed, 200; provisions, 200; debated, 201, 202, 204, 206 footnote, 213
Hale, Senator: 200, 202, 204, 209, 211
Hall, Frank: *History of State of Colorado*, 337
Hall, Jacob: 73, 115, 118
Halleck, General: 242, 248
Hamilton, Andrew: 20, 21
Hamilton, John: 21
Hamilton, Sam: 171
Hamilton, Surgeon: 263 footnote
Hanks: assistant to Little, 58, 62
Harness: make and cost of, 312
Harper, Hank: 250
Harris, Arnold: 39
Harrison, Benjamin: *This Country of Ours*, 337
Haslam, R. H. (Pony Bob): 172
Hauck, Louise Platt: "The Pony Express Celebration," 172 footnote
Hayes *Collection*: 61 footnote, 68 footnote, 98 footnote, 179 footnote, 225 footnote, 337
Hays, Colonel: 182
Haywood, mail contractor: 70
Head, Colonel: 250
Heap, G. H: *Central Route to Pacific*, 337
Hebard and Brininstool: *Bozeman Trail*, 269 footnote, 337
Heistand, J. A: 275
Helena (Montana): post route to, 324
Heywood, J. L: 56
Hinckley's Express: 160
History of Buchanan County and St. Joseph, Missouri: 179, 180 footnote
Hockaday and Liggett: 150, 151, 340

INDEX

Hockaday, John M: 109, 110 *footnote*, 114, 125, 150

Hodder, F. H: 80 *footnote*

Hodder, F. H: "Railroad Background of Kansas-Nebraska Act," 337

Holladay, Ben: 66 *footnote*, 227, 232, 260, 265, 276, 279, 280, 281, 282, 285, 286; sketch of, 295, 296; description of 299, 310, 317; sells mail line, 319, 340

Holt, Postmaster-general: appointed, 134; retrenchment by, 135; views presented, 136; 139, 140, 150, 157 *footnote*, 202, 206, 208, 213

Hostlers: 303

Hough, Emerson: *Passing of Frontier*, 337

Howbert, I: *Memories of Lifetime in Pike's Peak Region*, 256 *footnote*, 260 *footnote*, 262 *footnote*, 336

Hughes, Bela M: 218, 220, 221, 227 *footnote*, 235 *footnote*, 281, 282, 296

Hughes, B. M: *Letter to John Doniphan*, 337

Hulbert, A. B: *Crown Collection of American Maps*, 231 *footnote*, 337

Humboldt River (Nevada): mail route by, 64, 89, 111; railroad follows, 325

Hungate family: murdered by Indians, 256

Hunter, Senator: 133, 289

Hunter, W: 21

Hutton, N. H: 107 *footnote*

IDAHO: battle with Indians in, 249; gold discoveries in, 279; 280, 296, 319, 324

Independence (Missouri): 109, 110, 121, 135

Independence to Salt Lake City mail: private service by Mormons, 56; first government contract for, 57; experiences in conduct of, 58; complaints about service, 59; Kimball contract for, 62; interrupted by Utah War, 62, 109. See *Central mail route*

Independence to Santa Fe Mail: early service, 70; route, 71, 72; equipment for, 72; contract of 1854, 73

Indian troubles: 60, 64, 67, 68 *footnote*, 73, 74, 97, 98, 108, 116, 117, 118, 176, 177; Washoe Indian War, 181; 182, 224, 228, 230, 236, 237, 241, 242, 245, 246, 247, 248, 249, 250, 251, 252, 253, 254, 255, 256, 257, 258, 259, 260, 261, 262, 263, 264, 265, 266, 267, 268, 269, 280, 284; on Powder River, 318; of 1867, 320; policy toward, 321; peace commission, 322, 324

Inman, Henry: *Great Salt Lake Trail*, 337

Inman, Henry: *Old Santa Fe Trail*, 71 *footnote*, 236 *footnote*, 278 *footnote*, 337

JEFFERSON TERRITORY: 155, 160, 218 *footnote*

Johns, Colonel: 282

Johnson, Senator: 85

Jones, James H: 110 *footnote*

Jones, John S: 146, 150, 157, 219

Journal of American History: 20 *footnote*, 22 *footnote*, 335

Journals of Continental Congress: 23 *footnote*

Julesburg: 158, 159, 175, 223, 253, 257; sacked by Indians, 262, 263, 264; Indians burn, 265, 266, 268, 320

KANSAS: Pony Express station in, 172; 256

Kansas City: mail route from, 115; 121, 135, 141, 235, 278

Kansas City to Santa Fe Mail: 235, 237, 278, 322

Kansas City to Stockton route: postal feature secondary, 115; service and schedule on, 115; route de-

scribed, 116; first trip on, 117; 121, 135, 141
Keetley, J. H: 179 *footnote*
Kelly, Jay G: 172, 176 *footnote*
Kimball, Everett: *National Government of United States*, 337
Kimball, Hiram: 61
Kiowas: 253
Kuykendall, R. S: *History of Early California Journalism*, 45 *footnote*, 47 *footnote*, 337

LANE, Senator: 203
Laramie (Wyoming): 235
Larimer, William: 152
Larimer, W. H. H: 146, 156; *Reminiscences* cited, 145 *footnote*, 149 *footnote*, 152 *footnote*, 153 *footnote*, 156 *footnote*, 337
Las Vegas (Nevada): 69, 225
Latham, Senator: 99 *footnote*, 188, 199, 209, 211, 223
Law, George: 39
Leavenworth, Colonel: 248
Leavenworth: freighting equipment at, 147, 222; votes aid to Overland Despatch, 283
Leavenworth and Pike's Peak Express: inaugurated, 146; route of, 148, 149; route changed, 150; purchase Hockaday and Liggett line, 151; influence in Denver, 152; equipment and service, 153, 156
Leavenworth *Conservative*: 222 *footnote*
Leavenworth *Times*: 157
Leavenworth *Tribune*: 149
Lee, General: 292
Leech, Piper, and Montgomery (contractors): 324 *footnote*
Lewis, E. N: 269
Lincoln Highway: 231
Lincoln, President: 247, 250, 255, 296
Little, Feramorz: 58, 59, 62; *Mail Service across Plains*: footnotes on 57, 58, 59, 60, 62, 337

Little Rock *Gazette*: 70 *footnote*, 337
Livingston, John: 319
Los Angeles: mail in winter via, 65, 68, 93; mail station at, 97, 109, 113, 186, 217; mail service to, 279, 323
Los Angeles *Republican*: 323 *footnote*
Los Angeles *Southern Vineyard*: 337
Los Angeles *Star*: 225
Louisiana Tehuantepec Company: contract with, 119, 120
Lovelace, Governor: of New York, 20

McDONALD, William: *Select Documents*, 337
McDougall, Representative: 165 *footnote*
McIlvaine, Bowers: 39
McLane, Allan: 228 *footnote*
McLane, Louis: 287, 319
McMaster, J. B: *History of People of United States*, 31 *footnote*, 338
Magraw, W. M. F: 60, 61, 62
Mail contracts: compensation increased, 60; extra allowance by Congress, 138
Mail line increases: 103
Mail pouches: number of, 314
Mail steamer: arrival and departure of, 45. See *Ocean mail*
Majors, Alexander: 146, 151, 157, 190; *Seventy Years on Frontier* cited in *footnotes* on 147, 151, 169, 170, 172, 176, 178, 179, 190, 338
Marcy, Captain: 221 *footnote*
Mark Twain: describes passing of Pony Express, 178; *Roughing It* cited in *footnotes* on 179, 299, 300, 304, 305, 309
Maury, M. F: 56
Maynard, Congressman: 130
Memphis: 88; passenger fare from, 97; 111, 195, 200, 211
Mercereau's stage-wagon: 22
Messenger coach: 309
Miles, S. B: 63, 109
Mississippi Valley Historical Review: 80 *footnote*, 230 *footnote*, 335, 337

INDEX 355

Missouri: favors Postmaster-general Brown, 121; 150, 173, 196
Missouri and California Overland Mail and Transportation Company: 81
Missouri Commonwealth: 70
Mitchell, General: 255, 257
Mohave Indians: 116, 117
Montana: mail line to, 279; 280, 296, 319, 324
Moonlight, Colonel: 266
Moore's *Rebellion Record*: 289 footnote, 290 footnote, 338
Morehead: on origin of Pony Express, 165 footnote, 278
Mormons: 53, 56, 61, 62, 63, 66 footnote, 68, 175, 295
Mormon Trail to Los Angeles: mail upon, 64, 65
Mott, G. N: 250
Mud-wagon: 309, 310
Murphy, Captain: 266

NAVAJO: 250
Neale, Thomas: 20, 21
Neosho to Albuquerque mail: established, 117; service and difficulties, 118, 141
Nettels, Curtis: "The Overland Mail Issue during Fifties," 83 footnote, 92 footnote
Nevada: mines of, 277, 311; stage fare to, 312, 319; railroad built across, 325
New Granada Government: transported U. S. Mail across Isthmus of Panama, 42
New Mexico: 56, 71, 97, 236; Confederate army in, 246, 248, 256
New Orleans: mail from, 119; 120, 121, 199, 200, 208
New York *Tribune*: 274
Nicaragua route: 43
Nicolay, J: 255
Niles, Senator: 37

OCEAN Mail: to Oregon provided for, 38; first to and from California, 41; to California made semi-monthly, 42; arrival and departure, 45; amount of, 46; time in transit, 47; complaints about, 48; denounced in Congress, 86; compensation limited, 201, 202, 203; temporary contract for, 206; 210, 212, 228, 276
Ogden (Utah): 280
Oliver and Company's Express: 279, 280
Omaha: mail service from, established, 224; 258, 266, 296
Oregon: 208; mail to, 38, 278; steamship lines to, 296
Oregon Trail: 57, 145, 280
Ormsby, W. L: 93, 95
Osgood, Samuel: first Postmaster-general, 26
Ouray, Ute chief: 255
Overland Mail: pioneering agency, 86; promoter of union, 87
Overland Mail bill: introduced in Congress in 1856, 83; considered in Congress, 84; debated in Senate, 85; enacted, 87; defeated in Congress in 1860, 204
Overland Mail Company: 276, 279; in hands of Wells Fargo and Company, 286; merged with Wells Fargo, 319
Overland mail routes: receipts and expenditures upon, 134, 135; Holt against, 137; curtailed, 138
Overland route: advocated, 53
Overland Stage Line (Holladay's): chartered, 232, 248, 284, 285

PACIFIC MAIL STEAMSHIP COMPANY: incorporated, 40; first steamer to California, 41, 44; overcrowding steamers, 47; 48, 228
Pacific railroad: 79; surveys for, 80; 83; mail as precursor of, 91, 107, 108; 35th parallel recommended

for, 118; 123, 196; convention for at San Francisco, 197; bill for, 229; 317, 322, 325, 326
Pacific Stage and Express Company: 277
Pack, Mary: *Romance of Pony Express*, 178 footnote
Packhorses: 16, 23; used in winter, 109
Pamphlets of California Commerce: 319 footnote
Panama, Isthmus of: mail across, 42
Panama Railroad Company: mail contract with, 42, 48; denounced, 86
Parrish, R: *Great Plains*, 338
Passenger fare by stage: 54; Independence to Santa Fe, 73; on Butterfield Overland, 97; San Antonio to San Diego, 108; to Denver, 153, 160; 280, 312
Passengers by stage: conditions of travel, 97; cost of meals of, 98; equipment for, 98; 119, 120, 151, 153, 227, 245, 266, 277, 278; meals for, 304, 312; cost of meals for, 312, 313
Paxson, F. L: *Last American Frontier*, cited in footnotes on 299, 317, 318, 320, 322, 323, 325, 338; *History of American Frontier*, 338
Pearce, Senator: 140
Pence, G. W: 245
Phelps, John S: 118
Pierce, George: 65
Pioneer Stage Company: 277, 311, 319 footnote
Placerville (California): mail from, 65; 110, 111, 112, 113, 121, 135, 156, 161, 170; Pony Express at, 171; 175, 199, 204, 207, 212, 276 footnote, 300, 311, 312
Platte River: tributaries of, 148, 150; mail stations along, 153; 175, 218, 231; Indian depredations along, 254, 256; flood in, 280
Polk, President: 37

Pony Express: 161; purpose and origin of, 165, 166; Gwin to get government aid for, 169; preparations for, 170; first trip, 171; reception of first, 173; time made, 174; route, 175; stations, horses, riders, 176; rides and dress of riders, 179; letters and letter bags, 180; interrupted in Nevada, 182; made semiweekly, 182; best time made, 182; winter schedule and service, 185; time made in summer, 187; effort to subsidize, 188; aided by government, 189; rates on letters, 189; financially a failure, 190; value of, 190; 205; provided for by law, 212; 219, 223; private, 236, 279
Pope, General: 267
Portland (Oregon): 208, 278
Postage stamps: adopted by U. S. government, 30
Postal policy: liberal toward West, 27, 103, 104; mail as developer of country, 115; Holt for economy, 134; retrenchment, 135, 136, 137; for and against retrenchment, 139, 140, 141, 208; overland service charged to general treasury, 210; 329
Postal rates: to raise revenue, 21; low, 27; high, 28; increased as a war measure, 29; agitation for reduction, 29; to Pacific Coast, 30, 46; on newspapers, 31 footnote; in California, 55; increase proposed, 132; 133, 155, 156; on Pony Express letters, 180; 202; ten cent rate to Pacific Coast, 210; of 1863, 273 footnote
Postal reform: 132, 135, 136, 137, 139, 140, 141
Postal service: political agency, 15, 26; liberal policy toward, 16; extensive increases in routes and service, 121; as a pioneering agency, 129, 130; retrenchment, 131; policy

of Holt toward, 134; retrenchment, 135; reduced, 138
Postmaster-general of England: 21
Postmaster-general's report: of 1847, 38 *footnote*; of 1850 and 1856, 42 *footnote*, 43 *footnote*; of 1859, 46 *footnote*; of 1857, 89 *footnote*, 90 *footnote*, 91 *footnote*; of 1858, 93 *footnote*, 96 *footnote*, 113 *footnote*, 115 *footnote*, 119 *footnote*; of 1859, 117 *footnote*, 121, 134 *footnote*, 136 *footnote*, 137 *footnote*, 138 *footnote*; of 1860, 207 *footnote*, 208; of 1861, 214, 224 *footnote*; of 1862, 238; of 1863, 273 *footnote*, 275 *footnote*; of 1864, 276 *footnote*, 279 *footnote*; of 1865, 279, 287; of 1867, 280, 320; of 1866, 317, 322, 323 *footnote*; 324 *footnote*; 326 *footnote*, 340
Post Office Appropriation bill: of 1857 becomes law, 87; provisions of, 87, 88; 132, 133, 134, 138
Post Office Department: self-supporting at first, 28; growth of, to 1850, 32; should be self-supporting, 85, 129; should not be self-supporting, 130; embarrassed by failure of appropriations, 134; interference by Congress decried, 139; condition improving, 208
Post riders: 22
Post road: proposed from Fort Smith, Arkansas, to San Diego, California, 55
Post Route bill: of 1847, 38; passed without consideration, 104
Powder River: Indians leave for, 265; Indian disturbances on, 318
Powell, Major: 320
Prairie schooner: 53
Pritchard, Major: 283
Provo (Utah): 69, 222, 223
Pueblo (Colorado): 237

RAILROAD: see *Pacific railroad*
Reagan, J. H: 290

Red Cloud, Indian chief: 320
Reed, William: 245
Rees, James: *Footprints of letter carrier*, 338
Repair shops: 304
Republican Party: 139, 199, 204, 206 *footnote*
Republican River: mail route along, 148, 150; Indians leave for, 248; 254, 263
Rhodes, J. F: *History of United States since Compromise of 1850*, 31 *footnote*, 139 *footnote*, 338
Rice, Senator: 132, 199
Rich, W. E: *History of U. S. Post Office to Year 1829*, 20 *footnote*, 27 *footnote*
Richardson, A. D: *Beyond the Mississippi*, 338
Richardson, A. G: 278
Richardson, Billy: 172
Richardson, H: 172
Richardson, J. D: *Compilation of Messages and Papers of Presidents*, 27 *footnote*, 338; *Messages and Papers of Confederacy*, 290 *footnote*, 291 *footnote*, 338
Riley, William: 251 *footnote*
Rivalry among overland mail routes: 124, 125
Roberts, Marshall: 39
Rocky Mountains: emigration to, 147; gold fields of, 150; 202; route over, 229
Rocky Mountain News: cited in *footnotes* on following pages: 146, 148, 151, 153, 154, 155, 156, 157, 158, 159, 160, 161, 166, 169, 197, 218, 219, 220, 221, 222, 223, 228, 229, 230, 231, 232, 235, 236, 237, 242, 247, 248, 249, 250, 254, 256, 257, 258, 259, 260, 261, 262, 263, 264, 265, 266, 267, 268, 269, 280, 281, 282, 283, 284, 285
Roff, Harry: 171
Rogers, Phil: 245
Root and Connelley: *Overland Stage*

to *California*, cited in *footnotes* on 95, 147, 150, 161, 175, 178, 181, 182, 190, 261, 268, 280, 286, 288, 296, 300, 301, 304, 306, 309, 310, 312, 313, 314, 319, 326, 329, 338
Root, Frank: 149, 181, 261, 267 *footnote*, 285, 301, 306, 310, 313
Roper, Daniel C: *United States Post Office*, 20 *footnote*, 21 *footnote*, 25 *footnote*, 31 *footnote*, 338
Roper, Miss: captured by Indians, 258
Roundy, S: 54
Rupe, Captain: 165 *footnote*
Rusk, Senator: 60, 84, 86
Rusling, General: 280, 296, 302, 309, 310; *Across America*, 280 *footnote*, 296 *footnote*, 299 *footnote*, 300 *footnote*, 302 *footnote*, 309 *footnote*, 310 *footnote*, 311 *footnote*, 312 *footnote*, 313 *footnote*, 338
Russell, Majors and Waddell: 147, 165 *footnote*, 166 *footnote*, 169, 189, 205, 295
Russell, Robert R: 80 *footnote*
Russell, W. Green: 145, 283 *footnote*
Russell, W. H: 146, 147, 150, 152, 157, 162, 165 *footnote*, 166, 169, 170, 185, 218, 220, 221, 222, 281
Ryus, W. H: 235

SACRAMENTO: mail route from, 66; 85, 112; reception of Pony Express at, 173, 174, 175, 208, 286, 295, 314, 323
Sacramento *Placer Times*: 46
Sacramento *Union*: 80, 81 *footnote*, 89 *footnote*, 92, 106 *footnote*, 112, 113, 124, 338
St. Joseph: 112, 113, 125, 126, 160, 161, 170; Pony Express launched at, 172; 174, 179, 185, 186, 199, 204, 223, 267, 323
St. Joseph *Catholic Tribune*: 295 *footnote*
St. Joseph *Daily News*: 338
St. Louis: 88; route from, 92; 94, 95;

passenger fare from, 97; 111, 121, 124, 125, 195, 198, 200, 211
St. Louis *Republican*: 122
St. Paul to Puget Sound route: proposed, 131; 132, 200
Salt Lake Carrying Company: 54
Salt Lake City: first mail to, 56; 60, 62; mail from California reaches, 64; 65, 68, 70, 85, 89, 90, 109; service west of, 110; 111, 112, 113, 121, 122, 135, 150, 156, 170; Pony Express to, 172; 174, 175, 182, 199, 207, 212, 217, 218, 220, 222, 225, 229, 232, 248, 249, 250, 251, 261, 275 *footnote*, 276, 279, 280, 281, 282, 284, 285, 286, 287, 288, 295, 296, 300, 304, 312, 314, 324, 325, 327
Salt Lake City to California Mail: see *California to Salt Lake City mail*
San Antonio to San Diego mail: route established, 105; route described, 105, 106; supplies for, 106; developing the country, 107; passengers and equipment, 108; schedule changed, 108; 109, 121, 122, 135, 207
San Antonio: mail from, 74; 105, 121, 135, 199, 200, 207, 217
San Antonio to Santa Fé mail: schedule and service, 74; service improved, 75
San Bernardino: Mormon colony at, 69
Sanborn, General: 269
Sand Creek (Battle or massacre of): 262, 263
San Diego: 105, 108, 121, 122, 125, 207
Sanford, A. B: *Story of Bob Spotswood's Life*, 268 *footnote*, 338
Sanford, W. T. B: 69 *footnote*
San Francisco: reception of ocean mail at, 45; 70, 83; route to, 92; 93, 94; fare to, 97; 108, 111, 119, 120, 121, 124, 170; Pony Express from, 171; 173, 174, 175, 182, 185,

INDEX

186, 195; railroad convention at, 197; 208, 211, 212, 223, 237, 260, 261; newspapers of, defend overland mail, 274; 279, 314

San Francisco *Bulletin*: cited in footnotes on following pages: 43, 48, 68, 81, 93, 94, 96, 97, 98, 99, 106, 109, 110, 111, 112, 114, 115, 116, 117, 118, 119, 120, 121, 123, 124, 125, 126, 150, 161, 166, 169, 170, 171, 173, 174, 180, 181, 182, 185, 186, 187, 188, 189, 190, 196, 197, 198, 204, 205, 206, 224, 251, 253, 274, 275, 277, 278, 279, 289, 338

San Francisco *Herald*: 124, 338

Santa Fé: mail to, 70; 72, 115, 116, 117, 225, 235, 236, 237, 278, 284, 295, 322

Santa Fé to Independence Mail: see *Independence to Santa Fé mail*

Santa Fé to San Antonio mail: see *San Antonio to Santa Fé mail*

Santa Fé Trail: 71, 116, 145; wagons first employed on, 235, 278

Saunders, Jim: 145, 146

Seward, Senator: 130

Sherman, General: 318, 323

Sherman, Representative: 203

Shinn, C. H: *Story of Mine*, 65 footnote, 338

Sibley, General: 246

Sierra Nevada Mountains: crossed regularly in winter, 113; Pony Express crosses, 171, 175

Silver Age (Carson City, Nevada): 245

Simpson, J. H: *Report of Explorations across Great Basin*, 338

Simpson, J. S: 157

Simpson, W. R: 251

Sioux: 254, 255, 262, 320

Sleighs: for carriage of mail, 227, 325

Sloo, A. G: contract with for ocean mail service, 39

Smiley, J. C: *History of Colorado*, 254 footnote, 256 footnote, 338

Smith, Jedediah: 66 *footnote*, 69 *footnote*

Smith, Judge: 153

Smith, M. G: 159

Smith, William: "Colonial Post Office," 19 *footnote*, 20 *footnote*, 21 *footnote*, 23 *footnote*, 338

Smith, W. A: 231 *footnote*

Smoky Hill route: 283, 285 *footnote*, 296, 317

Sopris, S. T: 154, 339

South Pass: 60, 81, 89, 110, 175, 218, 223, 248, 249

Southern Pacific Railroad: 323

Southern Vineyard: 117 *footnote*

Spaids, Carlton: 326

Spotswood, Bob: 268

Stage-coaches: earliest, 22; required because of newspapers in mails, 27; on Butterfield route, 96; 109; on Tehuantepec route, 119; 147, 154, 208, 277; description of Concord, 306, 309; number and cost of, 310; 327, 328

Stage drivers: 153, 245, 301, 302, 303; whip of, 304; 311, 328

Stage stations: 62, 96; supplies for, 97; 148, 153, 170, 176, 219, 242; burned, 264, 280; home stations, 304; descriptions of, 305

Stage teams: 72; on Butterfield route, 96; average drive for, 97; mules, 108; 111, 116, 119, 147, 151, 153, 154, 245, 278, 310, 311

Stansbury, H: 230 *footnote*

Star Bids and service: 132, 137, 207

Steward, Captain: 182

Stimson, A. D: *History of Express Companies*, 319 *footnote*, 339

Stock tenders: 304

Stockton (California): 83, 115; second through mail at, 117; 121, 135, 141

Stockton to Kansas City route: see *Kansas City to Stockton route*

Street, David: 286

Supplies for overland mail: 305, 306

TAOS TRAIL: 236
Tehuantepec route: 44; contract for mail service on, 119; equipment, 120; 121, 122, 123, 135
Telegraph, overland: 182; termini of, 185; progress in building, 187 *footnote*; 212, 219, 249, 253, 264
Territorial Enterprise (Nevada): 176 *footnote*, 312 *footnote*, 325 *footnote*, 341
Texas: 106, favors mail line, 107, 210, 323
Texas Almanac: 105 *footnote*, 106 *footnote*, 107, 108 *footnote*, 339
Thatcher, George: 172
Thompson, "Snowshoe": 65
Thwaites, R. G: *Early Western Travels*, 339
Toombs, Senator: 123, 130, 131, 289
Tucson: 93, 217, 323
Tullidge, *History of Salt Lake City*: 62 *footnote*, 247, 339
Twitchell, R. E: *Leading Facts of New Mexico History*, 339

UNION PACIFIC RAILROAD: 231, 323, 325, 326 *footnote*
United States *Congressional Globe*: cited in *footnotes* on following pages: 37, 38, 61, 79, 80, 83, 84, 85, 86, 87, 103, 104, 122, 123, 130, 131, 132, 133, 134, 139, 140, 150, 166, 188, 198, 199, 200, 201, 202, 203, 207, 209, 210, 211, 213, 339
United States Constitution: provision regarding post offices and post roads, 25
United States Express Company: 286
United States *House Documents*: cited in *footnotes* on following pages: 44, 60, 61, 62, 63, 67, 73, 74, 105, 107, 108, 110, 117, 157, 160, 217, 235, 236, 275, 278, 289, 324, 326, 339
United States *House Reports*: 56 *footnote*, 340
United States *Senate Documents*: cited in *footnotes* on: 26, 28, 30, 32, 39, 40, 41, 42, 43, 44, 47, 66, 89, 106, 226, 340
United States *Statutes at Large*: cited in *footnotes* on: 25, 27, 29, 30, 31, 38, 42, 46, 55, 61, 70, 73, 81, 88, 189, 212, 340
Utah: first U. S. mail to, 57; territory created, 57; army invades, 63; "State of Deseret," 68; mail to, 151; militia to fight Indians, 247
Utah Records, Early: 57 *footnote*, 58 *footnote*, 64 *footnote*
Utes: 249, 250, 251, 252, 255

VAILE, Indian agent: 248
Vanderbilt, Cornelius: ocean service, 43, 135, 206
Van Voorlies, William: 55
Vasquez, Louis: 281 *footnote*
Villard, Henry: 299
Visscher's *The Pony Express*: 177 *footnote*, 178 *footnote*, 179 *footnote*, 180 *footnote*, 341

WADDELL, W. B: 157
Wagon roads: agitation for construction of, 81, 83; El Paso to Fort Yuma, 107
War of Rebellion, Official Record: 291 *footnote*, 292 *footnote*, 341
Ware, E. F: *Indian War of 1864*, 255 *footnote*, 266 *footnote*, 341
Wasatch Mountains: mail dragged over on foot, 60
Washburne, Congressman: 139
Washington, George: 22, 26
Wasson, David: 74
Weibling, H. G: 159
Weller, Senator: 83, 86, 130
Wells Fargo and Company: 68, 285, 286, 287; enlarged, 319, 326
Wells, Henry: 319
Wells, Lieutenant-general: 247
Western Stage Company: 160, 296
Wheeled vehicles: introduction of, 22
White River (Colorado): 222

Whitford, W. C: *Colorado Volunteers in Civil War*, 246, 341
Whitney, Asa: 79
Whitney, O. F: *History of Utah*, 54 footnote, 59 footnote, 63 footnote, 341; *Popular History of Utah*, 249, 341
Wickliffe, Postmaster-general: 29
Williams, B. D: 147, 148, 155
Williams, N. B: *American Post Office*, 341
Wilson, Senator: 202, 210
Winter Quarters (Nebraska Territory): mail to, from Salt Lake City, 57
Wood, Overland Mail employee: killed by Indians, 251 *footnote*
Woods, J. C: 105
Woodson, S. H: 57, 58
Woodward, Absalom: 63; killed, 64
Wynkoop, Major: 252, 262

YOUNG, Brigham: 57, 59, 61, 69 *footnote*, 246, 247, 281, 326 *footnote*
Young, Levi E: *Founding of Utah*, 56 *footnote*, 57 *footnote*, 341
Yulee, Senator: 132, 140, 202, 203, 289

www.ingramcontent.com/pod-product-compliance
Lightning Source LLC
Chambersburg PA
CBHW020731160426
43192CB00006B/192